SEVEN PILLARS OF WISDOM

ILLUSTRATIONS

SEVEN PILLARS
OF WISDOM

a triumph

T. E. LAWRENCE

VOLUME II

THE REPRINT SOCIETY
LONDON

facing: AUTHOR]

FIRST PUBLISHED 1935

NEW EDITION 1939
PUBLISHED BY THE REPRINT SOCIETY LTD.
BY ARRANGEMENT WITH
JONATHAN CAPE LTD.

PRINTED IN GREAT BRITAIN IN THE CITY OF OXFORD
AT THE ALDEN PRESS
PAPER BY JOHN DICKINSON & CO. LTD.

30TH SEPT. 1918

DAMASCUS

Kiswe

Nahr el Litani

Kuneitra

EL LEJA
HAURAN
Ezra'a
OR
J. DRUSE

Miskin
Sheikh Saad
Tafas
Ghazale
Arar
DERA
Burga

Sea of Galilee

HAIFA

Nazareth
Tell Shehab
Mezerib
Um Keis
Remthe
Taiyibe
Bosra
Salkhad

Afuleh
Nisib
Um el Surab

Beisan
Umtaiyeh
Um el Jemal

Tul-el-Keram
Abya
Mafrak

19TH SEPT. 1918

NABLUS
Dhuleil
Minifir
Abu Sawana

JAFFA
Zerga
Khau

R. Jordan

SALT

Ludd
Kissiro
AMMAN
AZRAK
Ramleh
JERICHO
Muaggar
Ziza

JERUSALEM
Amruh
Khanadeh

28TH OCT. 17
Madeba
Ammari

GAZA
Hebron
Themed
ATARA
Gaf

RAFAH
Atwi

Dead Sea
SAFRA
EL
JESHA

BEERSHEBA
Kerak
Ras Muheiwir
Um Kharug

Railway
Sultani
J. THLAITHUKHWAT

Faraifra

W. Hesa

Husb
GHOR
Hesa
Bair

Tafileh
Jurf

Rashidiya
Dana

HEJAZ

Shobek

Odroh
Jerdun

Petra
Jefer

W. Anab

Delagha
Waheida
MA'AN

Mreigha
Ghadir el Haj

Kuntilla
Aba el Lissan
Batra

IHTAR
Shedia

Guweira

Wadi Sirhan

W. es Sawan

LAWRENCE'S JOURNEYS
RAILWAYS, 1917-18
BRITISH FRONT LINE
SCALE OF MILES

50   100

W. Ithm
GULF OF AKABA
AKABA
Rumm
Shahm

NOTE – "J." denotes JEBEL (Mountain). "W." denotes WADI (Watercourse & Valley)

CHAPTER LXI

LEWIS, the Australian, at such an ambitious moment, said that he and Stokes would like to be of my party. A new, attractive idea. With them we should feel sure of our technical detachments, whilst attacking a garrisoned place. Also, the sergeants wanted to go very much, and their good work deserved reward. They were warned that their experiences might not at the moment seem altogether joyful. There were no rules; and there could be no mitigation of the marching, feeding, and fighting, inland. If they went they would lose their British Army comfort and privilege, to share and share with the Arabs (except in booty!) and suffer exactly their hap in food and discipline. If anything went wrong with me, they, not speaking Arabic, would be in a tender position.

Lewis replied that he was looking for just this strangeness of life. Stokes supposed that if we did it, he could. So they were lent two of my best camels (their saddle-bags tight with bully-beef and biscuits) and on September the seventh we went together up Wadi Itm, to collect our Howeitat from Auda in Guweira.

For the sergeants' sake, to harden them gently, things were made better than my word. We marched very easily for to-day, while we were our own masters. Neither had been on a camel before, and there was risk that the fearful heat of the naked granite walls of Itm might knock them out before the trip had properly begun. September was a bad month. A few days before, in the shade of the palm-gardens of Akaba beach, the thermometer had shown a hundred and twenty degrees. So we halted for midday under a cliff, and in the evening rode only ten miles to camp for the night.

We were comfortable with cans of hot tea, and rice and meat; and it was covertly enjoyable to watch the percussion of their surroundings on the two men. Each reacted to the type expected.

The Australian from the first seemed at home, and behaved freely towards the Arabs. When they fell into his spirit, and returned the fellowship, he was astonished: almost resentful: having never imagined that they would be misled by his kindness to forget the difference between a white man and a brown.

It added humour to the situation that he was browner by far than my new followers, of whom the youngest interested me most. He, Rahail, was quite a lad: a free-built, sturdy fellow, too fleshy for the life we were to lead, but for that the more tolerant of pains. His face was high-coloured; his cheeks a little full and low-pouched, almost pendent. The mouth was budded and small, the chin very pointed. This, added to the high, strong brows and antimony-enlarged eyes, gave him a mixed air of artifice and petulance, with weary patience self-imposed upon a base of pride. He was blowsy-spoken (mouthing his Arabic); vulgar in dialect; forward and impudent in speech; always thrusting, flaunting, restless and nervous. His spirit was not as strong as his body, but mercurial. When exhausted or cross he broke into miserable tears easily chased away by any interference; and after, was fit for more endurance. My followers, Mohammed and Ahmed, with Rashid and Assaf, the probationers, gave Rahail much licence of behaviour; partly because of his animal attractiveness, and of his tendency to advertise his person. He had to be checked once or twice for taking liberties with the sergeants.

Stokes, the Englishman, was driven by the Arab strangeness to become more himself, more insular. His shy correctness reminded my men in every movement that he was unlike them, and English. Such consideration elicited a return of respect. To them he was 'the sergeant', while Lewis was 'the long one'.

These were points of character, which all showed in their degree. It was humiliating to find that our book-experience of all countries and ages still left us prejudiced like washerwomen, but without their verbal ability to get on terms with strangers. The Englishmen in the Middle East divided into two classes. Class one, subtle and insinuating, caught the characteristics of the people about him, their speech, their conventions of thought, almost their manner. He directed men secretly, guiding them as he would. In such frictionless habit of influence his own nature lay hid, unnoticed.

Class two, the John Bull of the books, became the more rampantly English the longer he was away from England. He invented an Old

Country for himself, a home of all remembered virtues, so splendid in
the distance that, on return, he often found reality a sad falling off and
withdrew his muddle-headed self into fractious advocacy of the good
old times. Abroad, through his armoured certainty, he was a rounded
sample of our traits. He showed the complete Englishman. There was
friction in his track, and his direction was less smooth than that of the
intellectual type: yet his stout example cut wider swathe.

Both sorts took the same direction in example, one vociferously, the
other by implication. Each assumed the Englishman a chosen being,
inimitable, and the copying him blasphemous or impertinent. In this
conceit they urged on people the next best thing. God had not given it
them to be English; a duty remained to be good of their type. Consequently we admired native custom; studied the language; wrote books
about its architecture, folklore, and dying industries. Then one day, we
woke up to find this chthonic spirit turned political, and shook our
heads with sorrow over its ungrateful nationalism — truly the fine
flower of our innocent efforts.

The French, though they started with a similar doctrine of the
Frenchman as the perfection of mankind (dogma amongst them, not
secret instinct), went on, contrarily, to encourage their subjects to
imitate them; since, even if they could never attain the true level, yet
their virtue would be greater as they approached it. We looked upon
imitation as a parody; they as a compliment.

Next day, in the early heat, we were near Guweira, comfortably
crossing the sanded plain of restful pink with its grey-green undergrowth, when there came a droning through the air. Quickly we drove
the camels off the open road into the bush-speckled ground, where their
irregular colouring would not be marked by the enemy airmen; for the
loads of blasting gelatine, my favourite and most powerful explosive,
and the many ammonal-filled shells of the Stokes' gun would be ill
neighbours in a bombing raid. We waited there, soberly, in the saddle
while our camels grazed the little which was worth eating in the scrub,
until the aeroplane had circled twice about the rock of Guweira in
front of us, and planted three loud bombs.

We collected our caravan again on the path and paced gently into
camp. Guweira was thronged with life, and a mart for the Howeitat of

both hills and highlands. As far as the eye reached the plain was softly moving with herded camels, whose multitude drained the near water-holes each morning before dawn, so that late risers must travel many miles to drink.

This was little matter, for the Arabs had nothing to do but wait for the morning aeroplane; and after its passing, nothing but talk to kill time till night was full enough for sleep. The talk and leisure were too plentiful and had revived old jealousies. Auda was ambitious to take advantage of our dependence on his help to assort the tribes. He drew the bulk-wages for the Howeitat; and, by the money, sought to compel the smaller free-sections to his leadership.

They resented it, and were threatening either to retire into their hills or to re-open touch with the Turks. Feisal sent up Sherif Mastur as mediator. The thousands of Howeitat, in hundreds of sections, were uncompromising, hard-headed, greedy land-lawyers. To hold them content without angering Auda was task delicate enough for the most fastidious mind. Also, it was one hundred and ten degrees in the shade, and the shade was a surge of flies.

The three southern clans on whom we had been counting for our raid were among the dissidents. Mastur spoke to them, the chiefs of the Abu Tayi spoke, we all spoke, without effect. It seemed as though our plans were to break down at the start.

One day, going along before noon under the rock, Mastur met me with news that the southerners were mounting to desert our camp and movement. Full of vexation, I swung round into Auda's tent. He sat on its sand-floor, feeding on boiled bread with his latest wife, a jolly girl, whose brown skin was blue with the indigo dye from her new smock. When I suddenly burst in, the little woman whisked away through the back-flap like a rabbit. To gain ground with him, I began to jeer at the old man for being so old and yet so foolish like the rest of his race, who regarded our comic reproductive processes not as an unhygienic pleasure, but as a main business of life.

Auda retorted with his desire for heirs. I asked if he had found life good enough to thank his haphazard parents for bringing him into it? or selfishly to confer the doubtful gift upon an unborn spirit?

He maintained himself. 'Indeed, I am Auda,' said he, firmly, 'and you know Auda. My father (to whom God be merciful) was master, greater than Auda; and he would praise my grandfather. The world is greater as we go back.' 'But, Auda, we say honour our sons and daughters, the heirs of our accumulated worth, fulfillers of our broken wisdom. With each generation the earth is older, mankind more removed from its childhood . . .'

The old thing, not to-day to be teased, looked at me through his narrowed eyes with a benign humour, and pointed to Abu Tayi, his son, out on the plain before us trying a new camel, banging it on the neck with his stick in vain effort to make it pace like a thoroughbred. 'O world's imp,' said he, 'if God please he has inherited my worth, but thank God not yet my strength; and if I find fault with him I will redden his tail. No doubt you are very wise.' The upshot of our talk was that I should go off to a clean spot, to wait events. We hired twenty camels to carry the explosives; and the morrow, two hours after the aeroplane, was fixed for our start.

The aeroplane was the quaint regulator of public business in the Guweira camp. The Arabs, up as ever before dawn, waited for it: Mastur set a slave on the crag's peak to sound the first warning. When its constant hour drew near the Arabs would saunter, chatting in parade of carelessness, towards the rock. Arrived beneath it, each man climbed to the ledge he favoured. After Mastur would climb the bevy of his slaves, with his coffee on the brazier, and his carpet. In a shaded nook he and Auda would sit and talk till the little shiver of excitement tightened up and down the crowded ledges when first was heard the song of the engine over the pass of Shtar.

Everyone pressed back against the wall and waited stilly while the enemy circled vainly above the strange spectacle of this crimson rock banded with thousands of gaily-dressed Arabs, nesting like ibises in every cranny of its face. The aeroplane dropped three bombs, or four bombs, or five bombs, according to the day of the week. Their bursts of dense smoke sat on the sage-green plain compactly like cream-puffs; writhing for minutes in the windless air before they slowly spread and faded. Though we knew there was no menace in it, yet we could not but catch our breath when the sharp-growing cry of the falling bombs came through the loud engine overhead.

M*

CHAPTER LXII

GLADLY we left the noise and heart-burning of Guweira. So soon as we had lost our escort of flies we halted: indeed there was no need of haste, and the two unfortunate fellows with me were tasting of such heat as they had never known; for the stifling air was like a metal mask over our faces. It was admirable to see them struggle not to speak of it, that they might keep the spirit of the Akaba undertaking to endure as firmly as the Arabs; but by this silence the sergeants went far past their bond. It was ignorance of Arabic which made them so superfluously brave, for the Arabs themselves were loud against the tyrannous sun and the breathlessness; but the test-effect was wholesome; and, for effect, I played about, seeming to enjoy myself.

In the late afternoon we marched further and stopped for the night under a thick screen of tamarisk-trees. The camp was very beautiful, for behind us rose a cliff, perhaps four hundred feet in height, a deep red in the level sunset. Under our feet was spread a floor of buff-coloured mud, as hard and muffled as wood-paving, flat like a lake for half a mile each way: and on a low ridge to one side of it stood the grove of tamarisk-stems of brown wood, edged with a sparse and dusty fringe of green, which had been faded by drought and sunshine till it was nearly of the silvered grey below the olive-leaves about Les Baux, when a wind from the river-mouth rustled up the valley-grass and made the trees turn pale.

We were riding for Rumm, the northern water of the Beni Atiyeh: a place which stirred my thought, as even the unsentimental Howeitat had told me it was lovely. The morrow would be new with our entry to it: but very early, while the stars were yet shining, I was roused by Aid, the humble Harithi Sherif accompanying us. He crept to me, and said in a chilled voice, 'Lord, I am gone blind'. I made him lie down, and felt that he shivered as if cold; but all he could tell me was that in the night, waking up, there had been no sight, only pain in his eyes. The sun-blink had burned them out.

Day was still young as we rode between two great pikes of sandstone to the foot of a long, soft slope poured down from the domed hills in front of us. It was tamarisk-covered: the beginning of the Valley of Rumm, they said. We looked up on the left to a long wall of rock, sheering in like a thousand-foot wave towards the middle of the valley; whose other arc, to the right, was an opposing line of steep, red broken hills. We rode up the slope, crashing our way through the brittle undergrowth.

As we went, the brushwood grouped itself into thickets whose massed leaves took on a stronger tint of green the purer for their contrasted setting in plots of open sand of a cheerful delicate pink. The ascent became gentle, till the valley was a confined tilted plain. The hills on the right grew taller and sharper, a fair counterpart of the other side which straightened itself to one massive rampart of redness. They drew together until only two miles divided them: and then, towering gradually till their parallel parapets must have been a thousand feet above us, ran forward in an avenue for miles.

They were not unbroken walls of rock, but were built sectionally, in crags like gigantic buildings, along the two sides of their street. Deep alleys, fifty feet across, divided the crags, whose plans were smoothed by the weather into huge apses and bays, and enriched with surface fretting and fracture, like design. Caverns high up on the precipice were round like windows: others near the foot gaped like doors. Dark stains ran down the shadowed front for hundreds of feet, like accidents of use. The cliffs were striated vertically, in their granular rock; whose main order stood on two hundred feet of broken stone deeper in colour and harder in texture. This plinth did not, like the sandstone, hang in folds like cloth; but chipped itself into loose courses of scree, horizontal as the footings of a wall.

The crags were capped in nests of domes, less hotly red than the body of the hill; rather grey and shallow. They gave the finishing semblance of Byzantine architecture to this irresistible place: this processional way greater than imagination. The Arab armies would have been lost in the length and breadth of it, and within the walls a squadron of aeroplanes could have wheeled in formation. Our little caravan grew self-conscious, and fell dead quiet, afraid and ashamed to flaunt its smallness in the presence of the stupendous hills.

Landscapes, in childhood's dream, were so vast and silent. We looked backward through our memory for the prototype up which all men had walked between such walls toward such an open square as that in front where this road seemed to end. Later, when we were often riding inland, my mind used to turn me from the direct road, to clear my senses by a night in Rumm and by the ride down its dawn-lit valley towards the shining plains, or up its valley in the sunset towards that glowing square which my timid anticipation never let me reach. I would say, 'Shall I ride on this time, beyond the Khazail, and know it all?' But in truth I liked Rumm too much.

To-day we rode for hours while the perspectives grew greater and more magnificent in ordered design, till a gap in the cliff-face opened on our right to a new wonder. The gap, perhaps three hundred yards across, was a crevice in such a wall; and led to an amphitheatre, oval in shape, shallow in front, and long-lobed right and left. The walls were precipices, like all the walls of Rumm; but appeared greater, for the pit lay in the very heart of a ruling hill, and its smallness made the besetting heights seem overpowering.

The sun had sunk behind the western wall, leaving the pit in shadow; but its dying glare flooded with startling red the wings each side of the entry, and the fiery bulk of the further wall across the great valley. The pit-floor was of damp sand, darkly wooded with shrubs; while about the feet of all the cliffs lay boulders greater than houses, sometimes, indeed, like fortresses which had crashed down from the heights above. In front of us a path, pale with use, zigzagged up the cliff-plinth to the point from which the main face rose, and there it turned precariously southward along a shallow ledge outlined by occasional leafy trees. From between these trees, in hidden crannies of the rock, issued strange cries; the echoes, turned into music, of the voices of the Arabs watering camels at the springs which there flowed out three hundred feet above ground.

The rains, falling on the grey domes of the hill-top, seemed to have soaked slowly into the porous rock; and my mind followed them, filtering inch by inch downward through those mountains of sandstone till they came against the impervious horizontal layer of the plinth, and ran along its top under pressure, in jets which burst out on the cliff-face at the junction of the two rocky layers.

Mohammed turned into the amphitheatre's left hand lobe. At its far end Arab ingenuity had cleared a space under an overhanging rock: there we unloaded and settled down. The dark came upon us quickly in this high prisoned place; and we felt the water-laden air cold against our sunburnt skin. The Howeitat, who had looked after the loads of explosive collected their camel drove, and led them with echo-testing shouts up the hill-path to water against their early return to Guweira. We lit fires and cooked rice to add to the sergeants' bully-beef, while my coffee men prepared for the visitors who would come to us.

The Arabs in the tents outside the hollow of the springs had seen us enter, and were not slow to learn our news. In an hour we had the head men of the Darausha, Zelebani, Zuweida and Togatga clans about us; and there mounted great talk, none too happy. Aid, the Sherif, was too cast down in heart by his blindness to lift the burden of entertainment from my shoulders; and a work of such special require-ments was not to be well done by me. These smaller clans, angry with the Abu Tayi, suspected us of abetting Auda in his ambition to win a predominance over them. They were unwilling to serve the Sherif till assured of his support of their extremest claims.

Gasim abu Dumeik, the fine horseman who had led the highland men on the day of Aba el Lissan, seemed particularly vicious. He was a dark man with an arrogant face and thin-lipped smile: good enough at heart, but crusted. To-day, he flamed with jealousy of the Toweiha. Alone, I could never win him, so to make patent his hostility I took him as adversary and fought him fiercely with my tongue till he was silenced. In shame his audience deserted him and rallied ever so little to my side. Their flickering judgements began to murmur at the chiefs, and to advocate marching off with me. I took the chance to say that Zaal would be here in the morning, and that he and I would accept the help of all except the Dhumaniyeh; who, made impossible by Gasim's words, would be erased from Feisal's book and forfeit their earned goodwill and rewards. Gasim, swearing he would join the Turks at once, with-drew from the fireside in great anger, while cautious friends tried vainly to stop his mouth.

CHAPTER LXIII

NEXT morning there he was, with his men, ready to join or oppose us, as the whim went. While he hesitated Zaal arrived. Gasim's dourness soon clashed upon Zaal's metallic cruelty, and the pair had high words. We got between them before a fight could start, but enough passed to overthrow the weak arrangement of the night. The other clans, disgusted at Gasim's fierceness, came to us quietly in twos and threes, as volunteers; but begged me to make their loyalty known to Feisal before we started.

Their doubts determined me to communicate at once with him, partly that this trouble might be composed, and partly to raise camels for carrying the explosives. To hire Dhumaniyeh camels would not be fitting; and there were no others here. The best way was to go myself; because while Gasim might stop a messenger, he would not dare hinder me. The two sergeants were commended to Zaal, who swore to answer for their lives; and off went Ahmed and myself on stripped camels, meaning to hurry to Akaba and back.

We knew only the very long way by Wadi Itm. A short cut existed, but we could find no guide to it. Vainly we searched up and down the valley; and were in despair when a boy blurted out that we should go along the next valley to our right. By it, after an hour, we were on a watershed from which valleys trended away westward. They could lead only into Wadi Itm, for there was no other drainage hereabouts through the hills to the sea; and we raced down them, ever and again cutting at a venture across ridges on our right into parallel tributaries, to shorten the assumed line.

In the beginning it was clean sandstone country, of pleasant rock-shapes: but as we went spines of granite, the material of the shore, rose up in front of us, and after thirty miles of good trotting gradient we passed, by the southern Itm, into the main valley, just above the well of the surrender of Akaba. The journey took us only six hours.

In Akaba we rode straight to Feisal's house. My sudden return scared him, but a word explained the little drama which was being played at Rumm. After we had fed we took the necessary steps. The twenty baggage camels should start up in two days with enough of Feisal's camel-men to transport the explosives, and a few of his personal slaves to guard them. He would lend me Sherif Abdulla el Feir, the best of his henchmen now in camp, as mediator. The families of the men who rode with me to the railway should draw provisions from his stores on my certificate.

Abdulla and I went off before dawn, and in the afternoon, after a friendly ride, reached Rumm to find all safe: so anxiety was lifted. Sherif Abdulla at once got to work. Having collected the Arabs, including the recalcitrant Gasim, he began to smooth over their griefs with that ready persuasiveness which was the birthmark of an Arab leader, and which all his experience served to whet.

In the idleness forced on him by our absence, Lewis had explored the cliff, and reported the springs very good for washing in; so, to get rid of the dust and strain after my long rides, I went straight up the gully into the face of the hill, along the ruined wall of the conduit by which a spout of water had once run down the ledges to a Nabatæan well-house on the valley floor. It was a climb of fifteen minutes to a tired person, and not difficult. At the top, the waterfall, el Shellala as the Arabs named it, was only a few yards away.

Its rushing noise came from my left, by a jutting bastion of cliff over whose crimson face trailed long falling runners of green leaves. The path skirted it in an undercut ledge. On the rock-bulge above were clear-cut Nabathæan inscriptions, and a sunk panel incised with a monogram or symbol. Around and about were Arab scratches, including tribe-marks, some of which were witnesses of forgotten migrations: but my attention was only for the splashing of water in a crevice under the shadow of the overhanging rock.

From this rock a silver runlet issued into the sunlight. I looked in to see the spout, a little thinner than my wrist, jetting out firmly from a fissure in the roof, and falling with that clean sound into a shallow, frothing pool, behind the step which served as entrance. The walls and roof of the crevice dripped with moisture. Thick ferns and grasses of the finest green made it a paradise just five feet square.

Upon the water-cleansed and fragrant ledge I undressed my soiled body, and stepped into the little basin, to taste at last a freshness of moving air and water against my tired skin. It was deliciously cool. I lay there quietly, letting the clear, dark red water run over me in a ribbly stream, and rub the travel-dirt away. While I was so happy, a grey-bearded, ragged man, with a hewn face of great power and weariness, came slowly along the path till opposite the spring; and there he let himself down with a sigh upon my clothes spread out over a rock beside the path, for the sun-heat to chase out their thronging vermin.

He heard me and leaned forward, peering with rheumy eyes at this white thing splashing in the hollow beyond the veil of sun-mist. After a long stare he seemed content, and closed his eyes, groaning, 'The love is from God; and of God; and towards God'.

His low-spoken words were caught by some trick distinctly in my water pool. They stopped me suddenly. I had believed Semites unable to use love as a link between themselves and God, indeed, unable to conceive such a relation except with the intellectuality of Spinoza, who loved so rationally and sexlessly, and transcendently that he did not seek, or rather had not permitted, a return. Christianity had seemed to me the first creed to proclaim love in this upper world, from which the desert and the Semite (from Moses to Zeno) had shut it out: and Christianity was a hybrid, except in its first root not essentially Semitic.

Its birth in Galilee had saved it from being just one more of the innumerable revelations of the Semite. Galilee was Syria's non-Semitic province, contact with which was almost uncleanness for the perfect Jew. Like Whitechapel to London, it lay alien to Jerusalem. Christ by choice passed his ministry in its intellectual freedom; not among the mud-huts of a Syrian village, but in polished streets among fora and pillared houses and rococo baths, products of an intense if very exotic provincial and corrupt Greek civilization.

The people of this stranger-colony were not Greek — at least not in the majority — but Levantines of sorts, aping a Greek culture; and in revenge producing, not the correct banal Hellenism of the exhausted homeland, but a tropical rankness of idea, in which the rhythmical balance of Greek art and Greek ideality blossomed into novel shapes tawdry with the larded passionate colours of the East.

Gadarene poets, stuttering their verses in the prevailing excitement, held a mirror to the sensuality and disillusioned fatalism, passing into disordered lust, of their age and place; from whose earthiness the ascetic Semite religiosity perhaps caught the tang of humanity and real love that made the distinction of Christ's music, and fitted it to sweep across the hearts of Europe in a fashion which Judaism and Islam could not achieve.

And then Christianity had had the fortune of later architects of genius; and in its passage through time and clime had suffered sea-changes incomparably greater than the unchanging Jewry, from the abstraction of Alexandrian bookishness into Latin prose, for the mainland of Europe: and last and most terrible passing of all, when it became Teuton, with a formal synthesis to suit our chilly disputatious north. So remote was the Presbyterian creed from the Orthodox faith of its first or second embodiment that, before the war, we were able to send missionaries to persuade these softer Oriental Christians to our presentation of a logical God.

Islam, too, had inevitably changed from continent to continent. It had avoided metaphysics, except in the introspective mysticism of Iranian devotees: but in Africa it had taken on colours of fetishism (to express in a loose word the varied animalities of the dark continent), and in India, it had to stoop to the legality and literalism of its converts' minds. In Arabia, however, it had kept a Semitic character, or rather the Semitic character had endured through the phase of Islam (as through all the phases of the creeds with which the town-dwellers continually vested the simplicity of faith), expressing the monotheism of open spaces, the pass-through-infinity of pantheism and its everyday usefulness of an all-pervading, household God.

By contrast with this fixity, or with my reading of it, the old man of Rumm loomed portentous in his brief, single sentence, and seemed to overturn my theories of the Arab nature. In fear of a revelation, I put an end to my bath, and advanced to recover my clothes. He shut his eyes with his hands and groaned heavily. Tenderly I persuaded him to rise up and let me dress, and then to come with me along the crazy path which the camels had made in their climbing to and from the other water-springs. He sat down by our coffee-place, where Mohammed blew up the fire while I sought to make him utter doctrine.

When the evening meal was ready we fed him, so checking for some minutes his undercurrent of groans and broken words. Late at night, he rose painfully to his feet and tottered deafly into the night, taking his beliefs, if any, with him. The Howeitat told me that life-long he had wandered among them moaning strange things, not knowing day or night, not troubling himself for food or work or shelter. He was given bounty of them all, as an afflicted man: but never replied a word, or talked aloud, except when abroad by himself or alone among the sheep and goats.

CHAPTER LXIV

ABDULLA made progress with his settlement. Gasim, no longer defiant, but sulky, would not give public counsel: so about a hundred men of the smaller clans dared defy him by promising to ride with us. We talked it over with Zaal, and decided to try our fortune to the utmost of this power. By longer delay we risked adherents whom we now had, with little hope of getting others in the present temper of the tribes.

It was a tiny party, only a third of what had been hoped. Our weakness would modify our plans regrettably: also we lacked an assured leader. Zaal, as ever, showed himself capable of being chief prescient and active in all concrete preparations. He was a man of great mettle, but too close to Auda to suit the others; and his sharp tongue and the sneer hovering on his blue, wet lips fanned distrust and made men reluctant to obey even his good advice.

Next day the baggage camels came from Feisal, twenty of them in charge of ten freedmen, and guarded by four of his body-slaves. These were the trustiest attendants in the army, with a quite particular reading of the duties of personal service. They would have died to save their master hurt, or have died with him if he were hurt. We attached two to each sergeant, so that whatever happened to me their safe return would be assured. The loads needed for the reduced raid were sorted out and all made ready for an early start.

Accordingly at dawn on September the sixteenth we rode out from Rumm. Aid, the blind Sherif, insisted on coming, despite his lost sight; saying he could ride, if he could not shoot, and that if God prospered us he would take leave from Feisal in the flush of the success, and go home, not too sorry, to the blank life which would be left. Zaal led his twenty-five Nowasera, a clan of Auda's Arabs who called themselves my men, and were famous the desert over for their saddle-camels. My hard riding tempted them to my company.

Old Motlog el Awar, owner of el Jedha, the finest she-camel in North Arabia, rode her in our van. We looked at her with proud or greedy eyes, according to our relationship with him. My Ghazala was taller and more grand, with a faster trot, but too old to be galloped. However she was the only other animal in the party, or, indeed, in this desert, to be matched with the Jedha, and my honour was increased by her dignity.

The rest of our party strayed like a broken necklace. There were groups of Zuweida, Darausha, Togatga, and Zelebani; and it was on this ride that the virtue of Hammad el Tugtagi was first brought to my mind. Half an hour after we started there rode out from a side-valley some shame-faced men of the Dhumaniyeh, unable to endure others raiding while they idled with the women.

No one group would ride or speak with another, and I passed back and forth all day like a shuttle, talking first to one lowering sheikh, and then to another, striving to draw them together, so that before a cry to action came there might be solidarity. As yet they agreed only in not hearing any word from Zaal as to the order of our march; though he was admitted the most intelligent warrior, and the most experienced. For my private part he was the only one to be trusted further than eye-sight. Of the others, it seemed to me that neither their words nor their counsels, perhaps not their rifles, were sure.

Poor Sherif Aid's uselessness, even as nominal leader, forced me to assume the direction myself, against both principle and judgement; since the special arts of tribal raiding and the details of food-halts and pasturage, road-direction, pay, disputes, division of spoils, feuds and march order were much outside the syllabus of the Oxford School of Modern History. The need to vamp these matters kept me too busied to see the country, and prevented my worrying out how we must assault Mudowwara, and the best surprise uses of explosive.

We put our midday halt in a fertile place, where the late spring rain, falling on a sandy talus, had brought up a thick tufting of silvery grass which our camels loved. The weather was mild, perfect as an August in England, and we lingered in great content, recovered at last from the bickering appetites of the days before the start, and from that slight rending of nerve inevitable when leaving even a temporary settle-ment. Man, in our circumstances, took root so soon.

Late in the day we rode again, winding downhill in a narrow valley between moderate sandstone walls: till before sunset we were out on another flat of laid yellow mud, like that which had been so wonderful a prelude to Rumm's glory. By its edge we camped. My care had borne fruit, for we settled in only three parties, by bright fires of crackling, flaring tamarisk. At one supped my men; at the second Zaal; at the third the other Howeitat; and late at night, when all the chiefs had been well adjusted with gazelle meat and hot bread, it became possible to bring them to my neutral fire, and discuss sensibly our course for the morrow.

It seemed that about sunset we should water at Mudowwara well, two or three miles this side of the station, in a covered valley. Then, in the early night, we might go forward to examine the station and see if, in our weakness, we might yet attempt some stroke against it. I held strongly to this (against the common taste) for it was by so much the most critical point of the line. The Arabs could not see it, since their minds did not hold a picture of the long, linked Turkish front with its necessitous demands. However, we had reached internal harmony, and scattered confidently to sleep.

In the morning we delayed to eat again, having only six hours of march before us; and then pushed across the mud-flat to a plain of firm limestone rag, carpeted with brown, weather-blunted flint. This was succeeded by low hills, with occasional soft beds of sand, under the steeper slopes where eddying winds had dropped their dust. Through these we rode up shallow valleys to a crest; and then by like valleys down the far side, whence we issued abruptly, from dark, tossed stone-heaps into the sun-steeped wideness of a plain. Across it an occasional low dune stretched a drifting line.

We had made our noon halt at the first entering of the broken country; and, rightly, in the late afternoon came to the well. It was an open pool, a few yards square, in a hollow valley of large stone-slabs and flint and sand. The stagnant water looked uninviting. Over its face lay a thick mantle of green slime, from which swelled curious bladder-islands of floating fatty pink. The Arabs explained that the Turks had thrown dead camels into the pool to make the water foul; but that time had passed and the effect was grown faint. It would have been fainter had the criterion of their effort been my taste.

Yet it was all the drink we should get up here unless we took Mudowwara, so we set to and filled our water-skins. One of the Howeitat, while helping in this, slipped off the wet edge into the water. Its green carpet closed oilily over his head and hid him for an instant: then he came up, gasping vigorously, and scrambled out amid our laughter; leaving behind him a black hole in the scum from which a stench of old meat rose like a visible pillar, and hung about us and him and the valley, disconcertingly.

At dusk, Zaal and I, with the sergeants and others, crept forward quietly. In half an hour we were at the last crest, in a place where the Turks had dug trenches and stoned up an elaborate outpost of engrailed sangars which on this black new-moon night of our raid were empty. In front and below lay the station, its doors and windows sharply marked by the yellow cooking fires and lights of the garrison. It seemed close under our observation; but the Stokes gun would carry only three hundred yards. Accordingly we went nearer, hearing the enemy noises, and attentively afraid lest their barking dogs uncover us. Sergeant Stokes made casts out to left and right, in search of gun-positions, but found nothing that was satisfactory.

Meanwhile, Zaal and I crawled across the last flat, till we could count the unlighted tents and hear the men talking. One came out a few steps in our direction, then hesitated. He struck a match to light a cigarette, and the bold light flooded his face, so that we saw him plainly, a young, hollow-faced sickly officer. He squatted, busy for a moment, and returned to his men, who hushed as he passed.

We moved back to our hill and consulted in whispers. The station was very long, of stone buildings, so solid that they might be proof against our time-fused shell. The garrison seemed about two hundred. We were one hundred and sixteen rifles and not a happy family. Surprise was the only benefit we could be sure of.

So, in the end, I voted that we leave it, unalarmed, for a future occasion, which might be soon. But, actually, one accident after another saved Mudowwara; and it was not until August, 1918, that Buxton's Camel Corps at last measured to it the fate so long overdue.

CHAPTER LXV

QUIETLY we regained our camels and slept. Next morning we returned on our tracks to let a fold of the plain hide us from the railway, and then marched south across the sandy flat; seeing tracks of gazelle, oryx and ostrich; with, in one spot, stale padmarks of leopard. We were making for the low hills bounding the far side, intending to blow up a train; for Zaal said that where these touched the railway was such a curve as we needed for mine-laying, and that the spurs commanding it would give us ambush and a field of fire for our machine-guns.

So we turned east in the southern ridges till within half a mile of the line. There the party halted in a thirty-foot valley, while a few of us walked down to the line, which bent a little eastward to avoid the point of higher ground under our feet. The point ended in a flat table fifty feet above the track, facing north across the valley.

The metals crossed the hollow on a high bank, pierced by a two-arched bridge for the passage of rain-water. This seemed an ideal spot to lay the charge. It was our first try at electric mining and we had no idea what would happen; but it stood to our reason that the job would be more sure with an arch under the explosive because, whatever the effect on the locomotive, the bridge would go, and the succeeding coaches be inevitably derailed.

The ledge would make an admirable position for Stokes. For the automatics, it was rather high; but the enfilade would be masterful whether the train was going up or down the line. So we determined to put up with the disadvantages of plunging fire. It was good to have my two British responsibilities in one place, safe from surprise and with an independent retreat into the rough: for to-day Stokes was in pain with dysentery. Probably the Mudowwara water had upset his stomach. So few Englishmen seemed to have been endowed by their upbringing with any organic resistance to disease.

Back with our camels, we dumped the loads, and sent the animals to safe pasture near some undercut rocks from which the Arabs scraped salt. The freedmen carried down the Stokes gun with its shells; the Lewis guns; and the gelatine with its insulated wire, magneto and tools to the chosen place. The sergeants set up their toys on a terrace, while we went down to the bridge to dig a bed between the ends of two steel sleepers, wherein to hide my fifty pounds of gelatine. We had stripped off the paper wrapping of the individual explosive plugs and kneaded them together by help of the sun-heat into a shaking jelly in a sand-bag.

The burying of it was not easy. The embankment was steep, and in the sheltered pocket between it and the hill-side was a wind-laid bank of sand. No one crossed this but myself, stepping carefully; yet I left unavoidable great prints over its smoothness. The ballast dug out from the track I had to gather in my cloak for carriage in repeated journeys to the culvert, whence it could be tipped naturally over the shingle bed of the watercourse.

It took me nearly two hours to dig in and cover the charge: then came the difficult job of unrolling the heavy wires from the detonator to the hills whence we would fire the mine. The top sand was crusted and had to be broken through in burying the wires. They were stiff wires, which scarred the wind-rippled surface with long lines like the belly marks of preposterously narrow and heavy snakes. When pressed down in one place they rose into the air in another. At last they had to be weighted down with rocks which, in turn, had to be buried at the cost of great disturbance of the ground.

Afterwards it was necessary, with a sand-bag, to stipple the marks into a wavy surface; and, finally, with a bellows and long fanning sweeps of my cloak, to simulate the smooth laying of the wind. The whole job took five hours to finish; but then it was well finished: neither myself nor any of us could see where the charge lay, or that double wires led out underground from it to the firing point two hundred yards off, behind the ridge marked for our riflemen.

The wires were just long enough to cross from this ridge into a depression. There we brought up the two ends and connected them with the electric exploder. It was an ideal place both for it and for the man who fired it, except that the bridge was not visible thence.

However, this only meant that someone would have to press the handle at a signal from a point fifty yards ahead, commanding the bridge and the ends of the wires alike. Salem, Feisal's best slave, asked for this task of honour, and was yielded it by acclamation. The end of the afternoon was spent in showing him (on the disconnected exploder) what to do, till he was act-perfect and banged down the ratchet precisely as I raised my hand with an imaginary engine on the bridge.

We walked back to camp, leaving one man on watch by the line. Our baggage was deserted, and we stared about in a puzzle for the rest, till we saw them suddenly sitting against the golden light of sunset along a high ridge. We yelled to them to lie down or come down, but they persisted up there on their perch like a school of hooded crows, in full view of north and south.

At last we ran up and threw them off the skyline, too late. The Turks in a little hill-post by Hallat Ammar, four miles south of us, had seen them, and opened fire in their alarm upon the long shadows which the declining sun was pushing gradually up the slopes towards the post. Beduin were past masters in the art of using country, but in their abiding contempt for the stupidity of the Turks they would take no care to fight them. This ridge was visible at once from Mudowwara and Hallat Ammar, and they had frightened both places by their sudden ominous expectant watch.

However, the dark closed on us, and we knew we must sleep away the night patiently in hope of the morrow. Perhaps the Turks would reckon us gone if our place looked deserted in the morning. So we lit fires in a deep hollow, baked bread and were comfortable. The common tasks had made us one party, and the hill-top folly shamed everyone into agreement that Zaal should be our leader.

Day broke quietly, and for hours we watched the empty railway with its peaceful camps. The constant care of Zaal and of his lame cousin Howeimil, kept us hidden, though with difficulty, because of the insatiate restlessness of the Beduin, who would never sit down for ten minutes, but must fidget and do or say something. This defect made them very inferior to the stolid English for the long, tedious strain of a waiting war. Also it partly accounted for their uncertain stomachs in defence. To-day they made us very angry.

Perhaps, after all, the Turks saw us, for at nine o'clock some forty men came out of the tents on the hill-top by Hallat Ammar to the south and advanced in open order. If we left them alone, they would turn us off our mine in an hour; if we opposed them with our superior strength and drove them back, the railway would take notice, and traffic be held up. It was a quandary, which eventually we tried to solve by sending thirty men to check the enemy patrol gradually; and, if possible, to draw them lightly aside into the broken hills. This might hide our main position and reassure them as to our insignificant strength and purpose.

For some hours it worked as we had hoped; the firing grew desultory and distant. A permanent patrol came confidently up from the south and walked past our hill, over our mine and on towards Mudowwara without noticing us. There were eight soldiers and a stout corporal, who mopped his brow against the heat, for it was now after eleven o'clock and really warm. When he had passed us by a mile or two the fatigue of the tramp became too much for him. He marched his party into the shade of a long culvert, under whose arches a cool draught from the east was gently flowing, and there in comfort they lay on the soft sand, drank water from their bottles, smoked, and at last slept. We presumed that this was the noon-day rest which every solid Turk in the hot summer of Arabia took as a matter of principle, and that their allowing themselves the pause showed that we were disproved or ignored. However, we were in error.

CHAPTER LXVI

NOON brought fresh care. Through my powerful glasses we saw a hundred Turkish soldiers issue from Mudowwara Station and make straight across the sandy plain towards our place. They were coming very slowly, and no doubt unwillingly, for sorrow at losing their beloved midday sleep: but at their very worst marching and temper they could hardly take more than two hours before they reached us.

We began to pack up, preparatory to moving off, having decided to leave the mine and its leads in place on chance that the Turks might not find them, and we be able to return and take advantage of all the careful work. We sent a messenger to our covering party on the south, that they should meet us farther up, near those scarred rocks which served as screen for our pasturing camels.

Just as he had gone, the watchman cried out that smoke in clouds was rising from Hallat Ammar. Zaal and I rushed uphill and saw by its shape and volume that indeed there must be a train waiting in that station. As we were trying to see it over the hill, suddenly it moved out in our direction. We yelled to the Arabs to get into position as quick as possible, and there came a wild scramble over sand and rock. Stokes and Lewis, being booted, could not win the race; but they came well up, their pains and dysentery forgotten.

The men with rifles posted themselves in a long line behind the spur running from the guns past the exploder to the mouth of the valley. From it they would fire directly into the derailed carriages at less than one hundred and fifty yards, whereas the ranges for the Stokes and Lewis guns were about three hundred yards. An Arab stood up on high behind the guns and shouted to us what the train was doing — a necessary precaution, for if it carried troops and detrained them behind our ridge we should have to face about like a flash and retire fighting up the valley for our lives. Fortunately it held on at all the speed the two locomotives could make on wood fuel.

It drew near where we had been reported, and opened random fire into the desert. I could hear the racket coming, as I sat on my hillock by the bridge to give the signal to Salem, who danced round the exploder on his knees, crying with excitement, and calling urgently on God to make him fruitful. The Turkish fire sounded heavy, and I wondered with how many men we were going to have affair, and if the mine would be advantage enough for our eighty fellows to equal them. It would have been better if the first electrical experiment had been simpler.

However, at that moment the engines, looking very big, rocked with screaming whistles into view around the bend. Behind them followed ten box-waggons, crowded with rifle-muzzles at the windows and doors; and in little sand-bag nests on the roofs Turks precariously held on, to shoot at us. I had not thought of two engines, and on the moment decided to fire the charge under the second, so that however little the mine's effect, the uninjured engine should not be able to uncouple and drag the carriages away.

Accordingly, when the front 'driver' of the second engine was on the bridge, I raised my hand to Salem. There followed a terrific roar, and the line vanished from sight behind a spouting column of black dust and smoke a hundred feet high and wide. Out of the darkness came shattering crashes and long, loud metallic clangings of ripped steel, with many lumps of iron and plate; while one entire wheel of a loco-motive whirled up suddenly black out of the cloud against the sky, and sailed musically over our heads to fall slowly and heavily into the desert behind. Except for the flight of these, there succeeded a deathly silence, with no cry of men or rifle-shot, as the now grey mist of the explosion drifted from the line towards us, and over our ridge until it was lost in the hills.

In the lull, I ran southward to join the sergeants. Salem picked up his rifle and charged out into the murk. Before I had climbed to the guns the hollow was alive with shots, and with the brown figures of the Beduin leaping forward to grips with the enemy. I looked round to see what was happening so quickly, and saw the train stationary and dismembered along the track, with its waggon sides jumping under the bullets which riddled them, while Turks were falling out from the far doors to gain the shelter of the railway embankment.

As I watched, our machine-guns chattered out over my head, and the long rows of Turks on the carriage roofs rolled over, and were swept off the top like bales of cotton before the furious shower of bullets which stormed along the roofs and splashed clouds of yellow chips from the planking. The dominant position of the guns had been an advantage to us so far.

When I reached Stokes and Lewis the engagement had taken another turn. The remaining Turks had got behind the bank, here about eleven feet high, and from cover of the wheels were firing point-blank at the Beduin twenty yards away across the sand-filled dip. The enemy in the crescent of the curving line were secure from the machine-guns; but Stokes slipped in his first shell, and after a few seconds there came a crash as it burst beyond the train in the desert.

He touched the elevating screw, and his second shot fell just by the trucks in the deep hollow below the bridge where the Turks were taking refuge. It made a shambles of the place. The survivors of the group broke out in a panic across the desert, throwing away their rifles and equipment as they ran. This was the opportunity of the Lewis gunners. The sergeant grimly traversed with drum after drum, till the open sand was littered with bodies. Mushagraf, the Sherari boy behind the second gun, saw the battle over, threw aside his weapon with a yell, and dashed down at speed with his rifle to join the others who were beginning, like wild beasts, to tear open the carriages and fall to plunder. It had taken nearly ten minutes.

I looked up-line through my glasses and saw the Mudowwara patrol breaking back uncertainly towards the railway to meet the train-fugitives running their fastest northward. I looked south, to see our thirty men cantering their camels neck and neck in our direction to share the spoils. The Turks there, seeing them go, began to move after them with infinite precaution, firing volleys. Evidently we had a half hour respite, and then a double threat against us.

I ran down to the ruins to see what the mine had done. The bridge was gone; and into its gap was fallen the front waggon, which had been filled with sick. The smash had killed all but three or four and had rolled dead and dying into a bleeding heap against the splintered end. One of those yet alive deliriously cried out the word typhus. So I wedged shut the door, and left them there, alone.

Succeeding waggons were derailed and smashed: some had frames irreparably buckled. The second engine was a blanched pile of smoking iron. Its driving wheels had been blown upward, taking away the side of the fire-box. Cab and tender were twisted into strips, among the piled stones of the bridge abutment. It would never run again. The front engine had got off better: though heavily derailed and lying half-over, with the cab burst, yet its steam was at pressure, and driving-gear intact.

Our greatest object was to destroy locomotives, and I had kept in my arms a box of gun-cotton with fuse and detonator ready fixed, to make sure such a case. I now put them in position on the outside cylinder. On the boiler would have been better, but the sizzling steam made me fear a general explosion which would sweep across my men (swarming like ants over the booty) with a blast of jagged fragments. Yet they would not finish their looting before the Turks came. So I lit the fuse, and in the half-minute of its burning drove the plunderers a little back, with difficulty. Then the charge burst, blowing the cylinder to smithers, and the axle too. At the moment I was distressed with uncertainty whether the damage were enough; but the Turks later, found the engine beyond use and broke it up.

The valley was a weird sight. The Arabs, gone raving mad, were rushing about at top speed bareheaded and half-naked, screaming, shooting into the air, clawing one another nail and fist, while they burst open trucks and staggered back and forward with immense bales, which they ripped by the rail-side, and tossed through, smashing what they did not want. The train had been packed with refugees and sick men, volunteers for boat-service on the Euphrates, and families of Turkish officers returning to Damascus.

There were scores of carpets spread about; dozens of mattresses and flowered quilts, blankets in heaps, clothes for men and women in full variety; clocks, cooking-pots, food, ornaments and weapons. To one side stood thirty or forty hysterical women, unveiled, tearing their clothes and hair; shrieking themselves distracted. The Arabs without regard to them went on wrecking the household goods; looting their absolute fill. Camels had become common property. Each man frantically loaded the nearest with what it could carry and shooed it westward into the void, while he turned to his next fancy.

Seeing me tolerably unemployed, the women rushed, and caught at me with howls for mercy. I assured them that all was going well: but they would not get away till some husbands delivered me. These knocked their wives off and seized my feet in a very agony of terror of instant death. A Turk so broken down was a nasty spectacle: I kicked them off as well as I could with bare feet, and finally broke free.

Next a group of Austrians, officers and non-commissioned officers, appealed to me quietly in Turkish for quarter. I replied with my halting German; whereupon one, in English, begged a doctor for his wounds. We had none: not that it mattered, for he was mortally hurt and dying. I told them the Turks would return in an hour and care for them. But he was dead before that, as were most of the others (instructors in the new Skoda mountain howitzers supplied to Turkey for the Hejaz war), because some dispute broke out between them and my own bodyguard, and one of them fired a pistol shot at young Rahail. My infuriated men cut them down, all but two or three, before I could return to interfere.

So far as could be seen in the excitement, our side had suffered no loss. Among the ninety military prisoners were five Egyptian soldiers, in their underclothes. They knew me, and explained that in a night raid of Davenport's, near Wadi Ais, they had been cut off by the Turks and captured. They told me something of Davenport's work: of his continual pegging away in Abdulla's sector, which was kept alive by him for month after month, without any of the encouragement lent to us by success and local enthusiasm. His best helpers were such stolid infantrymen as these, whom I made lead the prisoners away to our appointed rallying place at the salt rocks.

CHAPTER LXVII

LEWIS and Stokes had come down to help me. I was a little anxious about them; for the Arabs, having lost their wits, were as ready to assault friend as foe. Three times I had had to defend myself when they pretended not to know me and snatched at my things. However, the sergeants' war-stained khaki presented few attractions. Lewis went out east of the railway to count the thirty men he had slain; and incidentally, to find Turkish gold and trophies in their haversacks. Stokes strolled through the wrecked bridge, saw there the bodies of twenty Turks torn to pieces by his second shell, and retired hurriedly.

Ahmed came up to me with his arms full of booty and shouted (no Arab could speak normally in the thrill of victory) that an old woman in the last waggon but one wished to see me. I sent him at once, empty-handed, for my camel and some baggage camels to remove the guns; for the enemy's fire was now plainly audible, and the Arabs, sated with spoils, were escaping one by one towards the hills, driving tottering camels before them into safety. It was bad tactics to leave the guns until the end: but the confusion of a first, overwhelmingly successful, experiment had dulled our judgement.

In the end of the waggon sat an ancient and very tremulous Arab dame, who asked me what it was all about. I explained. She said that though an old friend and hostess of Feisal, she was too infirm to travel and must wait her death there. I replied that she would not be harmed. The Turks were almost arrived and would recover what remained of the train. She accepted this, and begged me to find her old negress, to bring her water. The slave woman filled a cup from the spouting tender of the first engine (delicious water, from which Lewis was slaking his thirst), and then I led her to her grateful mistress. Months after there came to me secretly from Damascus a letter and a pleasant little Baluchi carpet from the lady Ayesha, daughter of Jellal el Lel, of Medina, in memory of an odd meeting.

Ahmed never brought the camels. My men, possessed by greed, had dispersed over the land with the Beduins. The sergeants and I were alone by the wreck, which had a strange silence now. We began to fear that we must abandon the guns and run for it, but just then saw two camels dashing back. Zaal and Howeimil had missed me and had returned in search.

We were rolling up the insulated cable, our only piece. Zaal dropped from his camel and would have me mount and ride; but, instead, we loaded it with the wire and the exploder. Zaal found time to laugh at our quaint booty, after all the gold and silver in the train. Howeimil was dead lame from an old wound in the knee and could not walk, but we made him couch his camel, and hoisted the Lewis guns, tied butt to butt like scissors, behind his saddle. There remained the trench mortars; but Stokes reappeared, unskilfully leading by the nose a baggage camel he had found straying. We packed the mortars in haste; put Stokes (who was still weak with his dysentery) on Zaal's saddle, with the Lewis guns, and sent off the three camels in charge of Howeimil, at their best pace.

Meanwhile, Lewis and Zaal, in a sheltered and invisible hollow behind the old gun-position, made a fire of cartridge boxes, petrol and waste, banked round it the Lewis drums and the spare small-arms ammunition; and, gingerly, on the top, laid some loose Stokes' shells. Then we ran. As the flames reached the cordite and ammonal there was a colossal and continuing noise. The thousands of cartridges exploded in series like massed machine-guns, and the shells roared off in thick columns of dust and smoke. The outflanking Turks, impressed by the tremendous defence, felt that we were in strength and strongly posted. They halted their rush, took cover, and began carefully to surround our position and reconnoitre it according to rule, while we sped panting into concealment among the ridges.

It seemed a happy ending to the affair, and we were glad to get off with no more loss than my camels and baggage; though this included the sergeants' cherished kits. However, there was food at Rumm, and Zaal thought perhaps we should find our property with the others, who were waiting ahead. We did. My men were loaded with booty, and had with them all our camels whose saddles were being suddenly delivered of spoils to look ready for our mounting.

Softly I explained what I thought of the two men who had been

N

ordered to bring up the camels when the firing ceased. They pleaded that the explosion had scattered everyone in fright, and afterwards the Arabs had appropriated each man any animal he saw. This was probably true; but my men also were able-bodied and might have helped themselves. We asked if anyone were hurt, and a voice said that the Shimt's boy — a very dashing fellow — had been killed in the first rush forward at the train. This rush was a mistake, made without instructions, as the Lewis and Stokes guns were sure to end the business if the mine worked properly. So I felt that his loss was not directly my reproach.

Three men had been slightly wounded. Then one of Feisal's slaves vouchsafed that Salem was missing. We called everyone together and questioned them. At last an Arab said that he had seen him lying hit, just beyond the engine. This reminded Lewis, who ignorant that he was one of us, had seen a negro on the ground there, badly hurt. I had not been told and was angry, for half the Howeitat must have known of it, and that Salem was in my charge. By their default now, for the second time, I had left a friend behind.

I asked for volunteers to come back and find him. After a little Zaal agreed, and then twelve of the Nowasera. We trotted fast across the plain towards the line. As we topped the last ridge but one we saw the train-wreck with Turks swarming over it. There must have been one hundred and fifty of them, and our attempt was hopeless. Salem would have been dead, for the Turks did not take Arab prisoners. Indeed, they used to kill them horribly; so, in mercy, we were finishing those of our badly wounded who would have to be left helpless on abandoned ground.

We must give up Salem; but to make some profit out of our return, I suggested to Zaal that we slip up-valley and recover the sergeants' kits. He was willing, and we rode till the Turks' shooting drove us to cover behind a bank. Our camp had been in the next hollow, across a hundred yards of flat. So, watching the time, one or two of the quicker youths nipped across to drag back the saddle-bags. The Turks were distant, and Turkish long-range fire was always bad; but for our third trip they got up a machine-gun, and the dusty splashes of the bullets on the dark flints let them group well about us.

I sent the running boys away, picked out what was light and best of the remaining baggage, and rejoined the party. We pounded down the slope and across. In the open the Turks could clearly count our fewness. They grew bold and ran forward on both flanks to cut us off. Zaal threw himself from his camel, climbed with five men to the peak of the ridge we had just crossed, and fired back at them. He was a marvellous shot, whom I had seen to bring down a running gazelle from the saddle with his second bullet at three hundred yards, and his fire checked them.

He called to us laden men to hurry across the next hollow and hold it while he fell back on us, and in this fashion we retired from ridge to ridge, putting up a good delay action and hitting thirteen or fourteen Turks at a cost of four camels wounded. At last, when we were only two ridges from our supports, and were feeling sure that we should do it easily, a solitary rider appeared, coming up. It was Lewis, with a Lewis gun held efficiently across his thighs. He had heard the rapid fire, and thought to see if we needed help.

He changed our strength very much, and my mind, for I was angry with the Turks, who had got Salem and had chased us breathless so far in dust and heat and streaming sweat. Therefore we took place to give our pursuers a knock; but either they suspected our silence, or they feared the distance they had come; anyway, we saw no more of them. After a few minutes we became cool, and wise-headed enough to ride off after the others.

They had marched very heavy-laden. Of our ninety prisoners, ten were friendly Medina women electing to go to Mecca by way of Feisal. There had been twenty-two riderless camels. The women had climbed on to five pack-saddles, and the wounded were in pairs on the residue. It was late in the afternoon. We were exhausted, the prisoners had drunk all our water. We must re-fill from the old well at Mudow-wara that night to sustain ourselves so far as Rumm.

As the well was close to the station, it was highly desirable that we get to it and away, lest the Turks divine our course and find us there defenceless. We broke up into little parties and struggled north. Victory always undid an Arab force, so we were no longer a raiding party, but a stumbling baggage caravan, loaded to breaking point with enough household goods to make rich an Arab tribe for years.

My sergeants asked me for a sword each, as souvenir of their first private battle. As I went down the column to look out something, suddenly I met Feisal's freedmen; and to my astonishment on the crupper behind one of them, strapped to him, soaked with blood, unconscious, was the missing Salem.

I trotted up to Ferhan and asked wherever he had found him. He told me that when the Stokes gun fired its first shell, Salem rushed past the locomotive, and one of the Turks shot him in the back. The bullet had come out near his spine, without, in their judgement, hurting him mortally. After the train was taken, the Howeitat had stripped him of cloak, dagger, rifle and head-gear. Mijbil, one of the freedmen, had found him, lifted him straight to his camel, and trekked off homeward without telling us. Ferhan, overtaking him on the road, had relieved him of Salem; who, when he recovered, as later he did, perfectly, bore me always a little grudge for having left him behind, when he was of my company and wounded. I had failed in staunchness. My habit of hiding behind a Sherif was to avoid measuring myself against the pitiless Arab standard, with its no-mercy for foreigners who wore its clothes, and aped its manners. Not often was I caught with so poor a shield as blind Sherif Aid.

We reached the well in three hours and watered without mishap. Afterwards we moved off another ten miles or so, beyond fear of pursuit. There we lay down and slept, and in the morning found ourselves happily tired. Stokes had had his dysentery heavy upon him the night before, but sleep and the ending of anxiety made him well. He and I and Lewis, the only unburdened ones, went on in front across one huge mud-flat after another till just before sunset we were at the bottom of Wadi Rumm.

This new route was important for our armoured cars, because its twenty miles of hard mud might enable them to reach Mudowwara easily. If so, we should be able to hold up the circulation of trains when we pleased. Thinking of this, we wheeled into the avenue of Rumm, still gorgeous in sunset colour; the cliffs as red as the clouds in the west, like them in scale and in the level bar they raised against the sky. Again we felt how Rumm inhibited excitement by its serene beauty. Such whelming greatness dwarfed us, stripped off the cloak of laughter in which we had ridden over the jocund flats.

Night came down, and the valley became a mind-landscape. The invisible cliffs boded as presences; imagination tried to piece out the plan of their battlements by tracing the dark pattern they cut in the canopy of stars. The blackness in the depth was very real — it was a night to despair of movement. We felt only our camels' labour, as hour after hour monotonously and smoothly they shouldered their puny way along the unfenced level, with the wall in front no nearer and the wall behind no further than at first.

About nine at night we were before the pit in which lay the water and our old camp. We knew its place because the deep darkness there grew humidly darker. We turned our camels to the right and advanced towards the rock, which reared its crested domes so high over us that the ropes of our head-cloths slipped back round our necks as we stared up. Surely if we stretched out even our camel-sticks in front of us we should touch the facing walls; yet for many paces more we crept in under their horns.

At last we were in the tall bushes: then we shouted. An Arab shouted back. The echoes of my voice rolling down from the cliff met his rising cry, and the sounds wrapped themselves together and wrestled among the crags. A flame flickered palely on the left, and we found Musa our watchman there. He lit a fire of powerfully scented wood, and by its light we broke open bully-beef and fed ravenously; gulping down, through our food, bowl after bowl of the delicious water, ice-cold, and heady after the foul drink of Mudowwara; which, for days had seared our throats.

We slept through the coming of the rest. Two days later we were at Akaba; entering in glory, laden with precious things, and boasting that the trains were at our mercy. From Akaba the two sergeants took hurried ship to Egypt. Cairo had remembered them and gone peevish because of their non-return. However, they could pay the penalty of this cheerfully. They had won a battle single-handed; had had dysentery; lived on camel-milk; and learned to ride a camel fifty miles a day without pain. Also Allenby gave them a medal each.

CHAPTER LXVIII

DAYS passed, talking politics, organization and strategy with Feisal, while preparations for a new operation went forward. Our luck had quickened the camp; and the mining of trains promised to become popular, if we were able to train in the technique of the work enough men for several parties. Captain Pisani was first volunteer. He was the experienced commander of the French at Akaba, an active soldier who burned for distinction — and distinctions. Feisal found me three young Damascenes of family, who were ambitious to lead tribal raids. We went to Rumm and announced that this raid was specially for Gasim's clan. Such coals of fire scorched them; but greed would not let them refuse. Everyone for days around flocked to join. Most were denied: nevertheless, we started out with one hundred and fifty men and a huge train of empty pack-camels for the spoils.

For variety we determined to work by Maan. So we rode up to Batra, climbing out of heat into cold, out of Arabia into Syria, from tamarisk to wormwood. As we topped the pass and saw the blood-red stain on the hills above the leech-infested wells, there met us a first breath of the northern desert; that air too fine to describe, which told of perfect loneliness, dried grass, and the sun on burning flints.

The guides said that Kilometre 475 would be good for mining: but we found it beset by blockhouses, and had to creep shyly away. We marched down the line till it crossed a valley on a high bank, pierced by bridges on each side and in the middle. There, after midnight, we laid an automatic mine of a new and very powerful lyddite type. The burying took hours, and dawn caught us as we worked. There was no perceptible lightening, and when we stared round to know where the dark was yielding, we could see no special onset of the day. Long minutes afterwards the sun disclosed itself, high above the earth's rim, over a vignetted bank of edgeless mist.

We retired a thousand yards up the valley's scrubby bed to ambush for the intolerable day. As the hours passed the sun increased, and shone so closely upon our radiant trench that we felt crowded by its rays. The men were a mad lot, sharpened to distraction by hope of success. They would listen to no word but mine, and brought me their troubles for judgement. In the six days' raid there came to a head, and were settled, twelve cases of assault with weapons, four camel-liftings, one marriage, two thefts, a divorce, fourteen feuds, two evil eyes, and a bewitchment.

These decisions were arrived at despite my imperfect knowledge of Arabic. The fraudulence of my business stung me. Here were more fruits, bitter fruits, of my decision, in front of Akaba, to become a principal of the Revolt. I was raising the Arabs on false pretences, and exercising a false authority over my dupes, on little more evidence than their faces, as visible to my eyes weakly watering and stinging after a year's exposure to the throb, throb of sunlight.

We waited that day, and night. At sunset a scorpion scuttled out of the bush by which I had lain down to make note of the day's weariness, and fastening on my left hand struck me it seemed repeatedly. The pain of my swollen arm kept me awake until the second dawn: to the relief of my overburdened mind, for its body became clamant enough to interrupt my self-questioning when the fire of some such surface injury swept the sluggish nerves.

Yet pain of this quality never endured long enough really to cure mind-sickness. After a night it would give way to that unattractive, and not honourable, internal ache which in itself provoked thought and left its victim yet weaker to endure. In such conditions the war seemed as great a folly as my sham leadership a crime; and, sending for our sheikhs, I was about to resign myself and my pretensions into their puzzled hands, when the fugleman announced a train.

It came down from Maan, a water-train, and passed over the mine without accident. The Arabs thanked me, for a booty of water was not their dream. The mine-action had failed; so at noon, with my pupils, I went down to lay an electric mine over the lyddite, that the detonation of one might fire the other. For concealment we trusted to the mirage and midday drowsiness of the Turks; justifiably, for there was no alarm in the hour we spent burying the charge.

From the southern bridge we brought the electric leads to the middle bridge, whose arch would conceal the exploder from a train overhead.

The Lewis guns we put under the northern bridge, to rake the far side of the train when the mine went off. The Arabs would line the bushes of a cross-channel of the valley three hundred yards our side of the railway. We waited afterwards throughout a day of sunlight and flies. Enemy patrols marched actively along the line, morning, afternoon and evening.

On the second day, about eight in the morning, a pillar of smoke left Maan. At the same time the first patrol approached. They were only half a dozen men, but their warning would deter the train; and we watched strainingly, in wonder which would win the race. The train was very slow, and sometimes the patrol halted.

We calculated they might be two or three hundred yards short of us when the train came. So we ordered everybody to stations. With twelve loaded wagons the engine panted on the up grade. However, it held on steadily. I sat by a bush in the stream-bed, a hundred yards from the mine; in view of it and of the exploder-party and of the machine-guns. When Faiz and Bedri heard the engine over their arch, they danced a war-dance round their little electric box. The Arabs in the ditch were hissing softly to me that it was time to fire: but not until the engine was exactly over the arch did I jump up and wave my cloak. Faiz instantly pressed his handle, and the great noise and dust and black-ness burst up, as at Mudowwara a week before, and enveloped me where I sat, while the green-yellow sickly smoke of lyddite hung sluggishly about the wreck. The Lewis guns rattled out suddenly, three or four short bursts: there was a yell from the Arabs, and, headed by Pisani sounding the women's vibrant battle-cry, they rushed in a wild torrent for the train.

A Turk appeared on the buffers of the fourth truck from the end, loosed the couplings, and let the tail of the train slip back down the gradient. I made a languid effort to get behind the wheel with a stone, but scarcely cared enough to do it well. It seemed fair and witty that this much of the booty should escape. A Turkish colonel from the window fired at me with a Mauser pistol, cutting the flesh of my hip. I laughed at his too-great energy, which thought, like a regular officer, to promote the war by the killing of an individual.

Our mine had taken out the near arch of the bridge. Of the loco-motive, the fire-box was torn open, and many tubes burst. The cab was cleared out, a cylinder gone, the frame buckled, two driving wheels and their journals shattered. The tender and first waggon had telescoped. About twenty Turks were dead, and others prisoners, including four officers, who stood by the line weeping for the life which the Arabs had no mind to take.

The contents of the trucks were food-stuffs, some seventy tons of them; 'urgently needed', according to the way-bill, in Medain Salih. We sent one way-bill to Feisal, as detailed report of our success, and left the other receipted in the van. We also kicked northward some dozen civilians, who had thought they were going to Medina.

Pisani superintended the carrying off or destruction of the booty. As before, the Arabs were now merely camel-drivers, walking behind laden pack-animals. Farraj held my camel, while Salem and Dheilan helped with the exploder and the too-heavy wire. Rescue parties of Turks were four hundred yards away when we had finished, but we rode off without a man killed or wounded.

My pupils practised the art of mining afterwards by themselves, and taught others. Rumour of their fortune rolled about the tribes in a growing wave: not always intelligently. 'Send us a lurens and we will blow up trains with it', wrote the Beni Atiyeh to Feisal. He lent them Saad, a cut-and-thrust Ageyli, by whose help they got an important train carrying Suleiman Rifada, our old nuisance of Wejh, with twenty thousand pounds in gold, and precious trophies. Saad repeated history by saving only the wire for his share.

In the next four months our experts from Akaba destroyed seventeen locomotives. Travelling became an uncertain terror for the enemy. At Damascus people scrambled for the back seats in trains, even paid extra for them. The engine-drivers struck. Civilian traffic nearly ceased; and we extended our threat to Aleppo by the mere posting a notice one night on Damascus Town Hall, that good Arabs would henceforward travel by the Syrian railway at their own risk. The loss of the engines was sore upon the Turks. Since the rolling stock was pooled for Palestine and Hejaz, our destructions not merely made the mass evacuation of Medina impossible, but began to pinch the army about Jerusalem, just as the British threat grew formidable.

Meanwhile Egypt had wired for me. An aeroplane carried me to

N*

G.H.Q., where Allenby by splendour of will was re-creating the broken British Army. He asked what our railway efforts meant; or rather if they meant anything beyond the melo-dramatic advertisement they gave Feisal's cause.

I explained my hope to leave the line just working, but only just, to Medina; where Fakhri's corps fed itself at less cost than if in prison at Cairo. The surest way to limit the line without killing it was by attacking trains. The Arabs put into mining a zest absent from their pure demolitions. We could not yet break the line, since railhead was the strongest point of a railway, and we preferred weakness in the nearest enemy neighbour till our regular army was trained and equipped and numerous enough to invest Maan.

He asked about Wadi Musa, because Turkish messages showed their intention to assault it at once. I explained that we had tried to provoke the Turks to attack Wadi Musa, and were about to be rewarded by their falling, foxed and fogged, into our trap. We went about in parties, not in stiff formation, and their aeroplanes failed to estimate us. No spies could count us, either, since even ourselves had not the smallest idea of our strength at any given moment.

On the other hand, we knew them exactly; each single unit, and every man they moved. They treated us as regulars, and before venturing a move against us calculated the total force we could meet them with. We, less orthodox, knew exactly what they would meet us with. This was our balance. For these years the Arab Movement lived on the exhilarating but slippery tableland between 'could' and 'would'. We allowed no margin for accident: indeed 'no margins' was the Akaba motto, continuously in the mouths of all.

When at last it came, Jemal's great attack on Wadi Musa made no noise. Maulud presided beautifully. He opened his centre, and with the greatest of humour let in the Turks until they broke their faces against the vertical cliffs of the Arab refuge. Then, while they were still puzzled and hurt, he came down simultaneously on both flanks. They never again attacked a prepared Arab position. Their losses had been heavy, but the loss of nerve at finding us invisible and yet full of back-lash cost them more than the casualties. Thanks to Maulud, Akaba became quit of all concern for its own present safety.

BOOK VI

THE RAID UPON THE BRIDGES

Chapters LXIX to LXXXI

By November, 1917, Allenby was ready to open a general attack against the Turks along his whole front. The Arabs should have done the same in their sector: but I was afraid to put everything on a throw, and designed instead the specious operation of cutting the Yarmuk Valley Railway, to throw into disorder the expected Turkish retreat. This half-measure met with the failure it deserved.

CHAPTER LXIX

OCTOBER, accordingly, was a month of anticipation for us, in the knowledge that Allenby, with Bols and Dawnay, was planning to attack the Gaza–Beersheba line; while the Turks, a quite small army strongly entrenched, with excellent lateral communications, had been puffed up by successive victories to imagine that all British generals were incompetent to keep what their troops had won for them by dint of sheer hard fighting.

They deceived themselves. Allenby's coming had re-made the English. His breadth of personality swept away the mist of private or departmental jealousies behind which Murray and his men had worked. General Lynden Bell made way for General Bols, Allenby's chief of staff, in France, a little, quick, brave, pleasant man; a tactical soldier, perhaps, but principally an admirable and effaced foil to Allenby, who used to relax himself on Bols. Unfortunately, neither of them had the power of choosing men; but Chetwode's judgement completed them with Guy Dawnay as third member of the staff.

Bols had never an opinion, nor any knowledge. Dawnay was mainly intellect. He lacked the eagerness of Bols, and the calm drive and human understanding of Allenby, who was the man the men worked for, the image we worshipped. Dawnay's cold, shy mind gazed upon our efforts with bleak eye, always thinking, thinking. Beneath this mathematical surface he hid passionate many-sided convictions, a reasoned scholarship in higher warfare, and the brilliant bitterness of a judgement disappointed with us, and with life.

He was the least professional of soldiers, a banker who read Greek history, a strategist unashamed, and a burning poet with strength over daily things. During the war he had had the grief of planning the attack at Suvla (spoiled by incompetent tacticians) and the battle for Gaza. As each work of his was ruined he withdrew further into the hardnesses of frosted pride, for he was of the stuff of fanatics.

Allenby, by not seeing his dissatisfaction, broke into him; and Dawnay replied by giving for the Jerusalem advance all the talent which he abundantly possessed. A cordial union of two such men made the Turks' position hopeless from the outset.

Their divergent characters were mirrored in the intricate plan. Gaza had been entrenched on a European scale with line after line of defences in reserve. It was so obviously the enemy's strongest point, that the British higher command had twice chosen it for frontal attack. Allenby, fresh from France, insisted that any further assault must be delivered by overwhelming numbers of men and guns, and their thrust maintained by enormous quantities of all kinds of transport. Bols nodded his assent.

Dawnay was not the man to fight a straight battle. He sought to destroy the enemy's strength with the least fuss. Like a master politician he used the bluff Chief as a cloak for the last depth of justifiable slimness. He advised a drive at the far end of the Turkish line, near Beersheba. To make his victory cheap he wanted the enemy main force behind Gaza, which would be best secured if the British concentration was hidden so that the Turks would believe the flank attack to be a shallow feint. Bols nodded his assent.

Consequently the movements were made in great secrecy; but Dawnay found an ally in his intelligence staff who advised him to go beyond negative precautions, and to give the enemy specific (and speciously wrong) information of the plans he matured.

This ally was Meinertzhagen, a student of migrating birds drifted into soldiering, whose hot immoral hatred of the enemy expressed itself as readily in trickery as in violence. He persuaded Dawnay: Allenby reluctantly agreed: Bols assented, and the work began.

Meinertzhagen knew no half measures. He was logical, an idealist of the deepest, and so possessed by his convictions that he was willing to harness evil to the chariot of good. He was a strategist, a geographer, and a silent laughing masterful man; who took as blithe a pleasure in deceiving his enemy (or his friend) by some unscrupulous jest, as in spattering the brains of a cornered mob of Germans one by one with his African knob-kerri. His instincts were abetted by an immensely powerful body and a savage brain, which chose the best way to its purpose, unhampered by doubt or habit. Meiner thought out false Army papers, elaborate and confidential, which to a trained staff officer would indicate wrong positions for Allenby's main formation, a wrong direction of the coming attack, and a date some days too late. This information was led up to by careful hints given in code wireless messages. When he knew the enemy had picked these up, Meinertz-hagen rode out with his note books, on reconnaissance. He pushed forward until the enemy saw him. In the ensuing gallop he lost all his loose equipment and very nearly himself, but was rewarded by seeing the enemy reserves held behind Gaza and their whole preparations swung towards the coast and made less urgent. Simultaneously, an Army order by Ali Fuad Pasha cautioned his staff against carrying documents into the line.

We on the Arab front were very intimate with the enemy. Our Arab officers had been Turkish officers, and knew every leader on the other side personally. They had suffered the same training, thought the same, took the same point of view. By practising modes of approach upon the Arabs we could explore the Turks: understand, almost get inside, their minds. Relation between us and them was universal, for the civil population of the enemy area was wholly ours without pay or persuasion. In consequence our intelligence service was the widest, fullest and most certain imaginable.

We knew, better than Allenby, the enemy hollowness, and the magnitude of the British resources. We under-estimated the crippling effect of Allenby's too plentiful artillery, and the cumbrous intricacy of his infantry and cavalry, which moved only with rheumatic slow-ness. We hoped Allenby would be given a month's fine weather; and, in that case, expected to see him take, not merely Jerusalem, but Haifa too, sweeping the Turks in ruin through the hills.

Such would be our moment, and we needed to be ready for it in the spot where our weight and tactics would be least expected and most damaging. For my eyes the centre of attraction was Deraa, the junction of the Jerusalem-Haifa-Damascus-Medina railways, the navel of the Turkish Armies in Syria, the common point of all their fronts; and, by chance, an area in which lay great untouched reserves of Arab fighting men, educated and armed by Feisal from Akaba. We could there use Rualla, Serahin, Serdiyeh, Khoreisha; and, far stronger than tribes, the settled peoples of Hauran and Jebel Druse.

I pondered for a while whether we should not call up all these

adherents and tackle the Turkish communications in force. We were
certain, with any management, of twelve thousand men: enough to
rush Deraa, to smash all the railway lines, even to take Damascus by
surprise. Any one of these things would make the position of the
Beersheba army critical: and my temptation to stake our capital
instantly upon the issue was very sore.

Not for the first or last time service to two masters irked me. I was
one of Allenby's officers, and in his confidence: in return, he expected
me to do the best I could for him. I was Feisal's adviser, and Feisal
relied upon the honesty and competence of my advice so far as often to
take it without argument. Yet I could not explain to Allenby the whole
Arab situation, nor disclose the full British plan to Feisal.

The local people were imploring us to come. Sheikh Talal el
Hareidhin, leader of the hollow country about Deraa, sent in repeated
messages that, with a few of our riders as proof of Arab support, he
would give us Deraa. Such an exploit would have done the Allenby
business, but was not one which Feisal could scrupulously afford unless
he had a fair hope of then establishing himself there. Deraa's sudden
capture, followed by a retreat, would have involved the massacre, or the
ruin of all the splendid peasantry of the district.

They could only rise once, and their effort on that occasion must be
decisive. To call them out now was to risk the best asset Feisal held for
eventual success, on the speculation that Allenby's first attack would
sweep the enemy before it, and that the month of November would be
rainless, favourable to a rapid advance.

I weighed the English army in my mind, and could not honestly
assure myself of them. The men were often gallant fighters, but their
generals as often gave away in stupidity what they had gained in
ignorance. Allenby was quite untried, sent to us with a not-blameless
record from France, and his troops had broken down in and been
broken by the Murray period. Of course, we were fighting for an
Allied victory, and since the English were the leading partners, the
Arabs would have, in the last resort, to be sacrificed for them. But was
it the last resort? The war generally was going neither well nor very
ill, and it seemed as though there might be time for another try next
year. So I decided to postpone the hazard for the Arabs' sake.

CHAPTER LXX

HOWEVER, the Arab Movement lived on Allenby's good pleasure, so it was needful to undertake some operation, less than a general revolt, in the enemy rear: an operation which could be achieved by a raiding party without involving the settled peoples; and yet one which would please him by being of material help to the British pursuit of the enemy. These conditions and qualifications pointed, upon consideration, to an attempted cutting of one of the great bridges in the Yarmuk valley.

It was by the narrow and precipitous gorge of the River Yarmuk that the railway from Palestine climbed to Hauran, on its way to Damascus. The depth of the Jordan depression, and the abruptness of the eastern plateau-face made this section of the line most difficult to build. The engineers had to lay it in the very course of the winding river-valley: and to gain its development the line had to cross and recross the stream continually by a series of bridges, the farthest west and the farthest east of which were hardest to replace.

To cut either of these bridges would isolate the Turkish army in Palestine, for one fortnight, from its base in Damascus, and destroy its power of escaping from Allenby's advance. To reach the Yarmuk we should need to ride from Akaba, by way of Azrak, some four hundred and twenty miles. The Turks thought the danger from us so remote that they guarded the bridges insufficiently.

Accordingly we suggested the scheme to Allenby, who asked that it be done on November the fifth, or one of the three following days. If it succeeded, and the weather held up afterwards for a fortnight, the odds were that no coherent unit of von Kress's army would survive its retreat to Damascus. The Arabs would then have their opportunity to carry their wave forward into the great capital, taking up at the half-way point from the British whose original impulse would then be nearly exhausted, with the exhaustion of their transport.

For such an eventuality we needed at Azrak an authority to lead the potential local adherents. Nasir, our usual pioneer, was absent: but out with the Beni Sakhr was Ali ibn el Hussein, the youthful and attractive Harith Sherif, who had distinguished himself in Feisal's early desperate days about Medina, and later had out-newcombed New-come about el Ula.

Ali, having been Jemal's guest in Damascus, had learned something of Syria: so I begged a loan of him from Feisal. His courage, his resource, and his energy were proven. There had never been any adventure, since our beginning, too dangerous for Ali to attempt, nor a disaster too deep for him to face with his high yell of a laugh.

He was physically splendid: not tall nor heavy, but so strong that he would kneel down, resting his forearms palm-up on the ground, and rise to his feet with a man on each hand. In addition, Ali could outstrip a trotting camel on his bare feet, keep his speed over half a mile and then leap into the saddle. He was impertinent, headstrong, conceited; as reckless in word as in deed; impressive (if he pleased) on public occasions, and fairly educated for a person whose native ambition was to excel the nomads of the desert in war and sport.

Ali would bring us the Beni Sakhr. We had good hopes of the Serahin, the tribe at Azrak. I was in touch with the Beni Hassan. The Rualla, of course, at this season were away at their winter quarters, so that our greatest card in the Hauran could not be played. Faiz el Ghusein had gone into the Lejah to prepare for action against the Hauran Railway if the signal came. Explosives were stored in desirable places. Our friends in Damascus were warned; and Ali Riza Pasha Rikabi, the city's military governor for the innocent Turks, and at the same time chief agent and conspirator for the Sherif, took quiet steps to retain control if the emergency arose.

My detailed plan was to rush from Azrak, under guidance of Rafa (that most gallant sheikh who had convoyed me in June), to Um Keis, in one or two huge marches with a handful of, perhaps, fifty men. Um Keis was Gadara, very precious with its memories of Menippus and of Meleager, the immoral Greek-Syrian whose self-expression marked the highest point of Syrian letters. It stood just over the westernmost of the Yarmuk bridges, a steel masterpiece whose destruction would fairly enrol me in the Gadarene school. Only half a dozen sentries were stationed actually on the girders and abutments. Reliefs for them were supplied from a garrison of sixty, in the station buildings of Hemme, where the hot springs of Gadara yet gushed out to the advantage of local sick. My hope was to persuade some of the Abu Tayi under Zaal to come with me. These men-wolves would make certain the actual storming of the bridge. To prevent enemy reinforcements coming up we would sweep the approaches with machine-guns, handled by Captain Bray's Indian volunteers from the cavalry division in France, under Jemadar Hassan Shah, a firm and experienced man. They had been months up country, rail-cutting, from Wejh, and might fairly be assumed to have become experts on camel-back, fit for the forced marches in prospect.

The demolition of great underslung girders with limited weights of explosive was a precise operation, and demanded a necklace of blasting gelatine, fired electrically. The *Humber* made us canvas straps and buckles, to simplify the fixing. None the less, the job remained a difficult one to do under fire. For fear of a casualty, Wood, the base engineer at Akaba, the only sapper available, was invited to come along and double me. He immediately agreed, though knowing he had been condemned medically for active service as the result of a bullet through the head in France. George Lloyd, who was spending a last few days in Akaba before going to Versailles on a regretted inter-allied Commission, said that he would ride up with us to Jefer: as he was one of the best fellows and least obtrusive travellers alive, his coming added greatly to our forlorn anticipation.

We were making our last preparations when an unexpected ally arrived in Emir Abd el Kader el Jezairi, grandson of the chivalrous defender of Algiers against the French. The exiled family had lived in Damascus for a generation. One of them, Omar, had been hanged by Jemal for treason disclosed in the Picot papers. The others had been deported, and Abd el Kader told us a long story of his escape from Brusa, and his journey, with a thousand adventures, across Anatolia to Damascus. In reality, he had been enlarged by the Turks upon request of the Khedive Abbas Hilmi, and sent down by him on private business to Mecca. He went there, saw King Hussein, and came back with a crimson banner, and noble gifts, his crazy mind half-persuaded of our right, and glowing jerkily with excitement.

To Feisal he offered the bodies and souls of his villagers, sturdy, hard-smiting Algerian exiles living compactly along the north bank of the Yarmuk. We seized at the chance this would give us to control for a little time the middle section of the Valley railway, including two or three main bridges, without the disability of raising the country-side; since the Algerians were hated strangers and the Arab peasantry would not join them. Accordingly, we put off calling Rafa to meet us at Azrak, and said not a word to Zaal, concentrating our thoughts instead on Wadi Khalid and its bridges.

While we were in this train of mind arrived a telegram from Colonel Bremond, warning us that Abd el Kader was a spy in pay of the Turks. It was disconcerting. We watched him narrowly, but found no proof of the charge, which was not to be accepted blindly, as from Bremond, who was more a liability than our colleague; his military temper might have carried away his judgement when he heard Abd el Kader's out-spoken public and private denunciations of France. The French conception of their country as a fair woman lent to them a national spitefulness against those who scorned her charms.

Feisal told Abd el Kader to ride with Ali and myself, and said to me, 'I know he is mad. I think he is honest. Guard your heads and use him'. We carried on, showing him our complete confidence, on the principle that a crook would not credit our honesty, and that an honest man was made a crook soonest by suspicion. As a matter of fact, he was an Islamic fanatic, half-insane with religious enthusiasm and a most violent belief in himself. His moslem susceptibilities were outraged by my undisguised christianity. His pride was hurt by our companion-ship; for the tribes greeted Ali as greater, and treated me as better, than himself. His bullet-headed stupidity broke down Ali's self-control twice or thrice into painful scenes: while his final effort was to leave us in the lurch at a desperate moment, after hindering our march and upsetting ourselves and our plans as far as he could.

CHAPTER LXXI

STARTING was as difficult as ever. For my bodyguard I took six recruits. Of these Mahmud was a native of the Yarmuk. He was an alert and hot-tempered lad of nineteen, with the petulance often accompanying curly hair. Another, Aziz, of Tafas, an older fellow, had spent three years with the Beduin in avoidance of military service. Though capable with camels, he was a shallow spirit, almost rabbit-mouthed, but proud. A third was Mustafa, a gentle boy from Deraa, very honest, who went about sadly by himself because he was deaf, and ashamed of his infirmity. One day on the beach, in a short word he had begged admittance to my bodyguard. So evidently did he expect to be refused that I took him; and it was a good choice for the others, since he was a mild peasant, whom they could bully into all the menial tasks. Yet he, too, was happy, for he was among desperate fellows, and the world would think him desperate. To balance his inefficiency on the march I enrolled Showak and Salem, two Sherari camel-herds, and Abd el Rahman, a runaway slave from Riyadth.

Of the old bodyguard I gave Mohammed and Ali a rest. They were tired after train-wrecking adventures; and, like their camels, needed to pasture quietly awhile. This left Ahmed the inevitable head man. His ruthless energy deserved promotion, but the obvious choice as ever failed. He misused his power and became oppressive; so it was his last march with me. I took Kreim for the camels; and Rahail, the lusty, conceited Haurani lad, for whom overwork was the grace which kept him continent. Matar, a parasite fellow of the Beni Hassan, attached himself to us. His fat peasant's buttocks filled his camel-saddle, and took nearly as large a share in the lewd or lurid jokes which, on march, helped pass my guards' leisure. We might enter Beni Hassan territory, where he had some influence. His unblushing greed made us sure of him, till his expectations failed.

My service was now profitable, for I knew my worth to the movement, and spent freely to keep myself safe. Rumour, for once in a helpful mood, gilded my open hand. Farraj and Daud, with Khidr and Mijbil, two Biasha, completed the party.

Farraj and Daud were capable and merry on the road, which they loved as all the lithe Ageyl loved it; but in camp their excess of spirit led them continually into dear affairs. This time they surpassed themselves by disappearing on the morning of our departure. At noon came a message from Sheikh Yusuf that they were in his prison, and would I talk to him about it? I went up to the house and found his bulk shaking between laughter and rage. He had just bought a cream-coloured riding-camel of purest blood. The beast had strayed in the evening into the palm-garden where my Ageyl were camped. They never suspected she belonged to the Governor, but laboured till dawn dyeing her head bright red with henna, and her legs blue with indigo, before turning her loose.

Akaba bubbled immediately in an uproar about this circus beast. Yusuf recognized her with difficulty and hurled all his police abroad to find the criminals. The two friends were dragged before the judgement seat, stained to the elbows with dye, and loudly protesting their entire innocence. Circumstances, however, were too strong; and Yusuf after doing his best with a palm-rib to hurt their feelings, put them in irons for a slow week's meditation. My concern made good his damage by the loan of a camel till his own should be respectable. Then I explained our instant need of the sinners, and promised another dose of his treatment for them when their skins were fit: so he ordered their release. They were delighted to escape the verminous prison on any terms, and rejoined us singing.

This business had delayed us. So we had an immense final meal in the luxury of camp, and started in the evening. For four hours we marched slowly: a first march was always slow, and both camels and men hated the setting out on a new hazard. Loads slipped, saddles had to be re-girthed, and riders changed. In addition to my own camels (Ghazala, the old grandmother, now far gone in foal, and Rima, a full-pointed Sherari camel which the Sukhur had stolen from the Rualla) and those of the bodyguard, I had mounted the Indians, and lent one to Wood (who was delicate in the saddle and rode a fresh animal nearly every day), and one to Thorne, Lloyd's yeomanry trooper, who sat his saddle like an Arab and looked workmanlike in a head-cloth, with a striped cloak over his khaki. Lloyd himself was on a thoroughbred Dheraiyeh which Feisul had lent him: a fine, fast-looking animal, but clipped after mange and thin.

Our party straggled. Wood fell behind, and my men, being fresh, and having much work to keep the Indians together, lost touch with him. So he found himself alone with Thorne, and missed our turn to the east, in the blackness which always filled the depths of the Itm gorge by night, except when the moon was directly overhead. They went on up the main track towards Guweira, riding for hours; but at last decided to wait for day in a side valley. Both were new to the country, and not sure of the Arabs, so they took turns to keep watch. We guessed what had happened when they failed to appear at our midnight halt, and before dawn Ahmed, Aziz and Abd el Rahman went back, with orders to scatter up the three or four practicable roads and bring the missing pair to Rumm.

I stayed with Lloyd and the main body as their guide across the curved slopes of pink sandstone and tamarisk-green valleys to Rumm. Air and light were so wonderful that we wandered without thinking in the least of to-morrow. Indeed, had I not Lloyd to talk to? The world became very good. A faint shower last evening had brought earth and sky together in the mellow day. The colours in cliffs and trees and soil were so pure, so vivid, that we ached for real contact with them, and at our tethered inability to carry anything of them away. We were full of leisure. The Indians proved bad camel-masters, while Farraj and Daud pleaded a new form of saddle-soreness, called 'Yusufiyeh', which made them walk mile after mile.

We entered Rumm at last, while the crimson sunset burned on its stupendous cliffs and slanted ladders of hazy fire down the walled avenue. Wood and Thorne were there already, in the sandstone amphitheatre of the springs. Wood was ill, and lying on the platform of my old camp. Abd el Rahman had caught them before noon, and persuaded them to follow him after a good deal of misunderstanding, for their few words of Egyptian did not help much with his clipped Aridh dialect or the Howeiti slang with which he eked it out. He had cut across the hills by a difficult path to their great discomfort.

Wood had been hungry and hot and worried, angry to the point of refusing the native mess which Abd el Rahman contrived them in a way-side tent. He had begun to believe that he would never see us again, and was ungrateful when we proved too overcome with the awe that Rumm compelled on her visitors to sympathize deeply with his sufferings. In fact, we stared and said 'Yes', and left him lying there while we wandered whispering about the wonder of the place. Fortunately Ahmed and Thorne thought more of food: and with supper friendly relations were restored.

Next day, while we were saddling, Ali and Abd el Kader appeared. Lloyd and I had a second lunch with them, for they were quarrelling, and to have guests held them in check. Lloyd was the rare sort of traveller who could eat anything with anybody, anyhow and at any time. Then, making pace, we pushed after our party down the giant valley, whose hills fell short of architecture only in design.

At the bottom we crossed the flat Gaa, matching our camels in a burst over its velvet surface, until we overtook the main body, and scattered them with the excitement of our gallop. The Indians' soberly laden camels danced like ironmongery till they had shed their burdens. Then we calmed ourselves, and plodded together gently up Wadi Hafira, a gash like a sword-cut into the plateau. At its head lay a stiff pass to the height of Batra; but to-day we fell short of this, and out of laziness and craving for comfort stopped in the sheltered bottom of the valley. We lit great fires, which were cheerful in the cool evening. Farraj prepared rice in his manner for me as usual. Lloyd and Wood and Thorne had brought with them bully beef in tins and British army biscuits. So we joined ranks and feasted.

Next day we climbed the zigzag broken pass, the grassy street of Hafira, below us framing a cone-hill in its centre, with, as background, the fantastic grey domes and glowing pyramids of the mountains of Rumm, prolonged to-day into wider fantasies by the cloud-masses brooding over them. We watched our long train wind upwards, till before noon the camels, Arabs, Indians and baggage had reached the top without accident. Contentedly we plumped ourselves down in the first green valley over the crest, sheltered from the wind, and warmed by the faint sunshine which tempered the autumn chill of this high tableland. Someone began to talk again about food.

CHAPTER LXXII

I WENT away north, scouting with Awad, a Sherari camel boy, engaged in Rumm without investigation. There were so many baggage camels in our party, and the Indians proved such novices at loading and leading them, that my bodyguard were being diverted from their proper duty of riding with me. So when Showakh introduced his cousin, a Khayal Sherari who would serve with me on any conditions, I accepted him at the glance: and now set out to measure his worth in a predicament.

We circled round Aba el Lissan to make sure that the Turks were in seemly idleness, for they had a habit of rushing a mounted patrol over the Batra sites at sudden notice, and I had no mind to put our party into unnecessary action yet. Awad, was a ragged brown-skinned lad of perhaps eighteen, splendidly built, with the muscles and sinews of an athlete, active as a cat, alive in the saddle (he rode magnificently) and not ill-looking, though with something of the base appearance of the Sherarat, and in his savage eye an air of constant and rather suspicious expectancy, as though he looked any moment for something new from life, and that something not of his seeking or ordering, nor wholly grateful.

These Sherarat helots were an enigma of the desert. Other men might have hopes or illusions. Sherarat knew that nothing better than physical existence was willingly permitted them by mankind in this world or another. Such extreme degradation was a positive base on which to build a trust. I treated them exactly like the others in my bodyguard. This they found astonishing; and yet pleasant, when they had learned that my protection was active and sufficient. While they served me they became wholly my property, and good slaves they were, for nothing practicable in the desert was beneath their dignity, or beyond their tempered strength and experience.

Awad before me showed himself confused and self-conscious, though with his fellows he could be merry and full of japes. His engagement was a sudden fortune beyond dreams, and he was pitifully determined to suit my mind. For the moment this was to wander across the Maan high road in order to draw the Turks' notice. When we had succeeded, and they trotted out in chase, we returned back, doubled again, and so tricked their mule-riders away northward out of the direction of danger. Awad took gleeful concern in the game and handled his new rifle well.

Afterwards I climbed with him to the top of a hill overlooking Batra, and the valleys which sloped to Aba el Lissan, and we lay there lazily till afternoon, watching the Turks riding in a vain direction, and our fellows asleep, and their pasturing camels, and the shadows of the low clouds seeming like gentle hollows as they chased over the grass in the pale sunlight. It was peaceful, chilly, and very far from the fretting world. The austerity of height shamed back the vulgar baggage of our cares. In the place of consequence it set freedom, power to be alone, to slip the escort of our manufactured selves; a rest and forgetfulness of the chains of being.

But Awad could not forget his appetite and the new sensation of power in my caravan to satisfy it regularly each day: so he fidgeted about the ground on his belly chewing innumerable stalks of grass, and talking to me of his animal joys in jerky phrases with averted face, till we saw Ali's cavalcade beginning to lip over the head of the pass. Then we ran down the slopes to meet them, and heard how he had lost four camels on the pass, two broken by falls, two failing through weakness as they mounted the rocky ledges. Also, he had fallen out again with Abd el Kader, from whose deafness and conceit and boorish manners he prayed God to deliver him. The Emir moved so cumbrously, having no sense of the road: and flatly refused to join with Lloyd and myself into one caravan, for safety.

We left them to follow us after dark, and as they had no guide, I loaned them Awad. We would meet again in Auda's tents. Then we moved forward over shallow valleys and cross-ridges till the sun set behind the last high bank, from whose top we saw the square box of the station at Ghadir el Haj breaking artificially out of the level, miles and miles away. Behind us in the valley were broom bushes, so we called a halt, and made our supper-fires. This evening Hassan Shah devised a pleasant notion (later to become a habit) of winding up our meal by an offering of his Indian tea. We were too greedy and grateful to refuse, and shamelessly exhausted his tea and sugar before fresh rations could be sent him from the base.

Lloyd and I marked the bearing of the railway where we purposed to cross just below Shedia. As the stars rose we agreed that we must march upon Orion. So we started and marched on Orion for hour after hour, with effect that Orion seemed no nearer, and there were no signs of anything between us and him. We had debouched from the ridges upon the plain, and the plain was never-ending, and mono-tonously striped by shallow wadi-beds, with low, flat, straight banks, which in the milky star-light looked always like the earthwork of the expected railway. The going underfoot was firm, and the cool air of the desert in our faces made the camels swing out freely.

Lloyd and I went in front to spy out the line, that the main body might not be involved if chance put us against a Turkish blockhouse or night-patrol. Our fine camels, lightly ridden, set too long a stride; so that, without knowing, we drew more and more ahead of the laden Indians. Hassan Shah the Jemadar threw out a man to keep us in sight, and then another, and after that a third, till his party was a hurrying string of connecting files. Then he sent up an urgent whisper to go slowly, but the message which reached us after its passage through three languages was unintelligible.

We halted and so knew that the quiet night was full of sounds, while the scents of withering grass ebbed and flowed about us with the dying wind. Afterwards we marched again more slowly, as it seemed for hours, and the plain was still barred with deceitful dykes, which kept our attention at unprofitable stretch. We felt the stars were shifting and that we were steering wrong. Lloyd had a compass somewhere. We halted and groped in his deep saddle-bags. Thorne rode up and found it. We stood around calculating on its luminous arrow-head, and deserted Orion for a more auspicious northern star. Then again interminably forward till as we climbed a larger bank Lloyd reined up with a gasp and pointed. Fair in our track on the horizon were two cubes blacker than the sky, and by them a pointed roof. We were bearing straight for Shedia station, nearly into it.

We swung to the right, and jogged hastily across an open space, a little nervous lest some of the caravan strung out behind us should miss the abrupt change of course: but all was well, and a few minutes later in the next hollow we exchanged our thrill in English and Turkish, Arabic and Urdu. Behind us broke out a faint pulse-quickening clamour of dogs in the Turkish camp.

We now knew our place, and took a fresh bearing to avoid the first blockhouse below Shedia. We led off confidently, expecting in a little to cross the line. Yet again time dragged and nothing showed itself. It was midnight, we had marched for six hours, and Lloyd began to speak bitterly of reaching Bagdad in the morning. There could be no railway here. Thorne saw a row of trees, and saw them move; the bolts of our rifles clicked, but they were only trees.

We gave up hope, and rode carelessly, nodding in our saddles, letting our tired eyes lid themselves. My Rima lost her temper suddenly. With a squeal she plunged sideways, nearly unseating me, pranced wildly over two banks and a ditch and flung herself flat in a dusty place. I hit her over the head, and she rose and paced forward nervously. Again the Indians lagged far behind our hasty selves; but after an hour the last bank of to-night loomed differently in front of us. It took straight shape, and over its length grew darker patches which might be the shadowed mouths of culverts. We spurred our minds to a fresh interest, and drove our animals swiftly and silently forward. When we were nearer it, the bank put up a fencing of sharp spikes along its edge. These were the telegraph poles. A white-headed figure checked us for a moment, but he never stirred, and so we judged him a kilometre post.

Quickly we halted our party and rode to one side and then straight in, to challenge what lay behind the quiet of the place, expecting the darkness to spout fire at us suddenly, and the silence to volley out in rifle shots. But there was no alarm. We reached the bank and found it deserted. We dismounted and ran up and down each way two hundred yards: nobody. There was room for our passage.

We ordered the others immediately over into the empty, friendly desert on the east, and sat ourselves on the metals under the singing wires, while the long line of shadowy bulks wavered up out of the dark, shuffled a little on the bank and its ballast, and passed down behind us into the dark in that strained noiselessness which was a night march of camels. The last one crossed. Our little group collected about a telegraph post. Out of a short scuffle Thorne rose slowly up the pole to catch the lowest wire and swing himself to its insulator-bracket. He reached for the top, and a moment later there was a loud metallic twang and shaking of the post as the cut wire leaped back each way into the air, and slapped itself free from six or more poles on either side. The second and third wires followed it, twisting noisily along the stony ground, and yet no answering sound came out of the night, showing that we had passed rightly in the empty distance of two blockhouses. Thorne, with splintery hands, slid down the tottering pole. We walked to our kneeling camels, and trotted after the company. Another hour, and we ordered a rest till dawn; but before then were roused by a brief flurry of rifle fire and the tapping of a machine-gun far away to the north. Little Ali and Abd el Kadir were not making so clean a crossing of the line.

Next morning, in a cheerful sunshine, we marched up parallel with the line to salute the first train from Maan, and then struck inland over the strange Jefer plain. The day was close, and the sun's power increased, making mirages on all the heated flats. Riding apart from our straggling party, we saw some of them drowned in the silver flood, others swimming high over its changing surface, which stretched and shrank with each swaying of the camel, or inequality of ground.

Early in the afternoon we found Auda camped unobtrusively in the broken, bushy expanse south-west of the wells. He received us with constraint. His large tent, with the women, had been sent away beyond reach of the Turkish aeroplanes. There were few Toweiha present: and those in violent dispute over the distribution of tribal wages. The old man was sad we should find him in such weakness.

I did my best tactfully to smooth the troubles by giving their minds a new direction and countervailing interests. Successfully too, for they smiled, which with Arabs was often half the battle. Enough advantage for the time; we adjourned to eat with Mohammed el Dheilan. He was a better diplomat, because less open than Auda; and would have looked cheerful if he thought proper, whatever the truth. So we were made very welcome to his platter of rice and meat and dried tomatoes. Mohammed, a villager at heart, fed too well.

After the meal, as we were wandering back over the grey dry

ditches, like mammoth-wallows, which floods had hacked deeply into the fibrous mud, I broached to Zaal my plans for an expedition to the Yarmuk bridges. He disliked the idea very much. Zaal in October was not the Zaal of August. Success was changing the hard-riding gallant of spring into a prudent man, whose new wealth made life precious to him. In the spring he would have led me anywhere; but the last raid had tried his nerve, and now he said he would mount only if I made a personal point of it.

I asked what party we could make up; and he named three of the men in the camp as good fellows for so desperate a hope. The rest of the tribe were away, dissatisfied. To take three Toweiha would be worse than useless, for their just conceit would inflame the other men, while they themselves were too few to suffice alone: so I said I would try elsewhere. Zaal showed his relief.

While we were still discussing what we ought to do (for I needed the advice of Zaal, one of the finest raiders alive, and most competent to judge my half-formed scheme), a scared lad rushed to our coffee-hearth and blurted that riders in a dust-cloud were coming up fast from the side of Maan. The Turks there had a mule-regiment and a cavalry regiment, and were always boasting that they would some day visit the Abu Tayi. So we jumped up to receive them.

Auda had fifteen men, of whom five were able-bodied, and the rest greybeards or boys, but we were thirty strong, and I pondered the hard luck of the Turkish commander who had chosen for his surprise the day on which there happened to be guesting with the Howeitat a section of Indian machine-gunners who knew their business. We couched and knee-haltered the camels in the deeper water-cuts, and placed the Vickers and Lewis in others of these natural trenches, admirably screened with alkali bushes, and commanding a flat field eight hundred yards each way. Auda dropped his tents, and threw out his riflemen to supplement our fire; and then we waited easily till the first horseman rode up the bank on to our level, and we saw they were Ali ibn el Hussein and Abd el Kadir, coming to Jefer from the enemy direction. We foregathered merrily, while Mohammed produced a second edition of tomato-rice for Ali's comfort. They had lost two men and a mare in the shooting on the railway in the night.

CHAPTER LXXIII

LLOYD was to go back from here to Versailles, and we asked Auda for a guide to take him across the line. About the man there was no difficulty, but great difficulty in mounting him; for the Howeitat camels were at pasture: and the nearest pasture lay a full day's journey south-east of these barren wells. I cut this difficulty by providing a mount for the new guide from my own beasts. Choice fell on my ancient Ghazala, whose pregnancy had proved more heavy than we thought. Before our long expedition ended she would be unfit for fast work. So, in honour of his good seat and cheerful spirit, Thorne was transferred to her, while the Howeitat stared open-mouthed. They esteemed Ghazala above all the camels of their desert and would have paid much for the honour of riding her, and here she was given to a soldier, whose pink face and eyes swollen with ophthalmia made him look feminine and tearful; a little, said Lloyd, like an abducted nun. It was a sorry thing to see Lloyd go. He was understanding, helped wisely, and wished our cause well. Also he was the only fully-taught man with us in Arabia, and in these few days together our minds had ranged abroad, discussing any book or thing in heaven or earth which crossed our fancy. When he left we were given over again to war and tribes and camels without end.

The night began with a surfeit of such work. The matter of the Howeitat must be put right. After dark we gathered round Auda's hearth, and for hours I was reaching out to this circle of fire-lit faces, playing on them with all the tortuous arts I knew, now catching one, now another (it was easy to see the flash in their eyes when a word got home); or again, taking a false line, and wasting minutes of precious time without response. The Abu Tayi were as hard-minded as they were hard-bodied, and the heat of conviction had burned out of them long since in stress of work.

Gradually I won my points, but the argument was yet marching near midnight when Auda held up his stick and called silence. We listened, wondering what the danger was, and after a while we felt a creeping reverberation, a cadence of blows too dull, too wide, too slow easily to find response in our ears. It was like the mutter of a distant, very lowly thunderstorm. Auda raised his haggard eyes towards the west, and said, 'The English guns'. Allenby was leading off in preparation, and his helpful sounds closed my case for me beyond dispute.

Next morning the atmosphere of the camp was serene and cordial. Old Auda, his difficulties over for this time, embraced me warmly, invoking peace upon us. At the last, whilst I was standing with my hand on my couched camel, he ran out, took me in his arms again, and strained me to him. I felt his harsh beard brush my ear as he whispered to me windily, 'Beware of Abd el Kader'. There were too many about us to say more.

We pushed on over the unending but weirdly beautiful Jefer flats, till night fell on us at the foot of a flint scarp, like a cliff above the plain. We camped there, in a snake-infested pocket of underwood. Our marches were short and very leisurely. The Indians had proved novices on the road. They had been for weeks inland from Wejh, and I had rashly understood that they were riders; but now, on good animals, and trying their best, they could average only thirty-five miles a day, a holiday for the rest of the party.

So for us each day was an easy movement, without effort, quite free from bodily strain. A golden weather of misty dawns, mild sunlight, and an evening chill added a strange peacefulness of nature to the peacefulness of our march. This week was a St. Martin's summer, which passed like a remembered dream. I felt only that it was very gentle, very comfortable, that the air was happy, and my friends content. Conditions so perfect must needs presage the ending of our time; but this certainty, because of its being unchallenged by any rebellious hope, served only to deepen the quiet of the autumnal present. There was no thought or care at all. My mind was as near stilled those days as ever in my life.

We camped for lunch and for a midday rest — the soldiers had to have three meals a day. Suddenly there was an alarm. Men on horses and camels appeared from the west and north and closed quickly on us. We snatched our rifles. The Indians, getting used to short notices, now carried their Vickers and Lewis mounted for action. After thirty seconds we were in complete posture of defence, though in this shallow country our position held little of advantage. To the front on each flank were my bodyguards in their brilliant clothes, lying spread out between the grey tufts of weed, with their rifles lovingly against their cheeks. By them the four neat groups of khaki Indians crouched about their guns. Behind them lay Sherif Ali's men, himself in their midst, bareheaded and keen, leaning easily upon his rifle. In the background the camel men were driving in our grazing animals to be under cover of our fire.

It was a picture that the party made. I was admiring ourselves and Sherif Ali was exhorting us to hold our fire till the attack became real, when Awad, with a merry laugh sprang up and ran out towards the enemy, waving his full sleeve over his head in sign of friendliness. They fired at, or over him, ineffectually. He lay down and shot back, one shot, aimed just above the head of the foremost rider. That, and our ready silence perplexed them. They pulled off in a hesitant group, and after a minute's discussion, flagged back their cloaks in half-hearted reply to our signal.

One of them rode towards us at a foot's pace. Awad, protected by our rifles, went two hundred yards to meet him, and saw that he was a Sukhurri, who, when he heard our names, feigned shock. We walked together to Sherif Ali, followed at a distance by the rest of the newcomers, after they had seen our peaceful greeting. They were a raiding party from the Zebn Sukhur, who were camped, as we had expected, in front at Bair.

Ali, furious with them, for their treacherous attack on us, threatened all sorts of pains. They accepted his tirade sullenly, saying that it was a Beni Sakhr manner to shoot over strangers. Ali accepted this as their habit, and a good habit in the desert, but protested that their unheralded appearance against us from three sides showed a premeditated ambush. The Beni Sakhr were a dangerous gang, not pure enough nomads to hold the nomadic code of honour or to obey the desert law in spirit, and not villagers enough to have abjured the business of rapine and raid.

Our late assailants went into Bair to report our coming. Mifleh, chief of their clan, thought it best to efface the ill-reception by a public show in which all men and horses in the place turned out to welcome us with wild cheers and gallopings and curvettings, and much firing of shots and shouting. They whirled round and round us in desperate chase, clattering over rocks with reckless horsemanship and small regard for our staidness, as they broke in and out of the ranks and let off their rifles under our camels' necks continually. Clouds of parching chalk dust arose, so that men's voices croaked.

Eventually the parade eased off, but then Abd el Kader, thinking the opinion even of fools desirable, felt it upon him to assert his virtue. They were shouting to Ali ibn el Hussein 'God give victory to our Sherif' and were reining back on their haunches beside me with 'Welcome, Aurans, harbinger of action'. So he climbed up his mare, into her high Moorish saddle, and with his seven Algerian servants behind him in stiff file, began to prance delicately in slow curves, crying out 'Houp, Houp', in his throaty voice, and firing a pistol unsteadily in the air.

The Bedu, astonished at this performance, gaped silently; till Mifleh came to us, and said, in his wheedling way, 'Lords pray call off your servant, for he can neither shoot nor ride, and if he hits someone he will destroy our good fortune of to-day'. Mifleh did not know the family precedent for his nervousness. Abd el Kader's brother held what might well be a world's record for three successive fatal accidents with automatic pistols in the circle of his Damascus friends. Ali Riza Pasha, chief local gladiator, had said 'Three things are notably impossible: One, that Turkey win this war; one, that the Mediterranean become champagne; one, that I be found in the same place with Mohammed Said, and he armed'.

We off-loaded by the ruins. Beyond us the black tents of the Beni Sakhr were like a herd of goats spotting the valley. A messenger bade us to Mifleh's tent. First, however, Ali had an inquiry to make. At the request of the Beni Sakhr, Feisal had sent a party of Bisha masons and well-sinkers to reline the blasted well from which Nasir and I had picked the gelignite on our way to Akaba. They had been for months in Bair and yet reported that the work was not nearly finished. Feisal had deputed us to inquire into the reasons for the costly delay. Ali found that the Bisha men had been living at ease and forcing the Arabs to provide them with meat and flour. He charged them with it. They

o

prevaricated, vainly, for Sherifs had a trained judicial instinct, and Mifleh was preparing a great supper for us. My men whispered excitedly that sheep had been seen to die behind his tent high on the knoll above the graves. So Ali's justice moved on wings before the food-bowls could be carried up. He heard and condemned the blacks all in a moment, and had judgement inflicted on them by his slaves inside the ruins. They returned a little self-conscious, kissed hands in sign of amenity and forgiveness, and a reconciled party knelt together to meat.

Howeitat feasts had been wet with butter; the Beni Sakhr were overflowing. Our clothes were splashed, our mouths running over, the tips of our fingers scalded with its heat. As the sharpness of hunger was appeased the hands dipped more slowly; but the meal was still far from its just end when Abd el Kader grunted, rose suddenly to his feet, wiped his hands on a handkerchief, and sat back on the carpets by the tent wall. We hesitated, but Ali muttered 'The fellah' and the work continued until all the men of our sitting were full, and the more frugal of us had begun to lick the stiff fat from our smarting fingers.

Ali cleared his throat, and we returned to our carpets while the second and third relays round the pans were satisfied. One little thing, of five or six, in a filthy smock, sat there stuffing solemnly with both hands from first to last, and, at the end, with swollen belly and face glistening with grease, staggered off speechlessly hugging a huge unpicked rib in triumph to its breast.

In front of the tent the dogs cracked the dry bones loudly, and Mifleh's slave in the corner split the sheep's skull and sucked out the brains. Meanwhile, Abd el Kader sat spitting and belching and picking his teeth. Finally, he sent one of his servants for his medicine chest, and poured himself out a draught, grumbling that tough meat was bad for his digestion. He had meant by such unmannerliness to make himself a reputation for grandeur. His own villagers could no doubt be browbeaten so, but the Zebn were too near the desert to be measured by a purely peasant-measure. Also to-day they had before their eyes the contrary example of Sherif Ali ibn el Hussein, a born desert-lord.

His fashion of rising all at once from the food was of the central deserts. On fringes of cultivation, among the semi-nomadic, each guest slipped aside as he was full. The Anazeh of the extreme north set the stranger by himself, and in the dark, that he be not ashamed of his appetite. All these were modes; but among the considerable clans the manner of the Sherifs was generally praised. So poor Abd el Kader was not understood.

He took himself off, and we sat in the tent-mouth, above the dark hollow, now set out in little constellations of tent-fires, seeming to mimic or reflect the sky above. It was a calm night, except when the dogs provoked one another to choral howlings, and as these grew rarer we heard again the quiet, steady thudding of the heavy guns preparing assault in Palestine.

To this artillery accompaniment we told Mifleh that we were about to raid the Deraa district, and would be glad to have him and some fifteen of his tribesmen with us, all on camels. After our failure with the Howeitat, we had decided not to announce our plain object, lest its forlorn character dissuade our partisans. However, Mifleh agreed at once, apparently with haste and pleasure, promising to bring with him the fifteen best men in the tribe and his own son. This lad, Turki by name, was an old love of Ali ibn el Hussein; the animal in each called to the other, and they wandered about inseparably, taking pleasure in a touch and silence. He was a fair, open-faced boy of perhaps seventeen; not tall, but broad and powerful, with a round freckled face, upturned nose, and very short upper lip, showing his strong teeth, but giving his full mouth rather a sulky look, belied by the happy eyes.

We found him plucky and faithful on two critical occasions. His good temper atoned for his having caught a little of the begging habit of his father, whose face was eaten up with greed. Turki's great anxiety was to be sure that he was reckoned a man among the men, and he was always looking to do something bold and wonderful which would let him flaunt his courage before the girls of his tribe. He rejoiced exceedingly in a new silk robe which I gave him at dinner, and walked, to display it, twice through the tent-village without his cloak, railing at those who seemed laggard from our meet.

CHAPTER LXXIV

DARK had fallen long before our caravan left Bair, after watering. We chiefs waited longer still while the Zebn got ready. Mifleh's preparations included a visit to Essad, the supposed ancestor of the clan, in his bedecked tomb near Annad's grave. The Beni Sakhr were already settled enough to have dressed themselves in the Semitic village-superstitions of sacred places, holy trees, and funerary shrines. Sheikh Mifleh thought the occasion warranted his adding another head-cord to the ragged collection looped round Essad's headstone, and characteristically asked us to provide the offering. I handed over one of my rich red-and-silk-silver Mecca ornaments, remarking that the virtue lay with the donor. The thrifty Mifleh pressed upon me one halfpenny in exchange, that he might plead purchase; and when I came past a few weeks later and saw that the gaud was gone, he cursed loudly in my hearing the sacrilege of some godless Sherari, who had robbed his ancestor. Turki would have told me more.

A steep old pathway took us out of Wadi Bair. Near the crest of a ridge we found the others camped for the night round a fire, but there passed no talk or coffee-making for this time. We lay close together, hushed and straining the ears to catch the throbbing of Allenby's guns. They spoke eloquently: and sheet lightning in the west made gun-flashes for them.

Next day we passed to the left of the Thlaithukhwat, the 'Three Sisters' whose clean white peaks were landmarks on their lofty water-shed for a day's journey all about; and went down the soft rolling slopes beyond them. The exquisite November morning had a softness in it like an English summer; but its beauty had to be fought off. I was spending the halts, and riding the stages, in the ranks of the Beni Sakhr teaching my ear their dialect, and storing in my memory the tribal, family or personal notes they let drop.

In the little-peopled desert every worshipful man knew every other; and instead of books they studied their generation. To have fallen short in such knowledge would have meant being branded either as ill-bred, or as a stranger; and strangers were not admitted to familiar intercourse or councils, or confidences. There was nothing so wearing, yet nothing so important for the success of my purpose, as this constant mental gymnastic of apparent omniscience at each time of meeting a new tribe.

At nightfall we camped in an affluent of Wadi Jesha, by some bushes of faint grey-green foliage, which pleased our camels and gave us fire-wood. That night the guns were very clear and loud, perhaps because the intervening hollow of the Dead Sea drummed the echoes up and over our high plateau. The Arabs whispered 'They are nearer; the English are advancing; God deliver the men under that rain'. They were thinking compassionately of the passing Turks, so long their weak oppressors; whom, for their weakness, though oppressors, they loved more than the strong foreigner with his blind indiscriminate justice.

The Arab respected force a little: he respected craft more, and often had it in enviable degree: but most of all he respected blunt sincerity of utterance, nearly the sole weapon God had excluded from his arma-ment. The Turk was all things by turn, and so commended himself to the Arabs for such while as he was not corporately feared. Much lay in this distinction of the corporate and the personal. There were Englishmen whom, individually, the Arabs preferred to any Turk, or foreigner; but, on the strength of this, to have generalized and called the Arabs pro-English, would have been a folly. Each stranger made his own poor bed among them.

We were up early, meaning to push the long way to Ammari by sunset. We crossed ridge after carpeted ridge of sun-burned flints, grown over with a tiny saffron plant so bright and close that all the view was gold. Safra el Jesha, the Sukhur called it. The valleys were only inches deep, their beds grained like morocco leather, in an intricate curving mesh, by innumerable rills of water after the last rain. The swell of every curve was a grey breast of sand set hard with mud, sometimes glistening with salt-crystals, and sometimes rough with the projecting brush of half-buried twigs which had caused it. These tailings of valleys running into Sirhan were always rich in grazing. When there was water in their hollows the tribes collected, and peopled them with tent-villages. The Beni Sakhr with us had so camped; and,

as we crossed the monotonous downs they pointed first to one in-
distinctive hollow with hearth and straight gutter-trenches and then to
another saying, 'There was my tent and there lay Hamdan el Saih.
Look at the dry stones for my bed-place, and for Tarfa's next it. God
have mercy upon her, she died the year of samh, in the Snainirat, of a
puff-adder.'

About noon a party of trotting camels appeared over the ridge,
moving fast, and openly towards us. Little Turki cantered out on his
old she-camel, with cocked carbine across his thighs, to find what they
meant. 'Ha,' cried Mifleh to me while they were still a mile off, 'that
is Fahad, on his Shaara, in the front. These are our kinsmen', and sure
enough they were. Fahad and Adhub, chief war-leaders of the Zebn,
had been camped west of the railway by Ziza, when a Gomani came in
with news of our march. They had saddled at once, and by hard riding
caught us only half-way on the road. Fahad, in courteous fashion,
chided me gently for presuming to ride their district on an adventure
while his father's sons lay in their tent.

Fahad was a melancholy, soft-voiced, little-spoken man of perhaps
thirty, with a white face, trim beard and tragic eyes. His young brother
Adhub was taller and stronger, yet not above middle height. Unlike
Fahad, he was active, noisy, uncouth-looking; with a snub nose, hairless
boy's face and gleaming green eyes flickering hungrily from object to
object. His commonness was pointed by his dishevelled hair and dirty
clothes. Fahad was neater, but still very plainly dressed, and the pair,
on their shaggy home-bred camels, looked as little like sheikhs of their
reputation as can be conceived. However, they were famous fighters.

At Ammari a high cold night wind was stirring the ashen dust of the
salt-ground about the wells into a haze, which gritted in our teeth like
the stale breath of an eruption; and we were ungrateful for the water.
It was on the surface, like so much of Sirhan, but most of the pools
were too bitter to drink. One notable one, however, called Bir el
Emir was thought very good by contrast. It lay in a little floor of bare
limestone among sand-hummocks.

The water (opaque and tasting of mixed brine and ammonia) was
just below the level of the rock-slab, in a stone bath with ragged undercut lips. Its depth Daud proved, by hurling Farraj fully-dressed into it.

He sank out of view in its yellowness, and afterwards rose quietly to the surface under the rock-edge where he could not be seen in the dusk. Daud waited a strained minute; but when his victim did not appear tore off his cloak and plunged after — to find him smiling under the overhanging ledge. Pearl-diving in the gulf had made them like fishes in the water.

They were dragged out, and then had a wild struggle in the sand beside the water-hole. Each sustained hurt, and they returned to my fire dripping wet, in rags, bleeding, with their hair and faces, legs, arms and bodies covered with mud and thorns, more like the devils of a whirlwind than their usual suave delicate presences. They said they had been dancing, and had tripped over a bush; it would be like my generosity to make them a gift of new clothes. I blasted their hopes, and sent them off to repair damages.

My bodyguard, more especially the Ageyl in it, were by nature foppish, and spent their wages on dress or ornaments, and much time in braiding their plaits of shining hair. Butter gave it the polish; and to keep down the vermin they frequently dragged the scalp with a fine-toothed comb, and sprinkled it with camel-staling. A German doctor at Beersheba, in their Turkish days (these were the men who one misty dawn rushed our Yeomanry in Sinai and wiped out a post) had taught them to be clean by prisoning the lousy ones in army latrines until they had swallowed their lice.

The wind became faint at dawn, and we moved forward for Azrak, half a march ahead. Hardly, however, were we clear of the drifts beside the wells when there was an alarm. Mounted men had been seen in the brushwood. This country was a tom-tiddler's ground of raiding parties. We drew together in the best place and halted. The Indian section chose a tiny ridge hacked about with narrow ruts of water-channels. They couched camels in the hollow behind, and had their guns mounted in due order in a moment Ali and Abd el Kader threw out their great crimson banners in the intermittent breeze Our skirmishers headed by Ahmed and Awad, ran out to right and left, and long shots were exchanged. All of it ended suddenly. The enemy broke cover and marched in line towards us, waving their cloaks and sleeves in the air and chanting their war-march of welcome. They were the fighting men of the Serhan tribe on their way to swear allegiance to Feisal. When they heard our news they turned back with us, rejoicing to be spared the road, for this tribe was not ordinarily warlike or nomadic. They made some little pomp over our joint entry to their tents at Ain el Beidha, a few miles east of Azrak, where the whole tribe was gathered; and our reception was loud, because there had been fear and lamentation among the women that morning when they saw their men march away on the hazard of rebellion.

However, here they were returning the same day, with a Sherif of their own, and Arab banners, and machine-guns, marching a ragged hundred men abreast, and singing as merrily as when they started out. My eyes were upon a notable red camel, perhaps a seven-year-old, under a Sirhani in the second line. The tall beast would not be put upon, but with a long, swinging pace, of which there was no equal, in the crowd of us, forged to the front and kept there. Ahmed slipped off to get acquainted with her owner.

In the camp the chief men distributed our party among their tents for the privilege of entertainment. Ali, Abd el Kader, Wood and myself were taken in by Mteir, the paramount sheikh of the tribe, an old, toothless, friendly thing, whose loose jaw sagged in his supporting hand all the while he talked. He gave us a fussy greeting and abundant hospitality of seethed sheep and bread. Wood and Abd el Kader were, perhaps, a little squeamish, for the Serahin seemed primitive in food-discipline, and at the common bowl there was more splashing and spluttering than was proper in the best tents. Afterwards, by constraint of Mteir's urgency, we lay on his rugs for the one night. Round our fresh bodies, for the change of food, collected all such local ticks, fleas and lice as were sick of a diet of unmitigated Serhan. Their delight made them so ravenous that with the best will in the world I could not go on feasting them. Nor apparently could Ali; for he, too, sat up and said that he felt wakeful. So we roused Sheikh Mteir, and sent for Mifleh ibn Bani, a young, active man, accustomed to command their battles. To them we explained Feisal's needs, and our plan to relieve him.

Gravely they heard us. The western bridge, they said, was quite impossible. The Turks had just filled its country with hundreds of military wood-cutters. No hostile party could slip through undetected. They professed great suspicion of the Moorish villages, and of Abd el Kader. Nothing would persuade them to visit the one under the guidance of the other. For Tell el Shehab, the nearest bridge, they feared lest the villagers, their inveterate enemies, attack them in the rear. Also if it rained the camels would be unable to trot back across the muddy plains by Remthe, and the whole party would be cut off and killed.

We were now in deep trouble. The Serahin were our last resource, and if they refused to come with us we should be unable to carry out Allenby's project by the appointed time. Accordingly Ali collected about our little fire more of the better men of the tribe, and fortified the part of courage by bringing in Fahad, and Mifleh, and Adhub. Before them we began to combat in words this crude prudence of the Serahin, which seemed all the more shameful to us after our long sojourn in the clarifying wilderness.

We put it to them, not abstractedly, but concretely, for their case, how life in mass was sensual only, to be lived and loved in its extremity. There could be no rest-houses for revolt, no dividend of joy paid out. Its spirit was accretive, to endure as far as the senses would endure, and to use each such advance as base for further adventure, deeper privation, sharper pain. Sense could not reach back or forward. A felt emotion was a conquered emotion, an experience gone dead, which we buried by expressing it.

To be of the desert was, as they knew, a doom to wage unending battle with an enemy who was not of the world, nor life, nor anything, but hope itself; and failure seemed God's freedom to mankind. We might only exercise this our freedom by not doing what it lay within our power to do, for then life would belong to us, and we should have mastered it by holding it cheap. Death would seem best of all our works, the last free loyalty within our grasp, our final leisure: and of these two poles, death and life, or less finally, leisure and subsistence, we should shun subsistence (which was the stuff of life) in all save its faintest degree, and cling close to leisure. Thereby we would serve to promote the not-doing rather than the doing. Some men, there might be, uncreative; whose leisure was barren; but the activity of these

o*

would have been material only. To bring forth immaterial things, things creative, partaking of spirit, not of flesh, we must be jealous of spending time or trouble upon physical demands, since in most men the soul grew aged long before the body. Mankind had been no gainer by its drudges.

There could be no honour in a sure success, but much might be wrested from a sure defeat. Omnipotence and the Infinite were our two worthiest foemen, indeed the only ones for a full man to meet, they being monsters of his own spirit's making; and the stoutest enemies were always of the household. In fighting Omnipotence, honour was proudly to throw away the poor resources that we had, and dare Him empty-handed; to be beaten, not merely by more mind, but by its advantage of better tools. To the clear-sighted, failure was the only goal. We must believe, through and through, that there was no victory except to go down into death fighting and crying for failure itself, calling in excess of despair to Omnipotence to strike harder, that by His very striking He might temper our tortured selves into the weapon of His own ruin.

This was a halting, half-coherent speech, struck out desperately, moment by moment, in our extreme need, upon the anvil of those white minds round the dying fire; and hardly its sense remained with me afterwards; for once my picture-making memory forgot its trade and only felt the slow humbling of the Serahin, the night-quiet in which their worldliness faded, and at last their flashing eagerness to ride with us whatever the bourne. Before daylight we called old Abd el Kader, and, taking him aside among the sandy thickets, screamed into his dense ear that the Serahin would start with us, under his auspices, for Wadi Khalid, after sunrise. He grunted that it was well: and we said to one another that never, if life and opportunity were prolonged for us, would we take a deaf man for a conspirator again.

CHAPTER LXXV

EXHAUSTED, we lay down a moment, but were astir again very early to review the camel-men of the Sirhan. They made a wild and ragged show, dashing past, but we thought them loose riders, and they blustered too much to be quite convincing. It was a pity they had no real leader. Mteir was too old for service, and ibn Bani was an indistinct man, ambitious rather as a politician than as a fighter. However, they were the force we had, so there was an end to it, and at three in the afternoon we mounted for Azrak, since another night in the tent would have left us picked to dry bones. Abd el Kader and his servants mounted their mares, as sign that the fighting line was near. They rode just behind us.

It was to be Ali's first view of Azrak, and we hurried up the stony ridge in high excitement, talking of the wars and songs and passions of the early shepherd kings, with names like music, who had loved this place; and of the Roman legionaries who languished here as garrison in yet earlier times. Then the blue fort on its rock above the rustling palms, with the fresh meadows and shining springs of water, broke on our sight. Of Azrak, as of Rumm, one said 'Numen inest'. Both were magically haunted: but whereas Rumm was vast and echoing and God-like, Azrak's unfathomable silence was steeped in knowledge of wandering poets, champions, lost kingdoms, all the crime and chivalry and dead magnificence of Hira and Ghassan. Each stone or blade of it was radiant with half-memory of the luminous silky Eden, which had passed so long ago.

At last Ali shook his rein, and his camel picked her careful way down the lava flow to the rich turf behind the springs. Our puckered eyes opened wide with relief that the bitterness of many weeks was gone out of the reflected sunlight. Ali screamed 'Grass', and flung himself off the saddle to the ground on hands and feet, his face bowed down among the harsh stems which seemed so kindly in the desert. He leaped up flushed, with his Harith war-cry, tore his head-cloth off, and raced along the marsh, bounding over the red channels where water clotted among the reeds. His white feet flashed beneath the tossed folds of his cash-mere robes. We in the West seldom experienced that added beauty when the body was seen lightly poised on bare feet; when the rhythm and grace of movement became visible, with the play of muscle and sinew pointing the mechanism of each stride and the balance of repose.

When we turned again to business there was no Abd el Kader. We looked for him in the castle, in the palm-garden, over by the spring. Eventually we sent our men away to search, and they came back with Arabs, who told us that from just after the start he had ridden off north-ward through the flaky hillocks, towards Jebel Druse. The rank and file did not know our plans, hated him, and had been glad to see him go: but it was bad news for us.

Of our three alternatives, Um Keis had been abandoned: without Abd el Kader, Wadi Khalid was impossible: this meant that we must necessarily attempt the bridge at Tell el Shehab. To reach it we had to cross the open land between Remthe and Deraa. Abd el Kader was gone up to the enemy, with information of our plans and strength. The Turks, if they took the most reasonable precautions, would trap us at the bridge. We took council with Fahad and decided to push on none the less, trusting to the usual incompetence of our enemy. It was not a confident decision. While we took it the sunshine seemed less lambent, and Azrak not so aloof from fear.

Next morning we wound pensively along a flinty valley and over a ridge into Wadi el Harith, whose green course had a sickening likeness to some lands at home. Ali rejoiced to see a rich pasture-valley bearing his family name, and was as glad as our camels when we found limpid pools of last week's rain-water in hollows among the bushes. We stopped and used the discovery for lunch, making a long halt. Adhub went off with Ahmed and Awad to look for gazelle. He came back with three. So we stopped yet longer and made a second lunch, like a feast, of meat gobbets roasted on ramrods till the outside was black as coal, while the heart remained juicily sweet. Sojourners in the desert loved its accidental bounty; also on this trip a reluctance weighed down our daily marching to make us glad of each delay.

Unhappily my rest time was spoiled by a bed of justice. The feud between Ahmed and Awad broke out during this gazelle chase into a duel. Awad shot off Ahmed's head-rope; Ahmed holed Awad's cloak. I disarmed them and gave loud order that the right thumb and fore-finger of each be cut off. The terror of this drove them into an instant, violent and public kissing of peace. A little later all my men went capital bail that the trouble had ended. I referred the case to Ali ibn el Hussein, who set them at liberty on probation, after sealing their promise with the ancient and curious nomad penance of striking the head sharply with the edge of a weighty dagger again and again till the issuing blood had run down to the waist belt. It caused painful but not dangerous scalp wounds, whose ache at first and whose scars later were supposed to remind the would-be defaulter of the bond he had given.

We pushed on again for miles over perfect going, through rich country for the camels, till at Abu Sawana we found a flinty hollow, brim-full of deliciously clear rain-water in a narrow channel two feet deep, and perhaps ten feet wide, but half a mile long. This would serve as starting point for our bridge-raid. To be sure of its safety, we rode a few yards further, to the top of a stony knoll; and there found ourselves looking down upon a retreating party of Circassian horsemen, sent out by the Turks to report if the waters were occupied. They had missed us, to our mutual benefit, by five minutes.

Next morning we filled our water-skins, since we should find nothing to drink between here and the bridge; and then marched leisurely until the desert ended in a three-foot depression at the edge of a clean plain, which extended flatly to the metals of the railway some miles off. We halted for dusk to make its crossing possible. Our plan was to slip over secretly, and hide in the further foothills, below Deraa. In the spring these hills were full of grazing sheep, for the rain cloaked their low sides in new grass and flowers. With the coming of summer they dried, and became deserted save for chance travellers on obscure errands. We might fairly calculate on lying in their folds for a day undisturbed.

We made our halt another opportunity of food, for we were reck-lessly eating all we could as often as we had the chance. It lightened our stores, and kept us from thinking: but even with this help the day was very long. At last sunset came. The plain shivered once, as the darkness, which for an hour had been gathering among the facing hills, flowed slowly out and drowned it. We mounted. Two hours later after a quick march over gravel, Fahad and myself, out scouting ahead, came to the railway; and without difficulty found a stony place where our caravan would make no signs of passage. The Turkish rail-guards were clearly at their ease, which meant that Abd el Kader had not yet caused a panic by what news he brought.

We rode the other side of the line for half an hour, and then dipped into a very slight rocky depression full of succulent plants. This was Ghadir el Abyadh, recommended by Mifleh as our ambush. We took his surprising word that we were in cover, and lay down among or alongside our loaded beasts for a short sleep. Dawn would show us how far we were safe and hidden.

As day was breaking Fahad led me to the edge of our pit, some fifteen feet above, and from it we looked straight across a slowly-dropping meadow to the railway, which seemed nearly within shot. It was most inconveniently close, but the Sukhur knew no better place. We had to stand-to all the day. Each time something was reported, our men ran to look at it, and the low bank would grow a serried frieze of human heads. Also, the grazing camels required many guards to keep them from straying into view. Whenever a patrol passed we had to be very gentle in controlling the beasts, since if one of them had roared or ruckled it would have drawn the enemy. Yesterday had been long: to-day was longer: we could not feed, as our water had to be husbanded with jealous care against the scarcity of to-morrow. The very knowledge made us thirsty.

Ali and I worked at the last arrangements for our ride. We were penned here until sunset; and must reach Tell el Shehab, blow up the bridge, and get back east of the railway by dawn. This meant a ride of at least eighty miles in the thirteen hours of darkness, with an elaborate demolition thrown in. Such a performance was beyond the capacity of most of the Indians. They were not good riders, and had broken up their camels in the march from Akaba. An Arab by saving his beast, could bring it home in fair condition after hard work. The Indians had done their best; but the discipline of their cavalry training had tired out them and the animals in our easy stages.

So we picked out the six best riders and put them on the six best camels, with Hassan Shah, their officer and greatest-hearted man, to lead them. He decided that this little party would be fittest armed with just one Vickers gun. It was a very serious reduction of our offensive power. The more I looked at it, the less fortunate seemed the development of this Yarmuk plan of ours.

The Beni Sakhr were fighting men; but we distrusted the Serahin. So Ali and I decided to make the Beni Sakhr, under Fahad, our storming party. We would leave some Serahin to guard the camels while the others carried the blasting gelatine in our dismounted charge upon the bridge. To suit the hurried carriage down steep hill-sides in the dark we changed the explosive loads into thirty-pound lumps, which were put, for visibility, each lump into its own white bag. Wood undertook to repack the gelatine, and shared the rare headache all got from handling it. This helped pass the time.

My bodyguard had to be carefully distributed. One good rider was told off to each of the less expert local men, whose virtue was that they knew the country: the pairs so made were attached to one or other of my foreign liabilities, with instructions to keep close to him all night. Ali ibn el Hussein took six of his servants, and the party was completed by twenty Beni Sakhr and forty Serahin. We left the lame and weak camels behind at Abyadh in charge of the balance of our men, with instructions to get back to Abu Sawana before dawn to-morrow and wait there for our news. Two of my men developed sudden illnesses, which made them feel unable to ride with us. I excused them for the night, and afterward from all duties whatsoever.

CHAPTER LXXVI

JUST at sunset we said good-bye to them, and went off up our valley, feeling miserably disinclined to go on at all. Darkness gathered as we rode over the first ridge and turned west, for the abandoned pilgrim road, whose ruts would be our best guide. We were stumbling down the irregular hill-side, when the men in front suddenly dashed forward. We followed and found them surrounding a terrified pedlar, with two wives and two donkeys laden with raisins, flour and cloaks. They had been going to Mafrak, the station just behind us. This was awkward; and in the end we told them to camp, and left a Sirhani to see they did not stir: he was to release them at dawn, and escape over the line to Abu Sawana.

We went plodding across country in the now absolute dark till we saw the gleam of the white furrows of the pilgrim road. It was the same road along which the Arabs had ridden with me on my first night in Arabia out by Rabegh. Since then in twelve months we had fought up it for some twelve hundred kilometres, past Medina and Hedia, Dizad, Mudowwara and Maan. There remained little to its head in Damascus where our armed pilgrimage should end.

But we were apprehensive of to-night: our nerves had been shaken by the flight of Abd el Kader, the solitary traitor of our experience. Had we calculated fairly we should have known that we had a chance in spite of him: yet a dispassionate judgement lay not in our mood, and we thought half-despairingly how the Arab Revolt would never perform its last stage, but would remain one more example of the caravans which started out ardently for a cloud-goal, and died man by man in the wilderness without the tarnish of achievement.

Some shepherd or other scattered these thoughts by firing his rifle at our caravan, seen by him approaching silently and indistinctly in the dark. He missed widely, but began to cry out in extremity of terror and, as he fled, to pour shot after shot into the brown of us.

Mifleh el Gomaan, who was guiding, swerved violently, and in a blind trot carried our plunging line down a slope, over a breakneck bottom, and round the shoulder of a hill. There we had peaceful unbroken night once more, and swung forward in fair order under the stars. The next alarm was a barking dog on the left, and then a camel unexpectedly loomed up in our track. It was, however, a stray, and riderless. We moved on again.

Mifleh made me ride with him, calling me 'Arab' that my known name might not betray me to strangers in the blackness. We were coming down into a very thick hollow when we smelt ashes, and the dusky figure of a woman leaped from a bush beside the track and rushed shrieking out of sight. She may have been a gipsy, for nothing followed. We came to a hill. At the top was a village which blazed at us while we were yet distant. Mifleh bore off to the right over a broad stretch of plough; we climbed it slowly, with creaking saddles. At the edge of the crest we halted.

Away to the north below our level were some brilliant clusters of lights. These were the flares of Deraa station, lit for army traffic: and we felt something reassuring perhaps, but also a little blatant in this Turkish disregard for us. [It was our revenge to make it their last illumination: Deraa was obscured from the morrow for a whole year until it fell.] In a close group we rode to the left along the summit and down a long valley into the plain of Remthe, from which village an occasional red spark glowed out, in the darkness to the north-west. The going became flat; but it was land half-ploughed, and very soft with a labyrinth of cony-burrows, so that our plunging camels sank fetlock-in and laboured. None the less, we had to put on speed, for the incidents and roughness of the way had made us late. Mifleh urged his reluctant camel into a trot.

I was better mounted than most, on the red camel which had led our procession into Beidha. She was a long, raking beast, with a huge piston-stride very hard to suffer: pounding, yet not fully mechanical, because there was courage in the persistent effort which carried her sailing to the head of the line. There, all competitors out-stripped, her ambition died into a solid step, longer than normal by some inches, but like any other animal's, except that it gave a confident feeling of immense reserves in strength and endurance. I rode back down the ranks and told them to press forward faster. The Indians, riding wooden, like horsemen, did their best, as did most of our number; but the ground was so bad that the greatest efforts were not very fruitful, and as hours went on first one and then another rider dropped behind. Thereupon I chose the rear position, with Ali ibn el Hussein who was riding a rare old racing camel. She may have been fourteen years old but never flagged nor jogged the whole night. With her head low she shuffled along in the quick, hang-kneed Nejd pace which was so easy for the rider. Our speed and camel-sticks made life miserable for the last men and camels.

Soon after nine o'clock we left the plough. The going should have improved: but it began to drizzle, and the rich surface of the land grew slippery. A Sirhani camel fell. Its rider had it up in a moment and trotted forward. One of the Beni Sakhr came down. He also was unhurt, and remounted hastily. Then we found one of Ali's servants standing by his halted camel. Ali hissed him on, and when the fellow mumbled an excuse cut him savagely across the head with his cane. The terrified camel plunged forward, and the slave, snatching at the hinder girth, was able to swing himself into the saddle. Ali pursued him with a rain of blows. Mustafa, my man, an inexperienced rider, fell off twice. Awad, his rank-man, each time caught his halter, and had helped him up before we overtook them.

The rain stopped, and we went faster. Downhill, now. Suddenly Mifleh, rising in his saddle, slashed at the air overhead. A sharp metallic contact from the night showed we were under the telegraph line to Mezerib. Then the grey horizon before us went more distant. We seemed to be riding on the camber of an arc of land, with a growing darkness at each side and in front. There came to our ears a faint sighing like wind among trees very far away, but continuous and slowly increasing. This must be from the great waterfall below Tell el Shehab, and we pressed forward confidently.

A few minutes later Mifleh pulled up his camel and beat her neck very gently till she sank silently on her knees. He threw himself off, while we reined up beside him on this grassy platform by a tumbled cairn. Before us from a lip of blackness rose very loudly the rushing of the river which had been long dinning our ears. It was the edge of the Yarmuk gorge, and the bridge lay just under us to the right.

We helped down the Indians from their burdened camels, that no sound betray us to listening ears; then mustered, whispering, on the clammy grass. The moon was not yet over Hermon, but the night was only half-dark in the promise of its dawn, with wild rags of tattered clouds driving across a livid sky. I served out the explosives to the fifteen porters, and we started. The Beni Sakhr under Adhub sank into the dark slopes before us to scout the way. The rainstorm had made the steep hill treacherous, and only by driving our bare toes sharply into the soil could we keep a sure foothold. Two or three men fell heavily.

When we were in the stiffest part, where rocks cropped out brokenly from the face, a new noise was added to the roaring water as a train clanked slowly up from Galilee, the flanges of its wheels screaming on the curves and the steam of its engine panting out of the hidden depths of the ravine in white ghostly breaths. The Serahin hung back. Wood drove them after us. Fahad and I leaped to the right, and in the light of the furnace-flame saw open trucks in which were men in khaki, perhaps prisoners going up to Asia Minor.

A little farther; and at last, below our feet, we saw a something blacker in the precipitous blackness of the valley, and at its other end a speck of flickering light. We halted to examine it with glasses. It was the bridge, seen from this height in plan, with a guard-tent pitched under the shadowy village-crested wall of the opposite bank. Everything was quiet, except the river; everything was motionless, except the dancing flame outside the tent.

Wood, who was only to come down if I were hit, got the Indians ready to spray the guard-tent if affairs became general; while Ali, Fahad, Mifleh and the rest of us, with Beni Sakhr and explosive porters, crept on till we found the old construction path to the near abutment. We stole along this in single file, our brown cloaks and soiled clothes blending perfectly with the limestone above us, and the depths below, until we reached the metals just before they curved to the bridge. There the crowd halted, and I crawled on with Fahad.

We reached the naked abutment, and drew ourselves forward on our faces in the shadow of its rails till we could nearly touch the grey skeleton of underhung girders, and see the single sentry leaning against the other abutment, sixty yards across the gulf. Whilst we watched, he began to move slowly up and down, up and down, before his fire, without ever setting foot on the dizzy bridge. I lay staring at him fascinated, as if planless and helpless, while Fahad shuffled back by the abutment wall where it sprang clear of the hill-side.

This was no good, for I wanted to attack the girders themselves; so I crept away to bring the gelatine bearers. Before I reached them there was the loud clatter of a dropped rifle and a scrambling fall from up the bank. The sentry started and stared up at the noise. He saw, high up, in the zone of light with which the rising moon slowly made beautiful the gorge, the machine-gunners climbing down to a new position in the receding shadow. He challenged loudly, then lifted his rifle and fired, while yelling the guard out.

Instantly all was complete confusion. The invisible Beni Sakhr, crouched along the narrow path above our heads, blazed back at random. The guard rushed into trenches, and opened rapid fire at our flashes. The Indians, caught moving, could not get their Vickers in action to riddle the tent before it was empty. Firing became general. The volleys of the Turkish rifles, echoing in the narrow place, were doubled by the impact of their bullets against the rocks behind our party. The Serahin porters had learned from my bodyguard that gelatine would go off if hit. So when the shots spattered about them they dumped the sacks over the edge and fled. Ali leaped down to Fahad and me, where we stood on the obscure abutment unperceived, but with empty hands, and told us that the explosives were now somewhere in the deep bed of the ravine.

It was hopeless to think of recovering them, with such hell let loose, so we scampered, without accident, up the hill-path through the Turkish fire, breathlessly to the top. There we met the disgusted Wood and the Indians, and told them it was all over. We hastened back to the cairn where the Serahin were scrambling on their camels. We copied them as soon as might be, and trotted off at speed, while the Turks were yet rattling away in the bottom of the valley. Turra, the nearest village, heard the clamour and joined in. Other villages awoke, and lights began to sparkle everywhere across the plain.

Our rush over-ran a party of peasants returning from Deraa. The Serahin, sore at the part they had played (or at what I said in the heat of running away) were looking for trouble, and robbed them bare.

The victims dashed off through the moonlight with their women, raising the ear-piercing Arab call for help. Remthe heard them. Its massed shrieks alarmed every sleeper in the neighbourhood. Their mounted men turned out to charge our flank, while settlements for miles about manned their roofs and fired volleys.

We left the Serahin offenders with their encumbering loot, and drove on in grim silence, keeping together in what order we could, while my trained men did marvellous service helping those who fell, or mounting behind them those whose camels got up too hurt to canter on. The ground was still muddy, and the ploughed strips more laborious than ever; but behind us was the riot, spurring us and our camels to exertion, like a pack hunting us into the refuge of the hills. At length we entered these, and cut through by a better road towards peace, yet riding our jaded animals as hard as we could, for dawn was near. Gradually the noise behind us died away, and the last stragglers fell into place, driven together, as on the advance, by the flail of Ali ibn el Hussein and myself in the rear.

The day broke just as we rode down to the railway, and Wood, Ali and the chiefs, now in front to test the passage, were amused by cutting the telegraph in many places while the procession marched over. We had crossed the line the night before to blow up the bridge at Tell el Shehab, and so cut Palestine off from Damascus, and we were actually cutting the telegraph to Medina after all our pains and risks! Allenby's guns, still shaking the air away there on our right, were bitter recorders of the failure we had been.

The grey dawn drew on with gentleness in it, foreboding the grey drizzle of rain which followed, a drizzle so soft and hopeless that it seemed to mock our broken-footed plodding towards Abu Sawana. At sunset we reached the long water-pool; and there the rejects of our party were curious after the detail of our mistakes. We were fools, all of us equal fools, and so our rage was aimless. Ahmed and Awad had another fight, young Mustafa refused to cook rice; Farraj and Daud knocked him about until he cried; Ali had two of his servants beaten: and none of us or of them cared a little bit. Our minds were sick with failure, and our bodies tired after nearly a hundred strained miles over bad country in bad conditions, between sunset and sunset, without halt or food.

CHAPTER LXXVII

FOOD was going to be our next preoccupation, and we held a council in the cold driving rain to consider what we might do. For lightness' sake we had carried from Azrak three days' rations, which made us complete until to-night; but we could not go back empty-handed. The Beni Sakhr wanted honour, and the Serahin were too lately disgraced not to clamour for more adventure. We had still a reserve bag of thirty pounds of gelatine, and Ali ibn el Hussein who had heard of the performances below Maan, and was as Arab as any Arab, said, 'Let's blow up a train'. The word was hailed with universal joy, and they looked at me: but I was not able to share their hopes, all at once.

Blowing up trains was an exact science when done deliberately, by a sufficient party, with machine-guns in position. If scrambled at it might become dangerous. The difficulty this time was that the available gunners were Indians; who, though good men fed, were only half-men in cold and hunger. I did not propose to drag them off without rations on an adventure which might take a week. There was no cruelty in starving Arabs; they would not die of a few days' fasting, and would fight as well as ever on empty stomachs; while, if things got too difficult, there were the riding-camels to kill and eat: but the Indians, though Moslems, refused camel-flesh on principle.

I explained these delicacies of diet. Ali at once said that it would be enough for me to blow up the train, leaving him and the Arabs with him to do their best to carry its wreck without machine-gun support. As, in this unsuspecting district, we might well happen on a supply train, with civilians or only a small guard of reservists aboard, I agreed to risk it. The decision having been applauded, we sat down in a cloaked circle, to finish our remaining food in a very late and cold supper (the rain had sodden the fuel and made fire not possible) our hearts somewhat comforted by chance of another effort.

At dawn, with the unfit of the Arabs, the Indians moved away for Azrak, miserably. They had started up country with me in hope of a really military enterprise, and first had seen the muddled bridge, and now were losing this prospective train. It was hard on them; and to soften the blow with honour I asked Wood to accompany them. He agreed, after argument, for their sakes; but it proved a wise move for himself, as a sickness which had been troubling him began to show the early signs of pneumonia.

The balance of us, some sixty men, turned back towards the railway. None of them knew the country, so I led them to Minifir, where, with Zaal, we had made havoc in the spring. The re-curved hill-top was an excellent observation post, camp, grazing ground and way of retreat, and we sat there in our old place till sunset, shivering and staring out over the immense plain which stretched map-like to the clouded peaks of Jebel Druse, with Um el Jemal and her sister-villages like ink-smudges on it through the rain.

In the first dusk we walked down to lay the mine. The rebuilt culvert of kilometre 172 seemed still the fittest place. While we stood by it there came a rumbling, and through the gathering darkness and mist a train suddenly appeared round the northern curve, only two hundred yards away. We scurried under the long arch and heard it roll over-head. This was annoying; but when the course was clear again we fell to burying the charge. The evening was bitterly cold, with drifts of rain blowing down the valley.

The arch was solid masonry, of four metres span, and stood over a shingle water-bed which took its rise on our hill-top. The winter rains had cut this into a channel four feet deep, narrow and winding, which served us as an admirable approach till within three hundred yards of the line. There the gully widened out and ran straight towards the culvert, open to the sight of anyone upon the rails.

We hid the explosive carefully on the crown of the arch, deeper than usual, beneath a tie, so that the patrols would not feel its jelly softness under their feet. The wires were taken down the bank into the shingle bed of the watercourse, where concealment was quick; and up it as far as they would reach. Unfortunately, this was only sixty yards, for there had been difficulty in Egypt over insulated cable and no more had been available when our expedition started. Sixty yards was plenty for the bridge, but little for a train: however, the ends happened to coincide with a little bush about ten inches high, on the edge of the watercourse, and we buried them beside this very convenient mark. It was impossible to leave them joined up to the exploder in the proper way, since the spot was evident to the permanent-way patrols as they made their rounds.

Owing to the mud the job took longer than usual, and it was very nearly dawn before we finished. I waited under the draughty arch till day broke, wet and dismal, and then I went over the whole area of disturbance, spending another half-hour in effacing its every mark, scattering leaves and dead grass over it, and watering down the broken mud from a shallow rain-pool near. Then they waved to me that the first patrol was coming, and I went up to join the others.

Before I had reached them they came tearing down into their prearranged places, lining the watercourse and spurs each side. A train was coming from the north. Hamud, Feisal's long slave, had the exploder; but before he reached me a short train of closed box-waggons rushed by at speed. The rainstorms on the plain and the thick morning had hidden it from the eyes of our watchman until too late. This second failure saddened us further and Ali began to say that nothing would come right this trip. Such a statement held risk as prelude of the discovery of an evil eye present; so, to divert attention, I suggested new watching posts be sent far out, one to the ruins on the north, one to the great cairn of the southern crest.

The rest, having no breakfast, were to pretend not to be hungry. They all enjoyed doing this, and for a while we sat cheerfully in the rain, huddling against one another for warmth behind a breastwork of our streaming camels. The moisture made the animals' hair curl up like a fleece, so that they looked queerly dishevelled. When the rain paused, which it did frequently, a cold moaning wind searched out the unprotected parts of us very thoroughly. After a time we found our wetted shirts clammy and comfortless things. We had nothing to eat, nothing to do and nowhere to sit except on wet rock, wet grass or mud. However, this persistent weather kept reminding me that it would delay Allenby's advance on Jerusalem, and rob him of his great possibility. So large a misfortune to our lion was a half-encouragement for the mice. We would be partners into next year.

In the best circumstances, waiting for action was hard. To-day it was beastly. Even enemy patrols stumbled along without care, perfunctorily against the rain. At last, near noon, in a snatch of fine weather, the watchmen on the south peak flagged their cloaks wildly in signal of a train. We reached our positions in an instant, for we had squatted the late hours on our heels in a streaming ditch near the line, so as not to miss another chance. The Arabs took cover properly. I looked back at their ambush from my firing point, and saw nothing but the grey hill-sides.

I could not hear the train coming, but trusted, and knelt ready for perhaps half an hour, when the suspense became intolerable, and I signalled to know what was up. They sent down to say it was coming very slowly, and was an enormously long train. Our appetites stiffened. The longer it was the more would be the loot. Then came word that it had stopped. It moved again.

Finally, near one o'clock, I heard it panting. The locomotive was evidently defective (all these wood-fired trains were bad), and the heavy load on the up-gradient was proving too much for its capacity. I crouched behind my bush, while it crawled slowly into view past the south cutting, and along the bank above my head towards the culvert. The first ten trucks were open trucks, crowded with troops. However, once again it was too late to choose, so when the engine was squarely over the mine I pushed down the handle of the exploder. Nothing happened. I sawed it up and down four times.

Still nothing happened; and I realized that it had gone out of order, and that I was kneeling on a naked bank, with a Turkish troop train crawling past fifty yards away. The bush, which had seemed a foot high, shrank smaller than a fig-leaf; and I felt myself the most distinct object in the country-side. Behind me was an open valley for two hundred yards to the cover where my Arabs were waiting and wondering what I was at. It was impossible to make a bolt for it, or the Turks would step off the train and finish us. If I sat still, there might be just a hope of my being ignored as a casual Bedouin.

So there I sat, counting for sheer life, while eighteen open trucks, three box-waggons, and three officers' coaches dragged by. The engine panted slower and slower, and I thought every moment that it would break down. The troops took no great notice of me, but the officers were interested, and came out to the little platforms at the ends of their carriages, pointing and staring. I waved back at them, grinning nervously, and feeling an improbable shepherd in my Meccan dress, with its twisted golden circlet about my head. Perhaps the mud-stains, the wet and their ignorance made me accepted. The end of the brake van slowly disappeared into the cutting on the north.

As it went, I jumped up, buried my wires, snatched hold of the wretched exploder, and went like a rabbit uphill into safety. There I took breath and looked back to see that the train had finally stuck. It waited, about five hundred yards beyond the mine, for nearly an hour to get up a head of steam, while an officers' patrol came back and searched very carefully, the ground where I had been seen sitting. However the wires were properly hidden: they found nothing: the engine plucked up heart again, and away they went.

CHAPTER LXXVIII

MIFLEH was past tears, thinking I had intentionally let the train through; and when the Serahin had been told the real cause they said 'Bad luck is with us'. Historically they were right; but they meant it for a prophecy, so I made sarcastic reference to their courage at the bridge the week before, hinting that it might be a tribal preference to sit on camel-guard. At once there was uproar, the Serahin attacking me furiously, the Beni Sakhr defending. Ali heard the trouble, and came running.

When we had made it up the original despondency was half forgotten. Ali backed me nobly, though the wretched boy was blue with cold and shivering in an attack of fever. He gasped that their ancestor the Prophet had given to Sherifs the faculty of 'sight', and by it he knew that our luck was turning. This was comfort for them: my first instalment of good fortune came when in the wet, without other tool than my dagger, I got the box of the exploder open and persuaded its electrical gear to work properly once more.

We returned to our vigil by the wires, but nothing happened, and evening drew down with more squalls and beastliness, everybody full of grumbles. There was no train; it was too wet to light a cooking fire; our only potential food was camel. Raw meat did not tempt anyone that night; and so our beasts survived to the morrow.

Ali lay down on his belly, which position lessened the hunger-ache, trying to sleep off his fever. Khazen, Ali's servant, lent him his cloak for extra covering. For a spell I took Khazen under mine, but soon found it becoming crowded. So I left it to him and went downhill to connect up the exploder. Afterwards I spent the night there alone by the singing telegraph wires, hardly wishing to sleep, so painful was the cold. Nothing came all the long hours, and dawn, which broke wet, looked even uglier than usual. We were sick to death of Minifir, of railways, of train watching and wrecking, by now. I climbed up to the main body while the early patrol searched the railway. Then the day cleared a little. Ali awoke, much refreshed, and his new spirit cheered

439

us. Hamud, the slave, produced some sticks which he had kept under his clothes by his skin all night. They were nearly dry. We shaved down some blasting gelatine, and with its hot flame got a fire going, while the Sukhur hurriedly killed a mangy camel, the best spared of our riding-beasts, and began with entrenching tools to hack it into handy joints.

Just at that moment the watchman on the north cried a train. We left the fire and made a breathless race of the six hundred yards down hill to our old position. Round the bend, whistling its loudest, came the train, a splendid two-engined thing of twelve passenger coaches, travelling at top speed on the favouring grade. I touched off under the first driving wheel of the first locomotive, and the explosion was terrific. The ground spouted blackly into my face, and I was sent spinning, to sit up with the shirt torn to my shoulder and the blood dripping from long ragged scratches on my left arm. Between my knees lay the exploder, crushed under a twisted sheet of sooty iron. In front of me was the scalded and smoking upper half of a man. When I peered through the dust and steam of the explosion the whole boiler of the first engine seemed to be missing.

I dully felt that it was time to get away to support; but when I moved, learnt that there was a great pain in my right foot, because of which I could only limp along, with my head swinging from the shock. Movement began to clear away this confusion, as I hobbled towards the upper valley, whence the Arabs were now shooting fast into the crowded coaches. Dizzily I cheered myself by repeating aloud in English 'Oh, I wish this hadn't happened'.

When the enemy began to return our fire, I found myself much between the two. Ali saw me fall, and thinking that I was hard hit, ran out, with Turki and about twenty men of his servants and the Beni Sakhr, to help me. The Turks found their range and got seven of them in a few seconds. The others, in a rush, were about me — fit models, after their activity, for a sculptor. Their full white cotton drawers drawn in, bell-like, round their slender waists and ankles; their hairless brown bodies; and the love-locks plaited tightly over each temple in long horns, made them look like Russian dancers.

We scrambled back into cover together, and there, secretly, I felt myself over, to find I had not once been really hurt; though besides the bruises and cuts of the boiler-plate and a broken toe, I had five different bullet-grazes on me (some of them uncomfortably deep) and my clothes ripped to pieces.

From the watercourse we could look about. The explosion had destroyed the arched head of the culvert, and the frame of the first engine was lying beyond it, at the near foot of the embankment, down which it had rolled. The second locomotive had toppled into the gap, and was lying across the ruined tender of the first. Its bed was twisted. I judged them both beyond repair. The second tender had disappeared over the further side; and the first three waggons had telescoped and were smashed in pieces.

The rest of the train was badly derailed, with the listing coaches butted end to end at all angles, zigzagged along the track. One of them was a saloon, decorated with flags. In it had been Mehmed Jemal Pasha, commanding the Eighth Army Corps, hurrying down to defend Jerusalem against Allenby. His chargers had been in the first waggon; his motor-car was on the end of the train, and we shot it up. Of his staff we noticed a fat ecclesiastic, whom we thought to be Assad Shukair, Imam to Ahmed Jemal Pasha, and a notorious pro-Turk pimp. So we blazed at him till he dropped.

It was all long bowls. We could see that our chances of carrying the wreck were slight. There had been some four hundred men on board, and the survivors, now recovered from the shock, were under shelter and shooting hard at us. At the first moment our party on the north spur had closed, and nearly won the game. Mifleh on his mare chased the officers from the saloon into the lower ditch. He was too excited to stop and shoot, and so they got away scathless. The Arabs following him had turned to pick up some of the rifles and medals littering the ground, and then to drag bags and boxes from the train. If we had had a machine-gun posted to cover the far side, according to my mining practice, not a Turk would have escaped.

Mifleh and Adhub rejoined us on the hill, and asked after Fahad. One of the Serahin told how he had led the first rush, while I lay knocked out beside the exploder, and had been killed near it. They showed his belt and rifle as proof that he was dead and that they had tried to save him. Adhub said not a word, but leaped out of the gully, and raced downhill. We caught our breaths till our lungs hurt us, watching him; but the Turks seemed not to see. A minute later he was dragging a body behind the left-hand bank.

Mifleh went back to his mare, mounted, and took her down behind a spur. Together they lifted the inert figure on to the pommel, and returned. A bullet had passed through Fahad's face, knocking out four teeth, and gashing the tongue. He had fallen unconscious, but had revived just before Adhub reached him, and was trying on hands and knees, blinded with blood to crawl away. He now recovered poise enough to cling to a saddle. So they changed him to the first camel they found and led him off at once.

The Turks, seeing us so quiet, began to advance up the slope. We let them come half-way, and then poured in volleys which killed some twenty and drove the others back. The ground about the train was strewn with dead, and the broken coaches had been crowded: but they were fighting under eye of their Corps Commander, and undaunted began to work round the spurs to outflank us.

We were now only about forty left, and obviously could do no good against them. So we ran in batches up the little stream-bed, turning at each sheltered angle to delay them by pot-shots. Little Turki much distinguished himself by quick coolness, though his straight-stocked Turkish cavalry carbine made him so expose his head that he got four bullets through his head-cloth. Ali was angry with me for retiring slowly. In reality my raw hurts crippled me, but to hide from him this real reason I pretended to be easy, interested in and studying the Turks. Such successive rests while I gained courage for a new run kept him and Turki far behind the rest.

At last we reached the hill-top. Each man there jumped on the nearest camel, and made away at full speed eastward into the desert, for an hour. Then in safety we sorted our animals. The excellent Rahail, despite the ruling excitement, had brought off with him, tied to his saddle-girth, a huge haunch of the camel slaughtered just as the train arrived. He gave us the motive for a proper halt, five miles farther on, as a little party of four camels appeared marching in the same direction. It was our companion, Matar, coming back from his home village to Azrak with loads of raisins and peasant delicacies.

So we stopped at once, under a large rock in Wadi Dhuleil, where was a barren fig-tree, and cooked our first meal for three days. There, also we bandaged up Fahad, who was sleepy with the lassitude of his severe hurt. Adhub, seeing this took one of Matar's new carpets, and, doubling it across the camel-saddle, stitched the ends into great pockets. In one they laid Fahad, while Adhub crawled into the other as make-weight: and the camel was led off southward towards their tribal tents.

The other wounded men were seen to at the same time. Mifleh brought up the youngest lads of the party, and had them spray the wounds with their piss, as a rude antiseptic. Meanwhile we whole ones refreshed ourselves. I bought another mangy camel for extra meat, paid rewards, compensated the relatives of the killed, and gave prize-money, for the sixty or seventy rifles we had taken. It was small booty, but not to be despised. Some Serahin, who had gone into the action without rifles, able only to throw unavailing stones, had now two guns apiece. Next day we moved into Azrak, having a great welcome, and boasting — God forgive us — that we were victors.

CHAPTER LXXIX

RAIN had set in steadily, and the country was sodden wet. Allenby had failed in his weather, and there could be no great advance this year. Nevertheless, for progress' sake we determined to hold to Azrak. Partly it would be a preaching base, from which to spread our movement in the North: partly it would be a centre of intelligence: partly it would cut off Nuri Shaalan from the Turks. He hesitated to declare himself only because of his wealth in Syria, and the possible hurt to his tribesmen if they were deprived of their natural market. We, by living in one of his main manors, would keep him ashamed to go in to the enemy. Azrak lay favourably for us, and the old fort would be convenient headquarters if we made it habitable, no matter how severe the winter.

So I established myself in its southern gate-tower, and set my six Haurani boys (for whom manual labour was not disgraceful) to cover with brushwood, palm-branches, and clay the ancient split stone rafters, which stood open to the sky. Ali took up his quarters in the south-east corner tower, and made that roof tight. The Indians weather-proofed their own north-west rooms. We arranged the stores on the ground floor of the western tower, by the little gate, for it was the soundest, driest place. The Biasha chose to live under me in the south gate. So we blocked that entry and made a hall of it. Then we opened a great arch from the court to the palm-garden, and made a ramp, that our camels might come inside each evening.

Hassan Shah we appointed Seneschal. As a good Moslem his first care was for the little mosque in the square. It had been half unroofed and the Arabs had penned sheep within the walls. He set his twenty men to dig out the filth, and wash the pavement clean. The mosque then became a most attractive house of prayer. What had been a place shut off, dedicated to God alone, Time had broken open to the Evanescent with its ministering winds and rain and sunlight; these entering into the worship taught worshippers how the two were one.

Our prudent Jemadar's next labour was to make positions for

machine-guns in the upper towers, from whose tops the approaches lay at mercy. Then he placed a formal sentry (a portent and cause of wonder in Arabia) whose main duty was the shutting of the postern gate at sundown. The door was a poised slab of dressed basalt, a foot thick, turning on pivots of itself, socketed into threshold and lintel. It took a great effort to start swinging, and at the end went shut with a clang and crash which made tremble the west wall of the old castle.

Meanwhile, we were studying to provision ourselves. Akaba was far off, and in winter the roads thither would be rigorous: so we prepared a caravan to go up to Jebel Druse, the neutral land, only a day off. Matar went in charge of this for us, with a long train of camels to carry back varieties of food for our motley party. Besides my bodyguard, who were taught to live on what they got, we had the Indians, for whom pepperless food was no food at all. Ali ibn el Hussein wanted sheep and butter and parched wheat for his men and the Biasha. Then there were the guests and refugees whom we might expect so soon as the news of our establishment was rumoured in Damascus. Till they came we should have a few days' repose, and we sat down to enjoy these dregs of autumn — the alternate days of rain and shine. We had sheep and flour, milk and fuel. Life in the fort, but for the ill-omened mud, went well enough.

Yet the peacefulness ended sooner than we thought. Wood, who had been ailing for some time, went down with a sharp attack of dysentery. This was nothing by itself, but the consequent weakness might have endangered him when winter set in earnestly. Besides, he was their base engineer at Akaba; and, except for the comfort of his companionship, I had no justification in keeping him longer. So we made up a party to go down with him to the coast, choosing as the escort, Ahmed, Abd el Rahman, Mahmoud, and Aziz. These were to return to Azrak forthwith from Akaba with a new caravan of stores, particularly comprising Indian rations. The rest of my men would stay in chilly idleness watching the situation develop.

Then began our flood of visitors. All day and every day they came, now in the running column of shots, raucous shouting and rush of camel-feet which meant a Bedouin parade, it might be of Rualla, or Sherarat, or Serahin, Serdiyeh, or Beni Sakhr, chiefs of great name like

P

ibn Zuhair, ibn Kaebir, Rafa el Khoreisha, or some little father of a family demonstrating his greedy goodwill before the fair eyes of Ali ibn el Hussein. Then it would be a wild gallop of horse: Druses, or the ruffling warlike peasants of the Arab plain. Sometimes it was a cautious, slow-led caravan of ridden camels, from which stiffly dismounted Syrian politicians or traders not accustomed to the road. One day arrived a hundred miserable Armenians, fleeing starvation and the suspended terror of the Turks. Again would come a spick and span group of mounted officers, Arab deserters from the Turkish armies, followed, often as not, by a compact company of Arab rank and file. Always they came, day after day, till the desert, which had been trackless when we came, was starred out with grey roads.

Ali appointed first one, then two, and at last three, guest-masters, who received the rising tide of these newcomers, sorted worshipful from curious, and marshalled them in due time before him or me. All wanted to know about the Sherif, the Arab army and the English. Merchants from Damascus brought presents: sweet-meats, sesame, caramel, apricot paste, nuts, silk clothes for ourselves, brocade cloaks, head-cloths, sheep-skins, felt rugs with coloured strands beaten into them in arabesques, Persian carpets. We returned them coffee and sugar, rice, and rolls of white cotton sheeting; necessities of which they had been deprived by war. Everybody learned that in Akaba there was plenty, coming across the open sea from all the markets of the world; and so the Arab cause which was theirs by sentiment, and instinct and inclination, became theirs by interest also. Slowly our example and teaching converted them: very slowly, by our own choice, that they might be ours more surely.

The greatest asset of Feisal's cause in this work up North was Sherif Ali ibn el Hussein. The lunatic competitor of the wilder tribesmen in their wildest feats was now turning all his force to greater ends. The mixed natures in him made of his face and body powerful pleadings, carnal, perhaps, except in so far as they were transfused by character. No one could see him without the desire to see him again; especially when he smiled, as he did rarely, with both mouth and eyes at once. His beauty was a conscious weapon. He dressed spotlessly, all in black or all in white; and he studied gesture.

Fortune had added physical perfection and unusual grace, but these qualities were only the just expression of his powers. They made obvious the pluck which never yielded, which would have let him be cut to pieces, holding on. His pride broke out in his war-cry, 'I am of the Harith', the two-thousand-year-old clan of freebooters; while the huge eyes, white with large black pupils slowly turning in them, emphasized the frozen dignity which was his ideal carriage, and to which he was always striving to still himself. But as ever the bubbling laugh would shriek out of him unawares; and the youth, boyish or girlish, of him, the fire and deviltry would break through his night like a sunrise.

Yet, despite this richness, there was a constant depression with him, the unknown longing of simple, restless people for abstract thought beyond their mind's supply. His bodily strength grew day by day, and hatefully fleshed over this humble something which he wanted more. His wild mirth was only one sign of the vain wearing-out of his desire. These besetting strangers underlined his detachment, his unwilling detachment, from his fellows. Despite his great instinct for confession and company, he could find no intimates. Yet he could not be alone. If he had no guests, Khazen, the servant, must serve his meals, while Ali and his slaves ate together.

In these slow nights we were secure against the world. For one thing, it was winter, and in the rain and the dark few men would venture either over the labyrinth of lava or through the marsh — the two approaches to our fortress; and, further, we had ghostly guardians. The first evening we were sitting with the Serahin, Hassan Shah had made the rounds, and the coffee was being pounded by the hearth, when there rose a strange, long wailing round the towers outside. Ibn Bani seized me by the arm and held to me, shuddering. I whispered to him, 'What is it?' and he gasped that the dogs of the Beni Hillal, the mythical builders of the fort, quested the six towers each night for their dead masters.

We strained to listen. Through Ali's black basalt window-frame crept a rustling, which was the stirring of the night-wind in the withered palms, an intermittent rustling, like English rain on yet-crisp fallen leaves. Then the cries came again and again and again, rising slowly in power, till they sobbed round the walls in deep waves to die away

choked and miserable. At such times our men pounded the coffee
harder while the Arabs broke into sudden song to occupy their ears
against the misfortune. No Bedouin would lie outside in wait for the
mystery, and from our windows we saw nothing but the motes of
water in the dank air which drove through the radiance of our firelight.
So it remained a legend: but wolves or jackals, hyænas, or hunting dogs,
their ghost-watch kept our ward more closely than arms could have done.

In the evening, when we had shut-to the gate, all guests would
assemble, either in my room or in Ali's, and coffee and stories would go
round until the last meal, and after it, till sleep came. On stormy nights
we brought in brushwood and dung and lit a great fire in the middle of
the floor. About it would be drawn the carpets and the saddle-sheep-
skins, and in its light we would tell over our own battles, or hear the
visitors' traditions. The leaping flames chased our smoke-ruffled
shadows strangely about the rough stone wall behind us, distorting
them over the hollows and projections of its broken face. When these
stories came to a period, our tight circle would shift over, uneasily, to
the other knee or elbow; while coffee-cups went clinking round, and a
servant fanned the blue reek of the fire towards the loophole with his
cloak, making the glowing ash swirl and sparkle with his draught. Till
the voice of the story-teller took up again, we would hear the rain-spots
hissing briefly as they dripped from the stone-beamed roof into the
fire's heart.

At last the sky turned solidly to rain, and no man could approach
us. In loneliness we learned the full disadvantages of imprisonment
within such gloomy ancient unmortared palaces. The rains guttered
down within the walls' thickness and spouted into the rooms from their
chinks. We set rafts of palm-branches to bear us clear of the streaming
floor, covered them with felt mats, and huddled down on them under
sheepskins, with another mat over us like a shield to throw off the
water. It was icy cold, as we hid there, motionless, from the murky
daylight until dark, our minds seeming suspended within these massive
walls, through whose every shot-window the piercing mist streamed
like a white pennant. Past and future flowed over us like an uneddying
river. We dreamed ourselves into the spirit of the place; sieges and
feasting, raids, murders, love-singing in the night.

This escape of our wits from the fettered body was an indulgence against whose enervation only change of scene could avail. Very painfully I drew myself again into the present, and forced my mind to say that it must use this wintry weather to explore the country lying round about Deraa.

As I was thinking how I would ride, there came to us, unheralded, one morning in the rain, Talal el Hareidhin, sheikh of Tafas. He was a famous outlaw with a price upon his head; but so great that he rode about as he pleased. In two wild years he had killed, according to report, some twenty-three of the Turks. His six followers were splendidly mounted, and himself the most dashing figure of a man in the height of Hauran fashion. His sheepskin coat was finest Angora covered in green broadcloth, with silk patches and designs in braid. His other clothes were silk; and his high boots, his silver saddle, his sword, dagger, and rifle matched his reputation.

He swaggered to our coffee-hearth, as a man sure of his welcome, greeting Ali boisterously (after our long sojourn with the tribes all peasants sounded boisterous), laughing broad-mouthed at the weather and our old fort and the enemy. He looked about thirty-five, was short and strong, with a full face, trimmed beard and long, pointed moustaches. His round eyes were made rounder, larger and darker by the antimony loaded on in villager style. He was ardently ours, and we rejoiced, since his name was one to conjure with in Hauran. When a day had made me sure of him, I took him secretly to the palm-garden, and told him my ambition to see his neighbourhood. The idea delighted him, and he companioned me for the march as thoroughly and cheerfully as only a Syrian on a good horse could. Halim and Faris, men specially engaged, rode with me as guards.

We went past Umtaiye, looking at tracks, wells and lava-fields, crossed the line to Sheikh Saad, and turned south to Tafas, where Talal was at home. Next day we went on to Tell Arar, a splendid position closing the Damascus railway and commanding Deraa. Afterwards we rode through tricky rolling country to Mezerib on the Palestine railway; planning, here also, for the next time; when with men, money and guns we should start the general rising to win inevitable victory. Perhaps the coming spring might see Allenby leap forward.

CHAPTER LXXX

PROPERLY to round off this spying of the hollow land of Hauran, it was necessary to visit Deraa, its chief town. We could cut it off on north and west and south, by destroying the three railways; but it would be more tidy to rush the junction first and work outwards. Talal, however, could not venture in with me since he was too well known in the place. So we parted from him with many thanks on both sides, and rode southward along the line until near Deraa. There we dismounted. The boy, Halim, took the ponies, and set off for Nisib, south of Deraa. My plan was to walk round the railway station and town with Faris, and reach Nisib after sunset. Faris was my best companion for the trip, because he was an insignificant peasant, old enough to be my father, and respectable.

The respectability seemed comparative as we tramped off in the watery sunlight, which was taking the place of the rain last night. The ground was muddy, we were barefoot, and our draggled clothes showed the stains of the foul weather to which we had been exposed. I was in Halim's wet things, with a torn Hurani jacket, and was yet limping from the broken foot acquired when we blew up Jemal's train. The slippery track made walking difficult, unless we spread out our toes widely and took hold of the ground with them: and doing this for mile after mile was exquisitely painful to me. Because pain hurt me so, I would not lay weight always on my pains in our revolt: yet hardly one day in Arabia passed without a physical ache to increase the corroding sense of my accessory deceitfulness towards the Arabs, and the legitimate fatigue of responsible command.

We mounted the curving bank of the Palestine Railway, and from its vantage surveyed Deraa Station: but the ground was too open to admit of surprise attack. We decided to walk down the east front of the defences: so we plodded on, noting German stores, barbed wire here and there, rudiments of trenches. Turkish troops were passing incuriously between the tents and their latrines dug out on our side.

At the corner of the aerodrome by the south end of the station we struck over towards the town. There were old Albatros machines in the sheds, and men lounging about. One of these, a Syrian soldier, began to question us about our villages, and if there was much 'government' where we lived. He was probably an intending deserter, fishing for a refuge. We shook him off at last and turned away. Someone called out in Turkish. We walked on deafly; but a sergeant came after, and took me roughly by the arm, saying 'The Bey wants you'. There were too many witnesses for fight or flight, so I went readily. He took no notice of Faris.

I was marched through the tall fence into a compound set about with many huts and a few buildings. We passed to a mud room, outside which was an earth platform, whereon sat a fleshy Turkish officer, one leg tucked under him. He hardly glanced at me when the sergeant brought me up and made a long report in Turkish. He asked my name: I told him Ahmed ibn Bagr, a Circassian from Kuneitra. 'A deserter?' 'But we Circassians have no military service'. He turned, stared at me, and said very slowly 'You are a liar. Enrol him in your section, Hassan Chowish, and do what is necessary till the Bey sends for him'.

They led me into a guard-room, mostly taken up by large wooden cribs, on which lay or sat a dozen men in untidy uniforms. They took away my belt, and my knife, made me wash myself carefully, and fed me. I passed the long day there. They would not let me go on any terms, but tried to reassure me. A soldier's life was not all bad. To-morrow, perhaps, leave would be permitted, if I fulfilled the Bey's pleasure this evening. The Bey seemed to be Nahi, the Governor. If he was angry, they said, I would be drafted for infantry training to the depot in Baalbek. I tried to look as though, to my mind, there was nothing worse in the world than that.

Soon after dark three men came for me. It had seemed a chance to get away, but one held me all the time. I cursed my littleness. Our march crossed the railway, where were six tracks, besides the sidings of the engine-shop. We went through a side gate, down a street, past a square, to a detached, two-storied house. There was a sentry outside, and a glimpse of others lolling in the dark entry. They took me upstairs to the Bey's room; or to his bedroom, rather. He was another bulky man, a Circassian himself, perhaps, and sat on the bed in a night-gown, trembling and sweating as though with fever. When I was pushed in he kept his head down, and waved the guard out. In a breathless voice he told me to sit on the floor in front of him, and after that was dumb; while I gazed at the top of his great head, on which the bristling hair stood up, no longer than the dark stubble on his cheeks and chin. At last he looked me over, and told me to stand up: then to turn round. I obeyed; he flung himself back on the bed, and dragged me down with him in his arms. When I saw what he wanted I twisted round and up again, glad to find myself equal to him, at any rate in wrestling.

He began to fawn on me, saying how white and fresh I was, how fine my hands and feet, and how he would let me off drills and duties, make me his orderly, even pay me wages, if I would love him.

I was obdurate, so he changed his tone, and sharply ordered me to take off my drawers. When I hesitated, he snatched at me; and I pushed him back. He clapped his hands for the sentry, who hurried in and pinioned me. The Bey cursed me with horrible threats: and made the man holding me tear my clothes away, bit by bit. His eyes rounded at the half-healed places where the bullets had flicked through my skin a little while ago. Finally he lumbered to his feet, with a glitter in his look, and began to paw me over. I bore it for a little, till he got too beastly; and then jerked my knee into him.

He staggered to his bed, squeezing himself together and groaning with pain, while the soldier shouted for the corporal and the other three men to grip me hand and foot. As soon as I was helpless the Governor regained courage, and spat at me, swearing he would make me ask pardon. He took off his slipper, and hit me repeatedly with it in the face, while the corporal braced my head back by the hair to receive the blows. He leaned forward, fixed his teeth in my neck and bit till the blood came. Then he kissed me. Afterwards he drew one of the men's bayonets. I thought he was going to kill me, and was sorry: but he only pulled up a fold of the flesh over my ribs, worked the point through, after considerable trouble, and gave the blade a half-turn. This hurt, and I winced, while the blood wavered down my side and dripped to the front of my thigh. He looked pleased and dabbled it over my stomach with his finger-tips.

In my despair I spoke. His face changed and he stood still, then controlled his voice with an effort, to say significantly, 'You must understand that I know: and it will be easier if you do as I wish'. I was dumbfounded, and we stared silently at one another, while the men who felt an inner meaning beyond their experience, shifted uncomfortably. But it was evidently a chance shot, by which he himself did not, or would not, mean what I feared. I could not again trust my twitching mouth, which faltered always in emergencies, so at last threw up my chin, which was the sign for 'No' in the East; then he sat down, and half-whispered to the corporal to take me out and teach me everything.

They kicked me to the head of the stairs, and stretched me over a guard-bench, pommelling me. Two knelt on my ankles, bearing down on the back of my knees, while two more twisted my wrists till they cracked, and then crushed them and my neck against the wood. The corporal had run downstairs; and now came back with a whip of the Circassian sort, a thong of supple black hide, rounded, and tapering from the thickness of a thumb at the grip (which was wrapped in silver) down to a hard point finer than a pencil.

He saw me shivering, partly I think, with cold, and made it whistle over my ear, taunting me that before his tenth cut I would howl for mercy, and at the twentieth beg for the caresses of the Bey; and then he began to lash me madly across and across with all his might, while I locked my teeth to endure this thing which lapped itself like flaming wire about my body.

To keep my mind in control I numbered the blows, but after twenty lost count, and could feel only the shapeless weight of pain, not tearing claws, for which I had prepared, but a gradual cracking apart of my whole being by some too-great force whose waves rolled up my spine till they were pent within my brain, to clash terribly together. Somewhere in the place a cheap clock ticked loudly, and it distressed me that their beating was not in its time. I writhed and twisted, but was held so tightly that my struggles were useless. After the corporal ceased, the men took up, very deliberately, giving me so many, and then an interval during which they would squabble for the next turn, ease themselves, and play unspeakably with me. This was repeated often, for what may

P*

have been no more than ten minutes. Always for the first of every new series, my head would be pulled round, to see how a hard white ridge, like a railway, darkening slowly into crimson, leaped over my skin at the instant of each stroke, with a bead of blood where two ridges crossed. As the punishment proceeded the whip fell more and more upon existing weals, biting blacker or more wet, till my flesh quivered with accumulated pain, and with terror of the next blow coming. They soon conquered my determination not to cry, but while my will ruled my lips I used only Arabic, and before the end a merciful sickness choked my utterance.

At last when I was completely broken they seemed satisfied. Somehow I found myself off the bench, lying on my back on the dirty floor, where I snuggled down, dazed, panting for breath, but vaguely comfortable. I had strung myself to learn all pain until I died, and no longer actor, but spectator, thought not to care how my body jerked and squealed. Yet I knew or imagined what passed about me.

I remembered the corporal kicking with his nailed boot to get me up; and this was true, for the next day my right side was dark and lacerated, and a damaged rib made each breath stab me sharply. I remembered smiling idly at him, for a delicious warmth, probably sexual, was swelling through me: and then that he flung up his arm and hacked with the full length of his whip into my groin. This doubled me half-over, screaming, or, rather, trying impotently to scream, only shuddering through my open mouth. One giggled with amusement. A voice cried, 'Shame, you've killed him'. Another slash followed. A roaring, and my eyes went black: while within me the core of life seemed to heave slowly up through the rending nerves, expelled from its body by this last indescribable pang.

By the bruises perhaps they beat me further: but I next knew that I was being dragged about by two men, each disputing over a leg as though to split me apart: while a third man rode me astride. It was momently better than more flogging. Then Nahi called. They splashed water in my face, wiped off some of the filth, and lifted me between them retching and sobbing for mercy, to where he lay: but he now rejected me in haste, as a thing too torn and bloody for his bed, blaming their excess of zeal which had spoilt me: whereas no doubt they had laid into me much as usual, and the fault rested mainly upon my indoor skin, which gave way more than an Arab's.

So the crestfallen corporal, as the youngest and best-looking of the guard, had to stay behind, while the others carried me down the narrow stair into the street. The coolness of the night on my burning flesh, and the unmoved shining of the stars after the horror of the past hour, made me cry again. The soldiers, now free to speak, warned me that men must suffer their officers' wishes or pay for it, as I had just done, with greater suffering.

They took me over an open space, deserted and dark, and behind the Government house to a lean-to wooden room, in which were many dusty quilts. An Armenian dresser appeared, to wash and bandage me in sleepy haste. Then all went away, the last soldier delaying by my side a moment to whisper in his Druse accent that the door into the next room was not locked.

I lay there in a sick stupor, with my head aching very much, and growing slowly numb with cold, till the dawn light came shining through the cracks of the shed, and a locomotive whistled in the station. These and a draining thirst brought me to life, and I found I was in no pain. Pain of the slightest had been my obsession and secret terror, from a boy. Had I now been drugged with it, to bewilderment? Yet the first movement was anguish: in which I struggled nakedly to my feet, and rocked moaning in wonder that it was not a dream, and myself back five years ago, a timid recruit at Khalfati, where something, less staining, of the sort had happened.

The next room was a dispensary. On its door hung a suit of shoddy clothes. I put them on slowly and unhandily, because of my swollen wrists: and from the drugs chose corrosive sublimate, as safeguard against recapture. The window looked on a long blank wall. Stiffly I climbed out, and went shaking down the road towards the village, past the few people already astir. They took no notice; indeed there was nothing peculiar in my dark broadcloth, red fez and slippers: but it was only by the full urge of my tongue silently to myself that I refrained from being foolish out of sheer fright. Deraa felt inhuman with vice and cruelty, and it shocked me like cold water when a soldier laughed behind me in the street.

By the bridge were the wells, with men and women about them. A side trough was free. From its end I scooped up a little water in my hands, and rubbed it over my face; then drank, which was precious to me; and afterwards wandered along the bottom of the valley, towards the south, unobtrusively retreating out of sight. This valley provided the hidden road by which our projected raid could attain Deraa town secretly, and surprise the Turks. So, in escaping I solved, too late, the problem which had brought me to Deraa.

Further on, a Serdi, on his camel, overtook me hobbling up the road towards Nisib. I explained that I had business there, and was already footsore. He had pity and mounted me behind him on his bony animal to which I clung the rest of the way, learning the feelings of my adopted name-saint on his gridiron. The tribe's tents were just in front of the village, where I found Faris and Halim anxious about me, and curious to learn how I had fared. Halim had been up to Deraa in the night, and knew by the lack of rumour that the truth had not been discovered. I told them a merry tale of bribery and trickery, which they promised to keep to themselves, laughing aloud at the simplicity of the Turks.

During the night I managed to see the great stone bridge by Nisib. Not that my maimed will now cared a hoot about the Arab Revolt (or about anything but mending itself): yet, since the war had been a hobby of mine, for custom's sake I would force myself to push it through. Afterwards we took horse, and rode gently and carefully towards Azrak, without incident, except that a raiding party of Wuld Ali let us and our horses go unplundered when they heard who we were. This was an unexpected generosity, the Wuld Ali being not yet of our fellowship. Their consideration (rendered at once, as if we had deserved men's homage) momently stayed me to carry the burden, whose certainty the passing days confirmed: how in Deraa that night the citadel of my integrity had been irrevocably lost.

CHAPTER LXXXI

XURY, the Druse Emir of Salkhad, reached our old castle just before me on his first visit to Sherif Ali. He told us the rest of the history of the Emir Abd el Kader, the Algerian. After stealing away from us he had ridden straight to their village, and entered in triumph, the Arab flag displayed, and his seven horsemen cantering about him, firing joy-shots. The people were astonished, and the Turkish Governor protested that such doings were an insult to him. He was introduced to Abd el Kader, who, sitting in pomp on the divan, made a bombastic speech, stating that the Sherif now took over Jebel Druse through his agency, and all existing officials were confirmed in their appointments.

Next morning he made a second progress through the district. The suffering Governor complained again. Emir Abd el Kader drew his gold-mounted Meccan sword, and swore that with it he would cut off Jemal Pasha's head. The Druses reproved him, vowing that such things should not be said in their house before his Excellency the Governor. Abd el Kader called them whoresons, ingle's accidents, sons of a bitch, profiteering cuckolds and pimps, jetting his insults broadcast to the roomfull. The Druses got angry. Abd el Kader flung raging out of the house and mounted, shouting that when he stamped his foot all Jebel Druse would rise on his side.

With his seven servants, he spurred down the road to Deraa Station, which he entered as he had entered Salkhad. The Turks, who knew his madness of old, left him to play. They disbelieved even his yarn that Ali and I would try the Yarmuk bridge that night. When, however, we did, they took a graver view, and sent him under custody to Damascus. Jemal's brutal humour was amused, and he enlarged him as a butt. Abd el Kader gradually became amenable. The Turks began to use him once more as *agent provocateur* and dissipator of the energy generated by their local Syrian nationalists.

The weather was now dreadful, with sleet and snow and storms continually; it was obvious that at Azrak there would be nothing but teaching and preaching in the next months. For this I was not eager. When necessary, I had done my share of proselytizing fatigues, converting as best I could; conscious all the time of my strangeness, and of the incongruity of an alien's advocating national liberty. The war for me held a struggle to side-track thought, to get into the people's attitude of accepting the revolt naturally and trustingly. I had to persuade myself that the British Government could really keep the spirit of its promises. Especially was this difficult when I was tired and ill, when the delirious activity of my brain tore to shreds my patience. And then, after the blunt Beduin who would thrust in, hailing me '*Ya Auruns*', and put their need without compliments, these smooth townspeople were maddening as they crawled for the favour of an audience with their Prince and Bey and Lord and Deliverer. Such imputed dignities, like body armour in a duel, were no doubt useful; but uncomfortable, and mean, too.

I had never been a lofty person; on the contrary I had tried to be accessible to everyone, even if it continually felt as though most of them came and saw me every day. I had striven as eloquently as I could by my own example to keep plain the standard of existence. I had had no tents, no cooks, no body-servants: just my guards, who were fighting men, not servile: and behold these Byzantine shopkeepers endeavouring to corrupt our simplicity! So I flung away from them in a rage, determined to go south and see if anything active could be done, in the cold weather, about the Dead Sea, which the enemy held as a trench dividing us from Palestine.

My remaining money was handed over to Sherif Ali, for his maintenance till the spring; and the Indians were commended to his care. Particularly we bought them fresh riding-camels, in case the need to move came suddenly upon them in the winter; though the daily news of a threat by the Turks against Azrak was scornfully discounted by young Ali. He and I took affectionate leave of one another. Ali gave me half his wardrobe: shirts, head-cloths, belts, tunics. I gave him an equivalent half of mine, and we kissed like David and Jonathan, each wearing the other's clothes. Afterwards, with Rahail only, on my two best camels, I struck away southward.

We left Azrak one evening, riding into a glowing west, while over our heads schools of cranes flew into the sunset like the out-drawn barbs of arrows. It was toilsome from the start. Night was deep by Wadi Butum, where the conditions became even worse. All the plain was wet, and our poor camels slithered and fell time and again. We fell as often as they did, but at least our part of sitting still, between falls, was easier than their part of movement. By midnight we had crossed the Ghadaf and the quag felt too awful for further progress. Also the mishandling at Deraa had left me curiously faint; my muscles seemed at once pappy and inflamed, and all effort frightened me in anticipation. So we halted.

We slept where we were, in the mud; rose up plated with it at dawn; and smiled crackily at one another. The wind blew, and the ground began to dry. It was important, for I wanted to reach Akaba before Wood's men had left it with the return caravan, and their eight days' start called for speed. My body's reluctance to ride hard was another (and perverse) reason for forcing the march. Until noon we made poor travelling, for the camels still broke through the loose crust of flints, and foundered in the red under-clay. After noon, on the higher ground, we did better, and began rapidly to close the white sky-tents which were the Thlaithakhwat peaks.

Suddenly shots rang out at close range, and four mouthing men dashed down the slope towards us. I stopped my camel peaceably. Seeing this they jumped off, and ran to us brandishing their arms. They asked who I was: volunteering that they were Jazi Howeitat. This was an open lie, because their camel-brands were Faiz. They covered us with rifles at four yards, and told us to dismount. I laughed at them, which was good tactics with Beduin at a crisis. They were puzzled. I asked the loudest if he knew his name. He stared at me, thinking I was mad. He came nearer, with his finger on the trigger, and I bent down to him and whispered that it must be 'Teras' since no other tradesman could be so rude. As I spoke, I covered him with a pistol hidden under my cloak.

It was a shooting insult, but he was so astonished that anyone should provoke an armed man, as to give up for the moment his thought of murdering us. He took a step back, and looked around, fearful that there was a reserve somewhere, to give us confidence. At once I rode off slowly, with a creepy feeling in my back, calling Rahail to follow.

They let him go too, unhurt. When we were a hundred yards away, they repented themselves, and began to shoot, but we dashed over the watershed into the next depression, and across it cantered more confidently into safe ground.

From the ridge at sunset we looked back for an instant upon the northern plain, as it sank away from us greyly, save that here and there glowed specks or great splashes of crimson fire, the reflection of the dying sun in shallow pools of rain-water on the flats. These eyes of a dripping bloody redness were so much more visible than the plain that they carried our sight miles into the haze, and seemed to hang detached in the distant sky, tilted up, like mirage.

We passed Bair long after dark, when only its latest tent-fires still shone. As we went we saw the stars mirrored in a valley bottom, and were able to water our breathless camels in a pool of yesterday's rain. After their drink, we eased them for half an hour. This night-journeying was hard on both men and animals. By day the camels saw the irregularities of their path, and undulated over them; and the rider could swing his body to miss the jerk of a long or short stride: but by night everything was blinded, and the march racked with shocks. I had a heavy bout of fever on me, which made me angry, so that I paid no attention to Rahail's appeals for rest. That young man had maddened all of us for months by his abundant vigour, and by laughing at our weaknesses; so this time I was determined to ride him out, showing no mercy. Before dawn he was blubbering with self-pity; but softly, lest I hear him.

Dawn in Jefer came imperceptibly through the mist like a ghost of sunlight, which left the earth untouched, and demonstrated itself as a glittering blink against the eyes alone. Things at their heads stood matt against the pearl-grey horizon, and at their feet melted softly into the ground. Our shadows had no edge: we doubted if that faint stain upon the soil below was cast by us or not. In the forenoon we reached Auda's camp; and stopped for a greeting, and a few Jauf dates. Auda could not provide us a relay of camels. We mounted again to get over the railway in the early night. Rahail was past protest now. He rode beside me white-faced, bleak and silent, wrought up only to outstay me, beginning to take a half pride in his pains.

Even had we started fair, he had the advantage anyhow over me in strength, and now I was nearly finished. Step by step I was yielding myself to a slow ache which conspired with my abating fever and the numb monotony of riding to close up the gate of my senses. I seemed at last approaching the insensibility which had always been beyond my reach: but a delectable land: for one born so slug-tissued that nothing this side fainting would let his spirit free. Now I found myself dividing into parts. There was one which went on riding wisely, sparing or helping every pace of the wearied camel. Another hovering above and to the right bent down curiously, and asked what the flesh was doing. The flesh gave no answer, for, indeed, it was conscious only of a ruling impulse to keep on and on; but a third garrulous one talked and wondered, critical of the body's self-inflicted labour, and contemptuous of the reason for effort.

The night passed in these mutual conversations. My unseeing eyes saw the dawn-goal in front; the head of the pass, below which that other world of Rumm lay out like a sunlit map; and my parts debated that the struggle might be worthy, but the end foolishness and a re-birth of trouble. The spent body toiled on doggedly and took no heed, quite rightly, for the divided selves said nothing which I was not capable of thinking in cold blood; they were all my natives. Telesius, taught by some such experience, split up the soul. Had he gone on, to the furthest limit of exhaustion, he would have seen his conceived regiment of thoughts and acts and feelings ranked around him as separate creatures; eyeing, like vultures, the passing in their midst of the common thing which gave them life.

Rahail collected me out of my death-sleep by jerking my head-stall and striking me, while he shouted that we had lost our direction, and were wandering toward the Turkish lines at Aba el Lissan. He was right, and we had to make a long cut back to reach Batra safely. We walked down the steeper portions of the pass, and then stumbled along Wadi Hafira. In its midst a gallant little Howeiti, aged perhaps fourteen, darted out against us, finger on trigger, and told us to stand and explain; which we did, laughing. The lad blushed, and pleaded that his father's camels kept him always in the field so that he had not known us either by sight or by description. He begged that we would not do him shame by betraying his error. The incident broke the tension between Rahail and myself; and, chatting, we rode out upon the Gaa. There under the tamarisk we passed the middle hour of the day in sleep, since by our slowness in the march over Batra we had lost the possibility of reaching Akaba within the three days from Azrak. The breaking of our intention we took quietly. Rumm's glory would not let a man waste himself in feverish regrets.

We rode up its valley in the early afternoon; easier now and exchanging jests with one another, as the long winter evening crept down. When we got past the Khazail in the ascent we found the sun veiled behind level banks of low clouds in the west, and enjoyed a rich twilight of the English sort. In Itm the mist steamed up gently from the soil, and collected into wool-white masses in each hollow. We reached Akaba at midnight, and slept outside the camp till breakfast, when I called on Joyce, and found the caravan not yet ready to start: indeed Wood was only a few days returned.

Later came urgent orders for me to go up at once to Palestine by air. Croil flew me to Suez. Thence I went up to Allenby's headquarters beyond Gaza. He was so full of victories that my short statement that we had failed to carry a Yarmuk bridge was sufficient, and the miserable details of failure could remain concealed.

While I was still with him, word came from Chetwode that Jerusalem had fallen; and Allenby made ready to enter in the official manner which the catholic imagination of Mark Sykes had devised. He was good enough, although I had done nothing for the success, to let Clayton take me along as his staff officer for the day. The personal Staff tricked me out in their spare clothes till I looked like a major in the British Army. Dalmeny lent me red tabs, Evans his brass hat; so that I had the gauds of my appointment in the ceremony of the Jaffa gate, which for me was the supreme moment of the war.

BOOK VII

THE DEAD SEA CAMPAIGN

Chapters LXXXII to XCI

AFTER *the capture of Jerusalem, Allenby, to relieve his right, assigned us a limited objective. We began well; but when we reached the Dead Sea, bad weather, bad temper and division of purpose blunted our offensive spirit and broke up our force.*

I had a misunderstanding with Zeid, threw in my hand, and returned to Palestine reporting that we had failed, and asking the favour of other employment. Allenby was in the hopeful midst of a great scheme for the coming spring. He sent me back at once to Feisal with new powers and duties.

CHAPTER LXXXII

S HAMEFACED with triumph – which was not so much a triumph as homage by Allenby to the mastering spirit of the place – we drove back to Shea's headquarters. The aides pushed about, and from great baskets drew a lunch, varied, elaborate and succulent. On us fell a short space of quiet, to be shattered by Monsieur Picot, the French political representative permitted by Allenby to march beside Clayton in the entry, who said in his fluting voice: 'And to-morrow, my dear general, I will take the necessary steps to set up civil government in this town.'

It was the bravest word on record; a silence followed, as when they opened the seventh seal in heaven. Salad, chicken mayonnaise and foie gras sandwiches hung in our wet mouths unmunched, while we turned to Allenby and gaped. Even he seemed for the moment at a loss. We began to fear that the idol might betray a frailty. But his face grew red: he swallowed, his chin coming forward (in the way we loved), whilst he said, grimly, 'In the military zone the only authority is that of the Commander-in-Chief – myself.' 'But Sir Grey, Sir Edward Grey' . . . stammered M. Picot. He was cut short. 'Sir Edward Grey referred to the civil government which will be established when I judge that the military situation permits.' And by car again, through the sunshine of a great thankfulness, we sped down the saluting mountain-side into our camp.

There Allenby and Dawnay told me the British were marched and fought nearly to a standstill, in the ledged and precipitous hills, shell-torn and bullet-spattered, amid which they wrestled with the Turks along a line from Ramleh to Jerusalem. So they would ask us in the lull to come north towards the Dead Sea until, if possible, we linked right up to its southern end, and renewed the continuous front. Fortunately, this had already been discussed with Feisal, who was preparing the convergent move on Tafileh, its necessary first step.

It was the moment to ask Allenby what he would do next. He thought he was immobilized till the middle of February, when he would push down to Jericho. Much enemy food was being lightered

464

up the Dead Sea, and he asked me to note this traffic as a second objective if the effort to Tafileh prevailed.

I, hoping to improve on this, replied that, should the Turks be continually shaken, we might join him at the north end of the Dead Sea. If he could put Feisal's fifty tons a day of supplies, stores and ammunition into Jericho, we would abandon Akaba and transfer our headquarters to the Jordan Valley. The Arab regulars, now some three thousand strong, would suffice to make our retention of the river's eastern bank reasonably secure.

This idea commended itself to Allenby and Dawnay. They could almost promise us such facilities when the railway reached Jerusalem some time towards the end of the coming January. We might be able to move our base two months after the line was through.

This talk left us a clear course of operations. The Arabs were to reach the Dead Sea as soon as possible; to stop the transport of food up it to Jericho before the middle of February; and to arrive at the Jordan before the end of March. Since the first movement would take a month to start, and all preliminaries were in hand, I could take a holiday. So I went down to Cairo, and stayed there a week experimenting with insulated cable and explosives.

After the week it seemed best to return to Akaba, where we arrived on Christmas Day; to find Snagge, as senior officer in Akaba, entertaining the British Community to dinner. He had screened-in the after deck and built tables, which took the hosts and the twenty-odd guests easily. Snagge stood godfather to the land, in hospitality, in the loan of his ship's doctor and workshop, and in cheerfulness.

In the early days of the revolt it had been the *Hardinge* which played his role of providence to us. Once, at Yenbo, Feisal had ridden in from the hills on a streaming day of winter, cold, wet, miserable and tired. Captain Linberry sent a launch ashore and invited him to the ship, where he found, waiting for him, a warm cabin, a peaceful meal, and a bountiful bath. Afterwards he lay back in an arm-chair, smoking one of his constant cigarettes, and remarked dreamily to me that now he knew what the furnishings of heaven would be.

Joyce told me that things were well. The situation had sensibly changed since Maulud's victory. The Turks had concentrated in Aba el Lissan. We were distracting them by raids against the line south of Maan. Abdulla and Ali were doing the same near Medina; and the Turks, being pinched to guard the railway had to draw men from Aba el Lissan to strengthen weak sections.

Maulud boldly threw out posts to places on the plateau, and began to harry the supply caravans from Maan. He was hampered by the intense cold, the rain and snow on the heights. Some of his ill-clad men actually died of exposure. But the Turks lost equally in men and much more in transport, since their mangy camels died off rapidly in the storms and mud. The loss straitened them in food-carrying and involved further withdrawals from Aba el Lissan.

At last they were too weak to hold the wide position, and, early in January, Maulud was able to force them out towards Mreigha. The Beduin caught the Turks moving, and cut up the hindmost battalion. This threw the Turks back precipitately, to Uheida, only six miles from Maan, and when we pressed after menacingly, they withdrew to Semna, the outpost line of Maan, three miles out. So by January the seventh Maulud was containing Maan directly.

Prosperity gave us ten days' leisure; and as Joyce and myself were rarely at liberty together we decided to celebrate the occasion by taking a car-trip down the mud-flats towards Mudowwara.

The cars were now at Guweira, in permanent camp. Gilman and Dowsett, with their crews and fifty Egyptian soldiers, had spent months in Wadi Itm, building, like engineers, a motor road through the gorge. It had been a great work, and was now in order to Guweira. So we took the Rolls tenders, filled them with spare tyres, petrol, and food for four days, and set off on our exploring trip.

The mud-flats were bone-dry and afforded perfect going. Our tyres left only a faint white scar across their velvet surface, as we twisted about the spacious smoothness at speed, skirting clumps of tamarisk and roaring along under the great sandstone crags. The drivers rejoiced for the first time in nine months, and flung forward abreast in a mad race. Their speedometers touched sixty-five; not bad for cars which had been months ploughing the desert with only such running repairs as the drivers had time and tools to give them.

Across the sandy neck from the first flat to the second we built a corduroy road of brushwood. When this was ready, the cars came steaming and hissing along it, dangerously fast to avoid getting stuck, rocking over hummocks in a style which looked fatal for springs. However, we knew it was nearly impossible to break a Rolls-Royce, and so were sorrier for the drivers, Thomas, Rolls and Sanderson. The jolts tore the steering-wheel from their grip, and left them breathless with bleeding hands after the crossing.

We lunched and rested, and then had another burst of speed, with a wild diversion in the middle when a gazelle was sighted over the flat and two of the great cars lurched aside in unavailing chase.

At the end of this second flat, the Gaa of Disi, we had a rough mile to the third flat of Abu Sawana, across which we had a final glorious sprint of fifteen miles, over the mud and over the equally firm flint plains beyond. We slept there that chilly night, happy with bully beef and tea and biscuit, with English talk and laughter round the fire, golden with its shower of sparks from the fierce brushwood. When these things tired, there was soft sand beneath our bodies and two blankets to wrap ourselves in. For me it was a holiday, with not an Arab near, before whom I must play out my tedious part.

In the morning we ran on nearly to Mudowwara, finding the ground-surface excellent to the watershed. So our reconnaissance had been a quick and easy success. At once we turned back, to fetch the armoured cars and undertake an immediate operation, with the help of the mountain gun section on Talbots.

This section was an oddment, which General Clayton had seen in Egypt, and had sent down to us in an inspired moment. Its six Talbots, specially geared for heavy work, carried two ten-pounders with British gunners. It was wicked to give good men such rotten tools; yet their spirit seemed hardly affected by the inferior weapons. Their commander, Brodie, was a silent Scotsman, never very buoyant and never too anxious; a man who found difficulties shameful to notice, and who stamped himself on his fellows. However hard the duty given them, they always attacked it with such untroubled determination that their will prevailed. On every occasion and in every crisis they would be surely in place at their moment, perspiring but imperturbable, with never a word in explanation or complaint.

Eight imposing cars drove off from Guweira next day, and reached our old stopping-place behind Mudowwara by sundown. This was excellent; and we camped, intending to find a road to the railway in the morning. Accordingly we set off early in a Rolls tender and searched through the very nasty low hills till evening, when we were in place behind the last ridge, above Tell Shahm, the second station northward from Mudowwara.

We had talked vaguely of mining a train, but the country was too open, and enemy blockhouses numerous. Instead we determined to attack a little entrenched work exactly opposite our hiding-place. So late in new year's morning, a day as cool as a good summer's day in England, after a pleasant breakfast we rolled gently over a stony plain to a hillock which overlooked the Turkish post. Joyce and I got out of our cars and climbed its summit, to look on.

Joyce was in charge, and for the first time I was at a fight as spectator. The novelty was most enjoyable. Armoured car work seemed fighting de luxe, for our troops, being steel-covered, could come to no hurt. Accordingly we made a field-day of it like the best regular generals, sitting in laconic conference on our hill-top and watching the battle intently through binoculars.

The Talbot battery opened the affair, coming spiritedly into action just below our point; while the three armoured cars crawled about the flanks of the Turkish earthwork like great dogs nosing out a trail. The enemy soldiers popped up their heads to gaze, and everything was very friendly and curious, till the cars slewed round their Vickers and began to spray the trenches. Then the Turks, realizing that it was an attack, got down behind their parapets and fired at the cars raggedly. It was about as deadly as trying to warm a rhinoceros with bird-shot: after a while they turned their attention to Brodie's guns and peppered the earth about them with bullets.

Obviously they did not mean to surrender, and obviously we had no means at disposal to compel them. So we drew off, contented with having prowled up and down the line, and proved the surface hard enough for car-operations at deliberate speed. However, the men looked for more, and to humour them we drove southward till opposite Shahm. There Brodie chose a gun-position at two thousand yards and began to throw shell after shell neatly into the station area.

Hating this, the Turks trickled off to a blockhouse, while the cars put leisurely bullets through the station doors and windows. They might have entered it safely, had there been point in doing so. As it was we called everybody off again, and returned into our hiding-hills. Our anxiety and forethought had been all to reach the railway through the manifold difficulties of the plains and hills. When we did reach it, we were entirely unready for action, with not a conception of what our tactics or method should be: yet we learned much from this very indecision.

The certainty that in a day from Guweira we could be operating along the railway, meant that traffic lay at our mercy. All the Turks in Arabia could not fight a single armoured car in open country. Thereby the situation of Medina, already bad, became hopeless. The German Staff saw it, and after Falkenhayn's visit to Maan, they repeatedly urged abandonment of everything south of that point; but the old Turk party valued Medina as the last remnant of their sovereignty in the Holy Places, their surviving claim upon the Caliphate. Sentiment swung them to the decision, against military expediency.

The British seemed curiously dense about Medina. They insisted that it must be captured, and lavished money and explosives on the operations which Ali and Abdulla continually undertook from their Yenbo base. When I pleaded to the contrary, they treated my view as a witty paradox. Accordingly, to excuse our deliberate inactivity in the north, we had to make a show of impotence, which gave them to understand that the Arabs were too poltroon to cut the line near Maan and keep it cut. This reason gratified their sense of fitness, for soldiers, always ready to believe ill of native action, took its inferiority as a compliment. So we battened on our ill reputation, which was an ungenerous stratagem, but the easiest. The staff knew so much more of war than I did that they refused to learn from me of the strange conditions in which Arab irregulars had to act; and I could not be bothered to set up a kindergarten of the imagination for their benefit.

ON our return to Akaba domestic affairs engaged the remaining free days. My part mostly concerned the bodyguard which I formed for private protection, as rumour gradually magnified my importance. On our first going up country from Rabegh and Yenbo, the Turks had been curious: afterwards they were annoyed; to the point of ascribing to the English the direction and motive force of the Arab Revolt, much as we used to flatter ourselves by attributing the Turkish efficiency to German influence.

However, the Turks said it often enough to make it an article of faith, and began to offer a reward of one hundred pounds for a British officer alive or dead. As time went on they not only increased the general figure, but made a special bid for me. After the capture of Akaba the price became respectable; while after we blew up Jemal Pasha they put Ali and me at the head of their list; worth twenty thousand pounds alive or ten thousand dead.

Of course, the offer was rhetorical; with no certainty whether in gold or paper, or that the money would be paid at all. Still, perhaps, it might justify some care. I began to increase my people to a troop, adding such lawless men as I found, fellows whose dash had got them into trouble elsewhere. I needed hard riders and hard livers; men proud of themselves, and without family. By good fortune three or four of this sort joined me at the first, setting a tone and standard.

One afternoon, I was quietly reading in Marshall's tent at Akaba (I lodged with Marshall, our Scottish doctor, as often as I was in camp) when there entered over the noiseless sand an Ageyly, thin, dark, and short, but most gorgeously dressed. He carried on his shoulder the richest Hasa saddle-bag I had ever seen. Its woollen tapestry of green and scarlet, white, orange and blue, had tassels woven over its sides in five rows, and from the middle and bottom hung five-foot streamers of geometric pattern, tasselled and fringed.

Respectfully greeting me, the young man threw the saddle-bag on my carpet, saying 'Yours' and disappeared suddenly, as he had come. Next day, he returned with a camel-saddle of equal beauty, the long brass horns of its cantles adorned with exquisite old Yemeni engraving. On the third day he reappeared empty-handed, in a poor cotton shirt, and sank down in a heap before me, saying he wished to enter my service. He looked odd without his silk robes; for his face, shrivelled and torn with smallpox, and hairless, might have been of any age; while he had a lad's supple body, and something of a lad's recklessness in his carriage.

His long black hair was carefully braided into three shining plaits down each cheek. His eyes were weak, closed up to slits. His mouth was sensual, loose, wet; and gave him a good-humoured, half cynical expression. I asked him his name; he replied Abdulla, surnamed el Nahabi, or the Robber; the nickname, he said was an inheritance from his respected father. His own adventures had been unprofitable. He was born in Boreida, and while young had suffered from the civil power for his impiety. When half-grown, a misfortune in a married woman's house had made him leave his native town, in a hurry, and take service with ibn Saud, Emir of Nejd.

In this service his hard swearing earned lashes and imprisonment. Consequently he deserted to Kuweit, where again he had been amorous. On his release he had moved to Hail, and enrolled himself among the retainers of ibn Rashid, the Emir. Unfortunately there he had disliked his officer to the point of striking him in public with a camel-stick. Return was made in kind; and, after a slow recovery in prison, he had once more been thrust friendless on the world.

The Hejaz Railway was being built, and to its works he had come in search of fortune; but a contractor docked his wages for sleeping at noonday. He retorted by docking the contractor of his head. The Turkish Government interfered, and he found life very hard in the prison at Medina. However, through a window, he came to Mecca, and for his proved integrity and camel-manship was made post-carrier between Mecca and Jidda. To this employ he settled down, laying aside his young extravagances, bringing to Mecca his father and mother and setting them up in a shop to work for him, with the capital provided by commission from merchants and robbers.

After a year's prosperity he was waylaid, losing his camel and its consignment. They seized his shop in compensation. From the wreck he saved enough to fit himself out as a man at arms, in the Sherifian camel-police. Merit made him a petty officer, but too much attention was drawn to his section by a habit of fighting with daggers, and by his foul mouth; a maw of depravity which had eaten filth in the stews of every capital in Arabia. Once too often his lips trembled with humour, sardonic, salacious, lying; and when reduced, he charged his downfall to a jealous Ateibi, whom he stabbed in Court before the eyes of the outraged Sherif Sharraf.

Sharraf's stern sense of public decency punished Abdulla by the severest of his chastisements, from which he very nearly died. When well enough, he entered Sharraf's service. On the outbreak of war he became orderly to ibn Dakhil, captain of the Ageyl with Feisal. His reputation grew: but the mutiny at Wejh turned ibn Dakhil into an ambassador. Abdulla missed the comradeship of the ranks, and ibn Dakhil had given him a written character to enter my service.

The letter said that for two years he had been faithful, but disrespectful; the wont of sons of shame. He was the most experienced Ageyli, having served every Arabian prince and having been dismissed each employment, after stripes and prison, for offences of too great individuality. Ibn Dakhil said that the Nahabi rode second to himself, was a master-judge of camels, and as brave as any son of Adam; easily since he was too blind-eyed to see danger. In fact, he was the perfect retainer and I engaged him instantly.

In my service only once did he taste cells. That was at Allenby's headquarters, when a despairing provost-marshal rang up to say that a wild man, with weapons, found sitting on the Commander-in-Chief's doorstep had been led without riot to the guard-room, where he was eating oranges as though for a wager, and proclaiming himself my son, one of Feisal's dogs. Oranges were running short.

So Abdulla experienced his first telephone conversation. He told the A.P.M. that such a fitting would be a comfort in all prisons, and took a ceremonious leave. He scouted absolutely the notion that he might walk about Ramleh unarmed, and was given a pass to make lawful his sword, dagger, pistol, and rifle. His first use of this pass was to re-visit the guard-room with cigarettes for the military police.

He examined the applicants for my service, and, thanks to him and to the Zaagi, my other commander (a stiff man of normal officer cut), a wonderful gang of experts grew about me. The British at Akaba called them cut-throats; but they cut throats only to my order. Perhaps in others' eyes it was a fault that they would recognize no authority but mine. Yet when I was away they were kind to Major Marshall, and would hold him in incomprehensible talk about points of camels, their breeds and ailments, from dawn till night time. Marshall was very patient; and two or three of them would sit attentive by his bedside, from the first daylight, waiting to continue his education as soon as he became conscious.

A good half (nearly fifty of the ninety) were Ageyl, the nervous limber Nejdi villagers who made the colour and the parade in Feisal's army, and whose care for their riding camels was such a feature of their service. They would call them by name, from a hundred yards away, and leave them in charge of the kit when they dismounted. The Ageyl, being mercenaries, would not do well unless well paid, and for lack of that condition had fallen into disrepute: yet the bravest single effort of the Arab war belonged to that one of them who twice swam down the subterranean water-conduit into Medina, and returned with a full report of the invested town.

I paid my men six pounds a month, the standard army wage for a man and camel, but mounted them on my own animals, so that the money was clear income: this made the service enviable, and put the eager spirits of the camp at my disposal. For my time-table's sake, since I was more busy than most, my rides were long, hard and sudden. The ordinary Arab, whose camel represented half his wealth, could not afford to founder it by travelling my speed: also such riding was painful for the man.

Consequently, I had to have with me picked riders, on my own beasts. We bought at long prices the fastest and strongest camels to be obtained. We chose them for speed and power, no matter how hard and exhausting they might be under the saddle: indeed, often we chose the hard-paced as the more enduring. They were changed or rested in our own camel-hospital when they became thin: and their riders were treated likewise. The Zaagi held each man bodily responsible for his mount's condition, and for the fitness of his saddlery.

Fellows were very proud of being in my bodyguard, which developed a professionalism almost flamboyant. They dressed like a bed of tulips, in every colour but white; for that was my constant wear, and they did not wish to seem to presume. In half an hour they would make ready for a ride of six weeks, that being the limit for which food could be carried at the saddle-bow. Baggage camels they shrank from as a disgrace. They would travel day and night at my whim, and made it a point of honour never to mention fatigue. If a new man grumbled, the others would silence him, or change the current of his complaint, brutally.

They fought like devils, when I wanted, and sometimes when I did not, especially with Turks or with outsiders. For one guardsman to strike another was the last offence. They expected extravagant reward and extravagant punishment. They made boast throughout the army of their pains and gains. By this unreason in each degree they were kept apt for any effort, any risk.

Abdulla and the Zaagi ruled them, under my authority, with a savagery palliated only by the power of each man to quit the service if he wished. Yet we had but one resignation. The others, though adolescents full of carnal passion, tempted by this irregular life, well-fed, exercised, rich, seemed to sanctify their risk, to be fascinated by their suffering. Servitude, like other conduct, was profoundly modified to Eastern minds by their obsession with the antithesis between flesh and spirit. These lads took pleasure in subordination; in degrading the body: so as to throw into greater relief their freedom in equality of mind: almost they preferred servitude as richer in experience than authority, and less binding in daily care.

Consequently the relation of master and man in Arabia was at once more free and more subject than I had experienced elsewhere. Servants were afraid of the sword of justice and of the steward's whip, not because the one might put an arbitrary term to their existence, and the other print red rivers of pain about their sides, but because these were the symbols and the means to which their obedience was vowed. They had a gladness of abasement, a freedom of consent to yield to their master the last service and degree of their flesh and blood, because their spirits were equal with his and the contract voluntary. Such boundless engagement precluded humiliation, repining and regret.

In this pledging of their endurance, it disgraced men, if from weakness of nerve or insufficiency of courage, they fell short of the call. Pain was to them a solvent, a cathartic, almost a decoration, to be fairly worn while they survived it. Fear, the strongest motive in slothful man, broke down with us, since love for a cause — or for a person — was aroused. For such an object, penalties were discounted, and loyalty became open-eyed, not obedient. To it men dedicated their being, and in its possession they had no room for virtue or vice. Cheerfully they nourished it upon what they were; gave it their lives; and, greater than that, the lives of their fellowship: it being many times harder to offer than to endure sacrifice.

To our strained eyes, the ideal, held in common, seemed to transcend the personal, which before had been our normal measure of the world. Did this instinct point to our happily accepting final absorption in some pattern wherein the discordant selves might find reasonable, inevitable purpose? Yet this very transcending of individual frailty made the ideal transient. Its principle became Activity, the primal quality, external to our atomic structure, which we could simulate only by unrest of mind and soul and body, beyond holding point. So always the ideality of the ideal vanished, leaving its worshippers exhausted: holding for false what they had once pursued.

However, for the time the Arabs were possessed, and cruelty of governance answered their need. Besides, they were blood enemies of thirty tribes, and only for my hand over them would have murdered in the ranks each day. Their feuds prevented them combining against me; while their unlikeness gave me sponsors and spies wherever I went or sent, between Akaba and Damascus, between Beersheba and Bagdad. In my service nearly sixty of them died.

With quaint justice, events forced me to live up to my bodyguard, to become as hard, as sudden, as heedless. The odds against me were heavy, and the climate cogged the die. In the short winter I outdid them, with my allies of the frost and snow: in the heat they outdid me. In endurance there was less disparity. For years before the war I had made myself trim by constant carelessness. I had learned to eat much one time; then to go two, three, or four days without food; and after to overeat. I made it a rule to avoid rules in food; and by a course of exceptions accustomed myself to no custom at all.

So, organically, I was efficient in the desert, felt neither hunger nor surfeit, and was not distracted by thought of food. On the march I could go dry between wells, and, like the Arabs, could drink greatly to-day for the thirst of yesterday and of to-morrow.

In the same way, though sleep remained for me the richest pleasure in the world, I supplied its place by the uneasy swaying in the saddle of a night-march, or failed of it for night after laborious night without undue fatigue. Such liberties came from years of control (contempt of use might well be the lesson of our manhood), and they fitted me peculiarly for our work: but, of course, in me they came half by training, half by trying, out of mixed choice and poverty, not effortlessly, as with the Arabs. Yet in compensation stood my energy of motive. Their less taut wills flagged before mine flagged, and by comparison made me seem tough and active.

Into the sources of my energy of will I dared not probe. The conception of antithetical mind and matter, which was basic in the Arab self-surrender, helped me not at all. I achieved surrender (so far as I did achieve it) by the very opposite road, through my notion that mental and physical were inseparably one: that our bodies, the universe, our thoughts and tactilities were conceived in and of the molecular sludge of matter, the universal element through which form drifted as clots and patterns of varying density. It seemed to me unthinkable that assemblages of atoms should cogitate except in atomic terms. My perverse sense of values constrained me to assume that abstract and concrete, as badges, did not denote oppositions more serious than Liberal and Conservative.

The practice of our revolt fortified the nihilist attitude in me. During it, we often saw men push themselves or be driven to a cruel extreme of endurance: yet never was there an intimation of physical break. Collapse rose always from a moral weakness eating into the body, which of itself, without traitors from within, had no power over the will. While we rode we were disbodied, unconscious of flesh or feeling: and when at an interval this excitement faded and we did see our bodies, it was with some hostility, with a contemptuous sense that they reached their highest purpose, not as vehicles of the spirit, but when, dissolved, their elements served to manure a field.

Q

REMOTE from the fighting line, in Akaba, during this pause, we saw the reverse of the shield, the corruption of our enthusiasm, which made the moral condition of the base unsatisfactory. We rejoiced when at last we were able to escape into the clean, fresh hills about Guweira. The early winter gave us days hot and sunny, or days overcast, with clouds massed about the head of the plateau nine miles away, where Maulud was keeping his watch in the mist and rain. The evenings held just enough of chill to add delightful value to a thick cloak and a fire.

We waited in Guweira for news of the opening of our operation against Tafileh, the knot of villages commanding the south end of the Dead Sea. We planned to tackle it from west, south, and east, at once; the east opening the ball by attacking Jurf, its nearest station on the Hejaz line. Conduct of this attack had been trusted to Sherif Nasir, the Fortunate. With him went Nuri Said, Jaafar's chief of staff, commanding some regulars, a gun, and some machine-guns. They were working from Jefer. After three days their post came in. As usual Nasir had directed his raid with skill and deliberation. Jurf, the objective, was a strong station of three stone buildings with outer-works and trenches. Behind the station was a low mound, trenched and walled, on which the Turks had set two machine-guns and a mountain gun. Beyond the mount lay a high, sharp ridge, the last spur of the hills which divided Jefer from Bair.

The weakness of the defence lay in this ridge, for the Turks were too few to hold both it and the knoll or station, and its crest overlooked the railway. Nasir one night occupied the whole top of the hill without alarm, and then cut the line above and below the station. A few minutes later, when it was light enough to see, Nuri Said brought his mountain gun to the edge of the ridge; and, with a third lucky shot, a direct hit, silenced the Turkish gun beneath his view.

Nasir grew greatly excited: the Beni Sakhr mounted their camels, swearing they would charge in forthwith. Nuri thought it madness while Turkish machine-guns were still in action from trenches: but his words had no effect upon the Bedu. In desperation he opened a rattling fire with all he had against the Turkish position, and the Beni Sakhr swept round the foot of the main ridge and up over the knoll in a flash. When they saw this camel-horde racing at them, the Turks flung away their rifles and fled into the station. Only two Arabs were fatally hurt.

Nuri ran down to the knoll. The Turkish gun was undamaged. He slewed it round and discharged it point blank into the ticket office. The Beni Sakhr mob yelled with joy to see the wood and stones flying, jumped again on their camels and loped into the station just as the enemy surrendered. Nearly two hundred Turks, including seven officers, survived as our prisoners.

The Bedu became rich: besides the weapons, there were twenty-five mules, and in the siding seven trucks of delicacies for the officers' messes of Medina. There were things the tribesmen had only heard of, and things they had never heard of: they were supremely happy. Even the unfortunate regulars got a share, and were able once more to enjoy olives, sesame paste, dried apricot, and other sweet or pickled products of their native, half-forgotten, Syria.

Nuri Said had artificial tastes, and rescued tinned meats and liquors from the wilder men. There was one whole truck of tobacco. As the Howeitat did not smoke, it was divided between the Beni Sakhr and the regulars. By its loss the Medina garrison became tobacco-less: their sad plight later so worked on Feisal, a confirmed smoker, that he loaded some pack-camels with cheap cigarettes and drove them into Tebuk with his compliments.

After the looting, the engineers fired charges under the two engines, against the water-tower, in the pump, and between the points of the sidings. They burned the captured trucks and damaged a bridge; but perfunctorily, for, as usual after victory, everyone was too loaded and too hot to care for altruistic labour. They camped behind the station, and about midnight had an alarm, when the noise and lights of a train came from the south and halted, clearly with foreknowledge, by the break of the evening before. Auda sent scouts to report.

Before they had returned a solitary sergeant walked into Nasir's camp as a volunteer for the Sherif's army. He had been sent out by the Turks to explore the station. His story was that there were only sixty men and a mountain gun on the relief train, which, if he went back with smooth news, might be surprised without a shot fired. Nasir called Auda, who called the Howeitat, and they went off silently to lay the trap: but just before they got there our scouts decided to do their unaided best, and opened fire against the coaches. In fear, the engine reversed, and rolled the train back, unhurt, to Maan. It was the only sorrow of Jurf.

After this raid the weather once more broke. For three successive days came falls of snow. Nasir's force with difficulty regained the tents at Jefer. This plateau about Maan lay between three and five thousand feet above sea level, open to all winds from north and east. They blew from Central Asia, or from Caucasus, terribly over the great desert to these low hills of Edom, against which their first fury broke. The surplus bitterness lipped the crest and made a winter, quite severe of its degree, below in Judæa and Sinai.

Outside Beersheba and Jerusalem the British found it cold; but our Arabs fled there to get warm. Unhappily the British supply staff realized too late that we were fighting in a little Alp. They would not give us tents for one-quarter of our troops, nor serge clothing, nor boots, nor blankets enough to issue two to each man of the mountain garrisons. Our soldiers, if they neither deserted nor died, existed in an aching misery which froze the hope out of them.

According to our plan the good news of Jurf was to send the Arabs of Petra, under Sherif Abd el Mayin, at once up their hills into the forest towards Shobek. It was an uncanny march in the hoar mist, that of these frozen-footed peasants in their sheepskins, up and down sharp valleys and dangerous hill-sides, out of whose snow-drifts the heavy trunks of junipers, grudging in leaves, jutted like castings in grey iron. The ice and frost broke down the animals, and many of the men; yet these hardy highlanders, used to being too cold throughout their winter, persisted in the advance.

The Turks heard of them as they struggled slowly nearer, and fled from the caves and shelters among the trees to the branch railhead, littering the roads of their panic with cast baggage and equipment.

Railhead of the forest railway, with its temporary sheds, was commanded from low ridges by the Arab gun-fire, and no better than a trap. The tribesmen, in a pack, tore the enemy to pieces as they ran out from their burning and falling walls. One disciplined company of proper troops, under an Albanian officer, fought their way to the main line; but the Arabs killed or took the others, and also the stores in Shobek, the old Crusader fort of Monreale, poised high on a chalk cone above its winding valley. Abd el Mayein put his headquarters there, and sent word to Nasir. Mastur, too, was told. He drew his Motalga horse and foot from the comfort of their tents in the sunny depths of Arabia and with them climbed the hill-pass eastward towards Tafileh.

However, the advantage lay with Nasir, who leaped in one day from Jefer, and after a whirlwind night appeared at dawn on the rocky brink of the ravine in which Tafileh hid, and summoned it to surrender on pain of bombardment: an idle threat, for Nuri Said with the guns had gone back to Guweira. There were only one hundred and eighty Turks in the village, but they had supporters in the Muhaisin, a clan of the peasantry; not for love so much as because Dhiab, the vulgar headman of another faction, had declared for Feisal. So they shot up at Nasir a stream of ill-directed bullets.

The Howeitat spread out along the cliffs to return the peasants' fire. This manner of going displeased Auda, the old lion, who raged that a mercenary village folk should dare to resist their secular masters, the Abu Tayi. So he jerked his halter, cantered his mare down the path, and rode out plain to view beneath the easternmost houses of the village. There he reined in, and shook a hand at them, booming in his wonderful voice: 'Dogs, do you not know Auda?' When they realized it was that implacable son of war their hearts failed them, and an hour later Sherif Nasir in the town-house was sipping tea with his guest the Turkish Governor, trying to console him for the sudden change of fortune.

At dark Mastur rode in. His Motalga looked blackly at their blood enemies the Abu Tayi, lolling in the best houses. The two Sherifs divided up the place, to keep their unruly followers apart. They had little authority to mediate, for by passage of time Nasir was nearly adopted into the Abu Tayi, and Mastur into the Jazi.

When morning came the factions were bickering; and the day passed anxiously; for besides these blood enemies, the Muhaisin were fighting for authority among the villagers, and further complications developed in two stranger elements: one a colony of freebooting Senussi from North Africa, who had been intruded by the Turks into some rich, but half derelict plough-land; the other a plaintive and active suburb of a thousand Armenians, survivors of an infamous deportation by the Young Turks in 1915.

The people of Tafileh went in deadly fear of the future. We were, as usual, short of food and short of transport, and they would remedy neither ill. They had wheat or barley in their bins; but hid it. They had pack-animals, asses and mules in abundance; but drove them away for safety. They could have driven us away too, but were, fortunately for us, short of the sticking point. Incuriousness was the most potent ally of our imposed order; for Eastern government rested not so much on consent or force, as on the common supinity, hebetude, lack-a-daisiness, which gave a minority undue effect.

Feisal had delegated command of this push towards the Dead Sea to his young half-brother Zeid. It was Zeid's first office in the north, and he set out eager with hope. As adviser he had Jaafar Pasha, our general. His infantry, gunners and machine-gunners stuck, for lack of food, at Petra; but Zeid himself and Jaafar rode on to Tafileh.

Things were almost at a break. Auda affected a magnanimity very galling to the Motalga boys, Metaab and Annad, sons of Abtan, whom Auda's son had killed. They, lithe, definite, self-conscious figures, began to talk big about revenge — tom-tits threatening a hawk. Auda declared he would whip them in the market-place if they were rude. This was very well, but their followers were two to every man of his, and we should have the village in a blaze. The young fellows, with Rahail, my ruffler, went flaunting in every street.

Zeid thanked and paid Auda and sent him back to his desert. The enlightened heads of the Muhaisin had to go as forced guests to Feisal's tent. Dhiab, their enemy, was our friend: we remembered regretfully the adage that the best allies of a violently-successful new regime were not its partisans, but its opponents. By Zeid's plenty of gold the economic situation improved. We appointed an officer-governor and organized our five villages for further attack.

CHAPTER LXXXV

NOTWITHSTANDING, these plans quickly went adrift. Before they had been agreed upon we were astonished by a sudden try of the Turks to dislodge us. We had never dreamed of this, for it seemed out of the question that they should hope to keep Tafileh, or want to keep it. Allenby was just in Jerusalem, and for the Turks the issue of the war might depend on their successful defence of the Jordan against him. Unless Jericho fell, or until it fell, Tafileh was an obscure village of no interest. Nor did we value it as a possession; our desire was to get past it towards the enemy. For men so critically placed as the Turks to waste one single casualty on its recapture appeared the rankest folly.

Hamid Fakhri Pasha, commanding the 48th Division and the Amman sector, thought otherwise, or had his orders. He collected about nine hundred infantry, made up of three battalions (in January 1918 a Turkish battalion was a poor thing) with a hundred cavalry, two mountain howitzers, and twenty-seven machine-guns, and sent them by rail and road to Kerak. There he impressed all the local transport, drew a complete set of civil officials to staff his new administration in Tafileh, and marched southward to surprise us.

Surprise us he did. We first heard of him when his cavalry feelers fell on our pickets in Wadi Hesa, the gorge of great width and depth and difficulty which cut off Kerak from Tafileh, Moab from Edom. By dusk he had driven them back, and was upon us.

Jaafar Pasha had sketched a defence position on the south bank of the great ravine of Tafileh; proposing, if the Turks attacked, to give them the village, and defend the heights which overhung it, behind. This seemed to me doubly unsound. The slopes were dead, and their defence as difficult as their attack. They could be turned from the east; and by quitting the village we threw away the local people, whose votes and hands would be for the occupiers of their houses.

However, it was the ruling idea — all Zeid had — and so about midnight he gave the order, and servants and retainers loaded up their stuff. The men-at-arms proceeded to the southern crest, while the baggage train was sent off by the lower road to safety. This move created panic in the town. The peasants thought we were running away (I think we were) and rushed to save their goods and lives. It was freezing hard, and the ground was crusted with noisy ice. In the blustering dark the confusion and crying through the narrow streets were terrible.

Dhiab the Sheikh had told us harrowing tales of the disaffection of the townspeople, to increase the splendour of his own loyalty; but my impression was that they were stout fellows of great potential use. To prove it I sat out on my roof, or walked in the dark up and down the steep alleys, cloaked against recognition, with my guards unobtrusively about me within call. So we heard what passed. The people were in a very passion of fear, nearly dangerous, abusing everybody and everything: but there was nothing pro-Turkish abroad. They were in horror of the Turks returning, ready to do all in their physical capacity to support against them a leader with fighting intention. This was satisfactory, for it chimed with my hankering to stand where we were and fight stiffly.

Finally, I met the young Jazi sheikhs Metaab and Annad, beautiful in silks and gleaming silver arms, and sent them to find their uncle, Hamd el Arar. Him I asked to ride away north of the ravine, to tell the peasantry, who, by the noise, were still fighting the Turks, that we were on our way up to help them. Hamd, a melancholy, courtly, gallant cavalier, galloped off at once with twenty of his relations, all that he could gather in the distracted moment.

Their passage at speed through the streets added the last touch required to perfect the terror. The housewives bundled their goods pell-mell out of doors and windows, though no men were waiting to receive them. Children were trampled on, and yelled, while their mothers were yelling anyhow. The Motalga during their gallop fired shot after shot into the air to encourage themselves, and, as though to answer them, the flashes of the enemy rifles became visible, outlining the northern cliffs in that last blackness of sky before the dawn. I walked up the opposite heights to consult with Sherif Zeid.

Zeid sat gravely on a rock, sweeping the country with field-glasses for the enemy. As crises deepened, Zeid drew detached, nonchalant. I was in a furious rage. The Turks should never, by the rules of sane generalship, have ventured back to Tafileh at all. It was simple greed, a dog-in-the-manger attitude unworthy of a serious enemy, just the sort of hopeless thing a Turk would do. How could they expect a proper war when they gave us no chance to honour them? Our morale was continually being ruined by their follies, for neither could our men respect their courage, nor our officers respect their brains. Also, it was an icy morning, and I had been up all night and was Teutonic enough to decide that they should pay for my changed mind and plan.

They must be few in number, judging by their speed of advance. We had every advantage, of time, of terrain, of number, of weather, and could checkmate them easily: but to my wrath that was not enough. We would play their kind of game on our pigmy scale; deliver them a pitched battle such as they wanted; kill them all. I would rake up my memory of the half-forgotten maxims of the orthodox army text-book, and parody them in action.

This was villainous, for with arithmetic and geography for allies we might have spared the suffering factor of humanity; and to make a conscious joke of victory was wanton. We could have won by refusing battle, foxed them by manœuvring our centre as on twenty such occasions before and since: yet bad temper and conceit united for this time to make me not content to know my power, but determined to give public advertisement of it to the enemy and to everyone. Zeid, now convinced of the inconvenience of the defence-line, was very ready to listen to the voice of the tempter.

First I suggested that Abdulla go forward with two Hotchkiss guns to test the strength and disposition of the enemy. Then we talked of what next; very usefully, for Zeid was a cool and gallant little fighter, with the temperament of a professional officer. We saw Abdulla climb the other bank. The shooting became intense for a time, and then faded into distance. His coming had stimulated the Motalga horsemen and the villagers, who fell on the Turkish cavalry and drove them over a first ridge, across a plain two miles wide, and over a ridge beyond it down the first step of the great Hesa depression.

Behind this lay the Turkish main body, just getting on the road

Q*

again after a severe night which had stiffened them in their places. They came properly into action, and Abdulla was checked at once. We heard the distant rolling of machine-gun fire, growing up in huge bursts, laced by a desultory shelling. Our ears told us what was happening as well as if we saw it, and the news was excellent. I wanted Zeid to come forward at once on that authority: but his caution stepped in and he insisted that we wait exact word from his advance-guard, Abdulla.

This was not necessary, according to book, but they knew I was a sham soldier, and took licence to hesitate over my advice when it came peremptorily. However, I held a hand worth two of that and went off myself for the front to prejudice their decision. On the way I saw my bodyguard, turning over the goods exposed for removal in the streets, and finding much of interest to themselves. I told them to recover our camels and to bring their Hotchkiss automatic to the north bank of the gorge in a hurry.

The road dipped into a grove of fig-trees, knots of blue snaky boughs; bare, as they would be long after the rest of nature was grown green. Thence it turned eastward, to wind lengthily in the valley to the crest. I left it, climbing straight up the cliffs. An advantage of going bare foot was a new and incredible sureness upon rock when the soles had got hard by painful insistence, or were too chilled to feel jags and scrapes. The new way, while warming me, also shortened my time appreciably, and very soon, at the top, I found a level bit, and then a last ridge overlooking the plateau.

This last straight bank, with Byzantine foundations in it, seemed very proper for a reserve or ultimate line of defence for Tafileh. To be sure, we had no reserve as yet — no one had the least notion who or what we would have anywhere — but, if we did have anybody, here was their place: and at that precise moment Zeid's personal Ageyl became visible, hiding coyly in a hollow. To make them move required words of a strength to unravel their plaited hair: but at last I had them sitting along the skyline of Reserve Ridge. They were about twenty, and from a distance looked beautiful, like 'points' of a considerable army. I gave them my signet as a token, with orders to collect there all new comers, especially my fellows with their gun.

As I walked northward towards the fighting, Abdulla met me, on his way to Zeid with news. He had finished his ammunition, lost five men from shell-fire, and had one automatic gun destroyed. Two guns, he thought the Turks had. His idea was to get up Zeid with all his men and fight: so nothing remained for me to add to his message; and there was no subtlety in leaving alone my happy masters to cross and dot their own right decision.

He gave me leisure in which to study the coming battlefield. The tiny plain was about two miles across, bounded by low green ridges, and roughly triangular, with my reserve ridge as base. Through it ran the road to Kerak, dipping into the Hesa valley. The Turks were fighting their way up this road. Abdulla's charge had taken the western or left-hand ridge, which was now our firing-line.

Shells were falling in the plain as I walked across it, with harsh stalks of wormwood stabbing into my wounded feet. The enemy fusing was too long, so that the shells grazed the ridge and burst away behind. One fell near me, and I learned its calibre from the hot cap. As I went they began to shorten range, and by the time I got to the ridge it was being freely sprinkled with shrapnel. Obviously the Turks had got observation somehow, and looking round I saw them climbing along the eastern side beyond the gap of the Kerak road. They would soon outflank us at our end of the western ridge.

'US' proved to be about sixty men, clustered behind the ridge in two bunches, one near the bottom, one by the top. The lower was made up of peasants, on foot, blown, miserable, and yet the only warm things I had seen that day. They said their ammunition was finished, and it was all over. I assured them it was just beginning and pointed to my populous reserve ridge, saying that all arms were there in support. I told them to hurry back, refill their belts and hold on to it for good. Meanwhile we would cover their retreat by sticking here for the few minutes yet possible.

They ran off, cheered, and I walked about among the upper group quoting how one should not quit firing from one position till ready to fire from the next. In command was young Metaab, stripped to his skimp riding-drawers for hard work, with his black love-curls awry, his face stained and haggard. He was beating his hands together and crying hoarsely with baffled vexation, for he had meant to do so well in this, his first fight for us.

My presence at the last moment, when the Turks were breaking through, was bitter; and he got angrier when I said that I only wanted to study the landscape. He thought it flippancy, and screamed something about a Christian going into battle unarmed. I retorted with a quip from Clausewitz, about a reguard effecting its purpose more by being than by doing: but he was past laughter, and perhaps with justice, for the little flinty bank behind which we sheltered was crackling with fire. The Turks, knowing we were there, had turned twenty machine-guns upon it. It was four feet high and fifty feet long, of bare flinty ribs, off which the bullets slapped deafeningly: while the air above so hummed or whistled with ricochets and chips that it felt like death to look over. Clearly we must leave very soon, and as I had no horse I went off first, with Metaab's promise that he would wait where he was if he dared, for another ten minutes.

The run warmed me. I counted my paces, to help in ranging the Turks when they ousted us; since there was only that one position for them, and it was poorly protected against the south. In losing this

Motalga ridge we would probably win the battle. The horsemen held on for almost their ten minutes, and then galloped off without hurt. Metaab lent me his stirrup to hurry me along, till we found ourselves breathless among the Ageyl. It was just noon, and we had leisure and quiet in which to think.

Our new ridge was about forty feet up, and a nice shape for defence. We had eighty men on it, and more were constantly arriving. My guards were in place with their gun; Lutfi, an engine-destroyer, rushed up hotly with his two, and after him came another hundred Ageyl. The thing was becoming a picnic, and by saying 'excellent' and looking overjoyed, we puzzled the men, and made them consider the position dispassionately. The automatics were put on the skyline, with orders to fire occasional shots, short, to disturb the Turks a little, but not too much, after the expedient of Massena in delaying enemy deployment. Otherwise a lull fell; I lay down in a sheltered place which caught a little sun, and no wind, and slept a blessed hour, while the Turks occupied the old ridge, extending over it like a school of geese, and about as wisely. Our men left them alone, being contented with a free exhibition of themselves.

In the middle of the afternoon Zeid arrived, with Mastur, Rasim and Abdulla. They brought our main body, comprising twenty mounted infantry on mules, thirty Motalga horsemen, two hundred villagers, five automatic rifles, four machine-guns and the Egyptian Army mountain gun which had fought about Medina, Petra and Jurf. This was magnificent, and I woke up to welcome them.

The Turks saw us crowding, and opened with shrapnel and machine-gun fire: but they had not the range and fumbled it. We reminded one another that movement was the law of strategy, and started moving. Rasim became a cavalry officer, and mounted with all our eighty riders of animals to make a circuit about the eastern ridge and envelop the enemy's left wing, since the books advised attack not upon a line, but upon a point, and by going far enough along any finite wing it would be found eventually reduced to a point of one single man. Rasim liked this, my conception of his target.

He promised, grinningly, to bring us that last man: but Hamd el Arar took the occasion more fittingly. Before riding off he devoted himself to the death for the Arab cause, drew his sword ceremoniously, and made to it, by name, a heroic speech. Rasim took five automatic guns with him; which was good.

We in the centre paraded about, so that their departure might be unseen of the enemy, who were bringing up an apparently endless procession of machine-guns and dressing them by the left at intervals along the ridge as though in a museum. It was lunatic tactics. The ridge was flint, without cover for a lizard. We had seen how, when a bullet struck the ground, it and the ground spattered up in a shower of deadly chips. Also we knew the range and elevated our Vickers guns carefully, blessing their long, old-fashioned sights; our mountain gun was propped into place ready to let go a sudden burst of shrapnel over the enemy when Rasim was at grips.

As we waited, a reinforcement was announced of one hundred men from Aima. They had fallen out with Zeid over war-wages the day previous, but had grandly decided to sink old scores in the crisis. Their arrival convinced us to abandon Marshal Foch and to attack from, at any rate, three sides at once. So we sent the Aima men, with three automatic guns, to outflank the right, or western wing. Then we opened against the Turks from our central position, and bothered their exposed lines with hits and ricochets.

The enemy felt the day no longer favourable. It was passing, and sunset often gave victory to defenders yet in place. Old General Hamid Fakhri collected his Staff and Headquarters, and told each man to take a rifle. 'I have been forty years a soldier, but never saw I rebels fight like these. Enter the ranks' . . . but he was too late. Rasim pushed forward an attack of his five automatic guns, each with its two-man crew. They went in rapidly, unseen till they were in position, and crumpled the Turkish left.

The Aima men, who knew every blade of grass on these, their own village pastures, crept, unharmed, within three hundred yards of the Turkish machine-guns. The enemy, held by our frontal threat, first knew of the Aima men when they, by a sudden burst of fire, wiped out the gun-teams and flung the right wing into disorder. We saw it, and cried advance to the camel men and levies about us.

Mohamed el Ghasib, comptroller of Zeyd's household, led them on his camel, in shining wind-billowed robes, with the crimson banner of the Ageyl over his head. All who had remained in the centre with us, our servants, gunners and machine-gunners, rushed after him in a wide vivid line.

The day had been too long for me, and I was now only shaking with desire to see the end: but Zeid beside me clapped his hands with joy at the beautiful order of our plan unrolling in the frosty redness of the setting sun. On the one hand Rasim's cavalry were sweeping a broken left wing into the pit beyond the ridge: on the other the men of Aima were bloodily cutting down fugitives. The enemy centre was pouring back in disorder through the gap, with our men after them on foot, on horse, on camel. The Armenians, crouching behind us all day anxiously, now drew their knives and howled to one another in Turkish as they leaped forward.

I thought of the depths between here and Kerak, the ravine of Hesa, with its broken, precipitous paths, the undergrowth, the narrows and defiles of the way. It was going to be a massacre and I should have been crying-sorry for the enemy; but after the angers and exertions of the battle my mind was too tired to care to go down into that awful place and spend the night saving them. By my decision to fight, I had killed twenty or thirty of our six hundred men, and the wounded would be perhaps three times as many. It was one-sixth of our force gone on a verbal triumph, for the destruction of this thousand poor Turks would not affect the issue of the war.

In the end we had taken their two mountain howitzers (Skoda guns, very useful to us), twenty-seven machine-guns, two hundred horses and mules, two hundred and fifty prisoners. Men said only fifty got back, exhausted fugitives, to the railway. The Arabs on their track rose against them and shot them ignobly as they ran. Our own men gave up the pursuit quickly, for they were tired and sore and hungry, and it was pitifully cold. A battle might be thrilling at the moment for generals, but usually their imagination played too vividly beforehand, and made the reality seem sham; so quiet and unimportant that they ranged about looking for its fancied core. This evening there was no glory left, but the terror of the broken flesh, which had been our own men, carried past us to their homes.

As we turned back it began to snow; and only very late, and by a last effort did we get our hurt men in. The Turkish wounded lay out, and were dead next day. It was indefensible, as was the whole theory of war: but no special reproach lay on us for it. We risked our lives in the blizzard (the chill of victory bowing us down) to save our own fellows; and if our rule was not to lose Arabs to kill even many Turks, still less might we lose them to save Turks.

Next day and the next it snowed yet harder. We were weather-bound, and as the days passed in monotony we lost the hope of doing. We should have pushed past Kerak on the heels of victory, frighting the Turks to Amman with our rumour: as it was, nothing came of all the loss and effort, except a report which I sent over to the British headquarters in Palestine for the Staff's consumption. It was meanly written for effect, full of quaint smiles and mock simplicities; and made them think me a modest amateur, doing his best after the great models; not a clown, leering after them where they with Foch, band-master, at their head went drumming down the old road of effusion of blood into the house of Clausewitz. Like the battle, it was nearly-proof parody of regulation use. Headquarters loved it, and innocently, to crown the jest, offered me a decoration on the strength of it. We should have more bright breasts in the Army if each man was able without witnesses, to write out his own despatch.

CHAPTER LXXXVII

HESA'S sole profit lay, then, in its lesson to myself. Never again were we combative, whether in jest, or betting on a certainty. Indeed, only three days later, our honour was partially redeemed by a good and serious thing we arranged through Abdulla el Feir, who was camped beneath us in the paradise of the Dead Sea's southern shore, a plain gushing with brooks of sweet water, and rich in vegetation. We sent him news of victory, with a project to raid the lake-port of Kerak and destroy the Turks' flotilla.

He chose out some seventy horsemen, of the Beersheba Beduin. They rode in the night along the shelf of track between the hills of Moab and the Sea's brim as far as the Turkish post; and in the first greyness, when their eyes could reach far enough for a gallop, they burst out of their undergrowth upon motor launch and sailing lighters, harboured in the northern bight, with the unsuspecting crews sleeping on the beach or in the reed-huts near by.

They were from the Turkish Navy, not prepared for land fighting, still less for receiving cavalry: they were awakened only by the drumming of our horses' hooves in the headlong charge: and the engagement ended at the moment. The huts were burned, the stores looted, the shipping taken out to deep sea and scuttled. Then, without a casualty, and with their sixty prisoners, our men rode back praising themselves. January the twenty-eighth; and we had attained our second objective — the stopping of Dead Sea traffic — a fortnight sooner than we had promised Allenby.

The third objective had been the Jordan mouth by Jericho, before the end of March; and it would have been a fair prospect, but for the paralysis which weather and distaste for pain had brought upon us since the red day of Hesa. Conditions in Tafileh were mended. Feisal had sent us ammunition and food. Prices fell, as men grew to trust our strength. The tribes about Kerak, in daily touch with Zeid, purposed to join him in arms so soon as he moved forward.

Just this, however, we could not do. The winter's potency drove leaders and men into the village and huddled them in a lack-lustre idleness against which counsels of movement availed little. Indeed, Reason, also, was within doors. Twice I ventured up to taste the snow-laden plateau, upon whose even face the Turkish dead, poor brown pats of stiffened clothes, were littered: but life there was not tolerable. In the day it thawed a little and in the night it froze. The wind cut open the skin: fingers lost power, and sense of feel: cheeks shivered like dead leaves till they could shiver no more, and then bound up their muscles in a witless ache.

To launch out across the snow on camels, beasts singularly inept on slippery ground, would be to put ourselves in the power of however few horsemen wished to oppose us; and, as the days dragged on, even this last possibility was withdrawn. Barley ran short in Tafileh, and our camels, already cut off by the weather from natural grazing, were now also cut off from artificial food. We had to drive them down into the happier Ghor, a day's journey from our vital garrison.

Though so far by the devious road, yet in direct distance the Ghor lay little more than six miles away, and in full sight, five thousand feet below. Salt was rubbed into our miseries by the spectacle of that near winter garden beneath us by the lake-side. We were penned in verminous houses of cold stone; lacking fuel, lacking food; storm-bound in streets like sewers, amid blizzards of sleet and an icy wind: while there in the valley was sunshine upon spring grass, deep with flowers, upon flocks in milk and air so warm that men went uncloaked.

My private party were more fortunate than most, as the Zaagi had found us an empty unfinished house, of two sound rooms and a court. My money provided fuel, and even grain for our camels, which we kept sheltered in a corner of the yard, where Abdulla, the animal lover, could curry them and teach every one by name to take a gift of bread, like a kiss, from his mouth, gently, with her loose lips, when he called her. Still, they were unhappy days, since to have a fire was to be stifled with green smoke, and in the window-spaces were only make-shift shutters of our own joinery. The mud roof dripped water all the day long, and the fleas on the stone floor sang together nightly, for praise of the new meats given them. We were twenty-eight in the two tiny rooms, which reeked with the sour smell of our crowd.

In my saddle-bags was a *Morte d'Arthur*. It relieved my disgust. The men had only physical resources; and in the confined misery their tempers roughened. Their oddnesses, which ordinary time packed with a saving film of distance, now jostled me angrily; while a grazed wound in my hip had frozen, and irritated me with painful throbbing. Day by day, the tension among us grew, as our state became more sordid, more animal.

At last Awad, the wild Sherari, quarrelled with little Mahmas; and in a moment their daggers clashed. The rest nipped the tragedy, so that there was only a slight wounding: but it broke the greatest law of the bodyguard, and as both example and guilt were blatant, the others went packing into the far room while their chiefs forthwith executed sentence. However, the Zaagi's shrill whip-strokes were too cruel for my taught imagination, and I stopped him before he was well warmed. Awad, who had lain through his punishment without complaint, at this release levered himself slowly to his knees and with bent legs and swaying head staggered away to his sleeping-place.

It was then the turn of the waiting Mahmas, a tight-lipped youth with pointed chin and pointed forehead, whose beady eyes dropped at the inner corners with an indescribable air of impatience. He was not properly of my guard, but a camel-driver; for his capacity fell far below his sense of it, and a constantly-hurt pride made him sudden and fatal in companionship. If worsted in argument, or laughed at, he would lean forward with his always handy little dagger and rip up his friend. Now he shrank into a corner showing his teeth, vowing, across his tears, to be through those who hurt him. Arabs did not dissect endurance, their crown of manhood, into material and moral, making allowance for nerves. So Mahmas' crying was called fear, and when loosed, he crept out disgraced into the night to hide.

I was sorry for Awad: his hardness put me to shame. Especially I was ashamed when, next dawn, I heard a limping step in the yard, and saw him attempting to do his proper duty by the camels. I called him in to give him an embroidered head-cloth as reward for faithful service. He came pitiably sullen, with a shrinking, mobile readiness for more punishment: my changed manner broke him down. By afternoon he was singing and shouting, happier than ever, as he had found a fool in Tafileh to pay him four pounds for my silken gift.

Such nervous sharpening ourselves on each other's faults was so revolting that I decided to scatter the party, and to go off myself in search of the extra money we should need when fine weather came. Zeid had spent the first part of the sum set aside for Tafileh and the Dead Sea; partly on wages, partly on supplies and in rewards to the victors of Seil Hesa. Wherever we next put our front line, we should have to enlist and pay fresh forces, for only local men knew the qualities of their ground instinctively; and they fought best, defending their homes and crops against the enemy.

Joyce might have arranged to send me money: but not easily in this season. It was surer to go down myself: and more virtuous than continued fœtor and promiscuity in Tafileh. So five of us started off on a day which promised to be a little more open than usual. We made good time to Reshidiya and as we climbed the saddle beyond, found ourselves momentarily above the clouds in a faint sunshine.

In the afternoon the weather drew down again and the wind hardened from the north and east, and made us sorry to be out on the bare plain. When we had forded the running river of Shobek, rain began to fall, first in wild gusts, but then more steadily, reeding down over our left shoulders and seeming to cloak us from the main bleakness of wind. Where the rain-streaks hit the ground they furred out whitely like a spray. We pushed on without halting and till long after sunset urged our trembling camels, with many slips, and falls across the greasy valleys. We made nearly two miles an hour, despite our difficulties; and progress was become so exciting and unexpected that its mere exercise kept us warm.

It had been my intention to ride all night: but, near Odroh, mist came down about us in a low ring curtain, over which the clouds, like tatters of a veil, spun and danced high up across the calmness of the sky. The perspective seemed to change, so that far hills looked small, and near hillocks great. We bore too much to the right.

This open country, though appearing hard, broke rottenly beneath their weight and let our camels in, four or five inches deep, at every stride. The poor beasts had been chilled all day, and had bumped down so often that they were stiff with bruises. Consequently, they made unwilling work of the new difficulties. They hurried for a few steps, stopped abruptly, looked round, or tried to dart off sideways.

We prevented their wishes, and drove them forward till our blind way met rocky valleys, with a broken skyline; dark to right and left, and in front apparent hills where no hills should be. It froze again, and the slabby stones of the valley became iced. To push farther, on the wrong road, through such a night was folly. We found a larger outcrop of rock. Behind it, where there should have been shelter, we couched our camels in a compact group, tails to wind: facing it, they might die of cold. We snuggled down beside them, hoping for warmth and sleep.

The warmth I, at least, never got, and hardly the sleep. I dozed once only to wake with a start when slow fingers seemed to stroke my face. I stared out into a night livid with large, soft snowflakes. They lasted a minute or two; but then followed rain, and after it more frost, while I squatted in a tight ball, aching every way but too miserable to move, till dawn. It was a hesitant dawn, but enough: I rolled over in the mud to see my men, knotted in their cloaks, cowering abandoned against the beasts' flanks. On each man's face weighed the most dolorous expression of resigned despair.

They were four southerners, whom fear of the winter had turned ill at Tafileh, and who were going to rest in Guweira till it was warm again: but here in the mist they had made up their minds, like he-camels, that death was upon them: and, though they were too proud to grumble at it, they were not above showing me silently that this which they made for my sake was a sacrifice. They did not speak or move in reply to me. Under a flung camel it was best to light a slow fire, to raise it: but I took the smallest of these dummies by the head-curls, and proved to him that he was still capable of feeling. The others got to their feet, and we kicked up the stiff camels. Our only loss was a water-skin, frozen to the ground.

With daylight the horizon had grown very close, and we saw that our proper road was a quarter of a mile to our left. Along it we struggled afoot. The camels were too done to carry our weight (all but my own died later of this march) and it was so muddy in the clay bottoms that we ourselves slid and fell like them. However, the Deraa trick helped, of spreading wide the toes and hooking them downward into the mud at each stride: and by this means, in a group, clutching and holding one another, we maintained progress.

The air seemed cold enough to freeze anything, but did not: the wind, which had changed during the night, swept into us from the west in hindering blizzards. Our cloaks bellied out and dragged like sails, against us. At last we skinned them off, and went easier, our bare shirts wrapped tightly about us to restrain their slapping tails. The whirling direction of the squalls was shown to our eyes by the white mist they carried across hill and dale. Our hands were numbed into insensibility, so that we knew the cuts on them only by red stains in their plastered mud: but our bodies were not so chill, and for hours quivered under the hailstones of each storm. We twisted ourselves to get the sharpness on an unhurt side, and held our shirts free from the skin, to shield us momentarily.

By late afternoon we had covered the ten miles to Aba el Lissan. Maulud's men were gone to ground, and no one hailed us; which was well, for we were filthy and miserable; stringy like shaven cats. Afterwards the going was easier, the last two miles to the head of Shtar being frozen like iron. We remounted our camels, whose breath escaped whitely through their protesting nostrils, and raced up to the first wonderful glimpse of the Guweira plain, warm, red and comfortable, as seen through the cloud-gaps. The clouds had ceiled the hollow strangely, cutting the mid-sky in a flat layer of curds at the level of the hill-top on which we stood: we gazed on them contentedly for minutes. Every little while a wisp of their fleecy sea-foam stuff would be torn away and thrown at us. We on the wall of bluffs would feel it slash across our faces; and, turning, would see a white hem draw over the rough crest, tear to shreds and vanish in a powdering of hoar grains or a trickle of water across the peat soil.

After having wondered at the sky we slid and ran gaily down the pass to dry sand in a calm mild air. Yet the pleasure was not vivid, as we had hoped. The pain of the blood fraying its passage once more about our frozen limbs and faces was much faster than the pain of its driving out: and we grew sensible that our feet had been torn and bruised nearly to pulp among the stones. We had not felt them tender while in the icy mud; but this warm, salty sand scoured the cuts. In desperation we climbed up our sad camels, and beat them woodenly towards Guweira. However, the change had made them happier, and they brought us home there sedately, but with success.

CHAPTER LXXXVIII

LAZY nights, three of them, in the armoured car tents at Guweira were pleasant, with Alan Dawnay, Joyce, and others talking, and Tafileh to boast about. Yet these friends were a little grieved at my luck, for their great expedition with Feisal a fortnight ago to overwhelm Mudowwara had turned out unprofitably. Partly it was the ancient problem of the co-operation of regulars with irregulars; partly it was the fault of old Mohammed Ali el Beidawi, who, put over the Beni Atiyeh, had come with them to water, cried, 'Noon-halt!' and sat there for two months, pandering to that hedonistic streak among the Arabs which made them helpless slaves of carnal indulgence. In Arabia, where superfluities lacked, the temptation of necessary food lay always on men. Each morsel which passed their lips might, if they were not watchful, become a pleasure. Luxuries might be as plain as running water or a shady tree, whose rareness and misuse often turned them into lusts. Their story reminded me of Apollonius' 'Come off it, you men of Tarsus, sitting on your river like geese, drunken with its white water!'

Then thirty thousand pounds in gold came up from Akaba for me and my cream camel, Wodheiha, the best of my remaining stud. She was Ateiba-bred and had won many races for her old owner: also, she was in splendid condition, fat but not too fat, her pads hardened by much practice over the northern flints, and her coat thick and matted. She was not tall, and looked heavy, but was docile and smooth to ride, turning left or right if the saddle-horn were tapped on the required side. So I rode her without a stick, comfortably reading a book when the march permitted.

As my proper men were at Tafileh or Azrak, or out on mission, I asked Feisal for temporary followers. He lent me his two Ateiba horsemen, Serj and Rameid; and, to help carry my gold, added to the party Sheikh Motlog, whose worth we had discovered when our armoured cars explored the plains below Mudowwara for Tebuk.

Motlog had gone as sponsor, pointing out the country from a perch high on the piled baggage of a box-Ford. They were dashing in and out of sand-hills at speed, the Fords swaying like launches in a swell. At one bad bend they skidded half-round on two wheels crazily. Motlog was tossed out on his head. Marshall stopped the car and ran back contrite, with ready excuses for the driving; but the Sheikh, ruefully rubbing his head, said gently 'Don't be angry with me. I have not learnt to ride these things'.

The gold was in thousand-pound bags. I gave two bags each to fourteen of Motlog's twenty men, and took the last two myself. A bag weighed twenty-two pounds, and in the awful road-conditions two were weight enough for a camel, and swung fairly on either side in the saddle-bags. We started at noon, hoping to make a good first stage before getting into the trouble of the hills: but unfortunately it turned wet after half an hour, and a steady rain soaked us through and through, and made our camels' hair curl like a wet dog's.

Motlog at that precise stage saw a tent, Sherif Fahad's, in the corner of a sandstone pike. Despite my urging, he voted to spend the night there, and see what it looked like on the hills to-morrow. I knew this would be a fatal course, wasting days in indecision: so I said farewell to him and rode on with my two men, and with six Shobek-bound Howeitat, who had joined our caravan.

The argument had delayed us, and consequently we only reached the foot of the pass at dark. By the sad, soft rain we were made rather sorry for our virtue, inclined to envy Motlog his hospitality with Fahad, when suddenly a red spark to our left drew us across to find Saleh ibn Shefia camped there in a tent and three caves, with a hundred of his freed-men fighters from Yenbo. Saleh, the son of poor old Mohammed, our jester, was the proper lad who had carried Wejh by assault on Vickery's field-day.

'Cheyf ent?' ('How are you?') said I earnestly twice or thrice. His eyes sparkled at the Juheina manner. He came near me and with bowed head and intense voice poured out a string of twenty 'Cheyf ents' before drawing breath. I disliked being outdone, so replied with a dozen as solemnly. He took me up with another of his long bursts, many more than twenty this time. So I gave up trying to learn how many are the possible repetitions of salutations in Wadi Yenbo.

He welcomed me, in spite of my drenched condition, to his own carpet in his tent and gave me a new garment of his mother's sewing, while waiting for the hot stew of meat and rice. Then we lay down and slept a full night of great satisfaction, hearing the patter of rain on the double canvas of his Meccan tent.

In the morning we were off at dawn, munching a handful of Saleh's bread. As we set foot on the ascent, Serj looked up and said, 'The mountain wears his skull-cap'. There was a white dome of snow on every crest; and the Ateiba pushed quickly and curiously up the pass to feel this new wonder with their hands. The camels, too, were ignorant, and stretched their slow necks down to sniff its whiteness twice or thrice in tired inquiry; but then drew their heads away and looked forward without life-interest, once more.

Our inactivity lasted only another moment; for, as we put our heads over the last ridge, a wind from the north-east took us in the teeth, with a cold so swift and biting that we gasped for breath and turned hurriedly back into shelter. It seemed as if it would be fatal to face it; but that we knew was silly: so we pulled ourselves together and rode hard through its first extreme to the half-shelter of the valley. Serj and Rameid, terrified by these new pains in their lungs, thought they were strangling; and to spare them the mental struggle of passing a friendly camp, I led our little party aside behind Maulud's hill, so that we saw nothing of his weather-beaten force.

These men of Maulud's had been camped in this place, four thousand feet above the sea, for two months without relief. They had to live in shallow dug-outs on the hill-side. They had no fuel except the sparse, wet wormwood, over which they were just able to bake their necessary bread every other day. They had no clothes but khaki drill uniform of the British summer sort. They slept in their rain-sodden verminous pits on empty or half-empty flour-sacks, six or eight of them together in a knotted bunch, that enough of the worn blankets might be pooled for warmth.

Rather more than half of them died or were injured by the cold and wet; yet the others maintained their watch, exchanging shots daily with the Turkish outposts, and protected only by the inclement weather from crushing counter-attack. We owed much to them, and more to Maulud, whose fortitude stiffened them in their duty.

The old scarred warrior's history in the Turkish army was a catalogue of affairs provoked by his sturdy sense of Arab honour and nationality, a creed for which three or four times he had sacrificed his prospects. It must have been a strong creed which enabled him to endure cheerfully three winter months in front of Maan and to share out enough spirit among five hundred ordinary men to keep them stout-heartedly about him.

We, for our one day, had a fill of hardship. Just on the ridge about Aba el Lissan the ground was crusted with frost, and only the smart of the wind in our eyes hindered us: but then our troubles began. The camels came to a standstill in the slush at the bottom of a twenty-foot bank of slippery mud, and lowed at it helplessly, as if to say that they could not carry us up that. We jumped off to help them, and slid back ourselves just as badly. At last we took off our new, cherished boots, donned to armour us against the winter; and hauled the camels up the glacis barefoot, as on the journey down.

That was the end of our comfort, and we must have been off twenty times before sunset. Some of the dismounts were involuntary, when our camels side-slipped under us, and came down with the jingle of coin ringing through the hollow rumble of their cask-like bellies. While they were strong this falling made them as angry as she-camels could be: afterwards they grew plaintive, and finally afraid. We also grew short with one another, for the foul wind gave us no rest. Nothing in Arabia could be more cutting than a north wind at Maan, and to-day's was of the sharpest and strongest. It blew through our clothes as if we had none, fixed our fingers in claws not able to hold either halter or riding-stick, and cramped our legs so that we had no grip of the saddle-pin. Consequently, when thrown from our falling beasts we pitched off, to crash stiffly on the ground, still frozen-brittle in the cross-legged attitude of riding.

However, there was no rain, and the wind felt like a drying one, so we held on steadily to the north. By evening we had almost made the rivulet of Basta. This meant that we were travelling more than a mile an hour; and for fear lest on the morrow we and our camels would both be too tired to do so well, I pushed on in the dark across the little stream.

It was swollen, and the beasts jibbed at it, so that we had to lead the way on foot, through three feet of chilly water.

Over the high ground, beyond, the wind buffeted us like an enemy: at about nine o'clock the others flung themselves crying down on the ground and refused to go further. I, too, was very near crying; sustained, indeed, only by my annoyance with their open lamentations; and therefore reluctantly glad at heart to yield to their example. We built up the nine camels in a phalanx, and lay between them in fair comfort, listening to the driving wrack clashing about us as loud as the surges by night round a ship at sea. The visible stars were brilliant, seeming to change groups and places waywardly between the clouds which scudded over our heads. We had each two army blankets, and a packet of cooked bread; so we were armed against evil and could sleep securely in the mud and cold.

CHAPTER LXXXIX

AT dawn we went forward refreshed: but the weather had turned soft, with a greyness through which loomed the sad wormwood-covered hills. Upon their slopes the limestone ribs of this very old earth stood wearily exposed. In their hollows our difficulties increased with the mud. The misty valleys were sluggish streams of melting snow: and at last new thick showers of wet flakes began to fall. We reached the desolate ruins of Odroh in a midday like twilight: a wind was blowing and dying intermittently, and slow-moving banks of cloud and drizzle closed us about.

I bore right, to avoid the Beduin between us and Shobek: but our Howeitat companions led us straight upon their camp. We had ridden six miles in seven hours, and they were exhausted. The two Ateiba were not only exhausted, but demoralized, and swore mutinously that nothing in the world should keep us from the tribal tents. We wrangled by the roadside under the soft drift.

For myself I felt quite fresh and happy, averse from the delay of needless tribal hospitality. Zeid's penniless state was excellent pretext for a trial of strength with the Edomite winter. Shobek was only ten miles further, and daylight had yet five hours to run. So I decided to go on alone. It would be quite safe, for in such weather neither Turk nor Arab was abroad, and the roads were mine. I took their four thousand pounds from Serj and Rameid, and cursed them into the valley for cowards: which really they were not. Rameid was catching his breath in great sobs, and Serj's nervous pain marked each lurch of his camel with a running moan. They raved with miserable rage when I dismissed them and turned away.

The truth was that I had the best camel. The excellent Wodheiha struggled gamely forward under the weight of the extra gold. In flat places I rode her: at ascents and descents we used to slide together side by side with comic accidents, which she seemed rather to enjoy.

By sunset the snow-fall ceased; we were coming down to the river of Shobek, and could see a brown track straggling over the opposite hill towards the village. I tried a short cut, but the frozen crust of the mud-banks deceived me, and I crashed through the cat-ice (which was sharp, like knives) and bogged myself so deeply that I feared I was going to pass the night there, half in and half out of the sludge: or wholly in which would be a tidier death.

Wodheiha, sensible beast, had refused to enter the morass: but she stood at a loss on the hard margin, and looked soberly at my mud-larking. However, I managed, with the still-held head-stall, to per-suade her a little nearer. Then I flung my body suddenly backward against the squelching quag, and, grabbing wildly behind my head, laid hold of her fetlock. She was frightened, and started back: and her purchase dragged me clear. We crawled farther down the bed to a safe place, and there crossed: after I had hesitatingly sat in the stream and washed off the weight of stinking clay.

Shiveringly I mounted again. We went over the ridge and down to the base of the shapely cone, whose mural crown was the ring-wall of the old castle of Monreale, very noble against the night sky. The chalk was hard, and it was freezing; snow-drifts lay a foot deep each side of the spiral path which wound up the hill. The white ice crackled desolately under my naked feet as we neared the gate, where, to make a stage entry, I climbed up by Wodheiha's patient shoulder into the saddle. Then I repented, since only by throwing myself sideways along her neck did I avoid the voussoirs of the arch as she crashed underneath in half-terror of this strange place.

I knew that Sherif Abd el Main should be still at Shobek, so rode boldly up the silent street in the reeded starlight, which played with the white icicles and their underlying shadow among the walls and snowy roofs and ground. The camel stumbled doubtfully over steps hidden beneath a thick covering of snow: but I had no care of that, having reached my night's goal, and having so powdery a blanket to fall on. At the crossways I called out the salutation of a fair night: and after a minute, a husky voice protested to God through the thick sacking which stuffed a loophole of the mean house on my right. I asked for Abd el Mayein, and was told 'in the Government house' which lay at the further end of the old castle's enceinte.

Arrived there I called again. A door was flung open, and a cloud of smoky light streamed recklessly across, whirling with motes, through which black faces peered to know who I was. I hailed them friendly, by name, saying that I was come to eat a sheep with the master: upon which these slaves ran out, noisy with astonishment, and relieved me of Wodheiha, whom they led into the reeking stable where themselves lived. One lit me with a flaming spar up the stone outside stairs to the house door, and between more servants, down a winding passage dripping with water from the broken roof, into a tiny room. There lay Abd el Muein upon a carpet, face down, breathing the least smoky level of air.

My legs were shaky, so I dropped beside him, and gladly copied his position to avoid the choking fumes of a brass brazier of flaming wood which crackled in a recessed shot-window of the mighty outer wall. He searched out for me a waist-cloth, while I stripped off my things and hung them to steam before the fire, which became less smarting to the eyes and throat as it burned down into red coals. Meanwhile Abd el Mayin clapped his hands for supper to be hastened and served 'Fauzan' (tea in Harith slang, so named from his cousin, governor of their village) hot and spiced and often, till the mutton, boiled with raisins in butter, was carried in.

He explained, with his blessings on the dish, that next day they would starve or rob, since he had here two hundred men, and no food or money, and his messengers to Feisal were held up in the snow. Whereat I, too, clapped hands, commanding my saddle-bags, and presented him with five hundred pounds on account, till his subsidy came. This was good payment for the food, and we were very merry over my oddness of riding alone, in winter, with a hundredweight and more of gold for baggage. I repeated that Zeid, like himself, was straitened; and told of Serj and Rameid with the Arabs. The Sherif's eyes darkened and he made passes in the air with his riding-stick. I explained, in extenuation of their failure, that the cold did not trouble me, since the English climate was of this sort most of the year. 'God forbid it', said Abd el Muyein.

After an hour he excused himself, because he had just married a Shobek wife. We talked of their marriage, whose end was the bearing of children: I withstood it, quoting old Dionysus of Tarsus.

At his sixty years without marriage they were shocked, holding procreation and evacuation alike as inevitable movements of the body; they repeated their half of the commandment to honour parents. I asked how they could look with pleasure on children, embodied proofs of their consummated lust? And invited them to picture the minds of the children, seeing crawl wormlike out of the mother that bloody, blinded thing which was themselves! It sounded to him a most excellent joke, and after it we rolled up in the rugs and slept warmly. The fleas were serried, but my nakedness, the Arab defence against a verminous bed, lessened their plague: and the bruises did not prevail because I was too tired.

In the morning I rose with a splitting headache, and said I must go on. Two men were found to ride with me, though all said we should not reach Tafileh that night. However, I thought it could not be worse than yesterday; so we skated timorously down the rapid path to the plain across which still stretched the Roman road with its groups of fallen milestones, inscribed by famous emperors.

From this plain the two faint-hearts with me slipped back to their fellows on the castle-hill. I proceeded, alternately on and off my camel, like the day before, though now the way was all too slippery, except on the ancient paving, the last footprint of Imperial Rome which had once so much more preciously, played the Turk to the desert dwellers. On it I could ride: but I had to walk and wade the dips where the floods of fourteen centuries had washed the road's foundations out. Rain came on, and soaked me, and then it blew fine and freezing till I crackled in armour of white silk, like a theatre knight: or like a bridal cake, hard iced.

The camel and I were over the plain in three hours; wonderful going: but our troubles were not ended. The snow was indeed as my guides had said, and completely hid the path, which wound uphill between walls and ditches, and confused piles of stone. It cost me an infinity of pain to turn the first two corners. Wodheiha, tired of wading to her bony knees in useless white stuff, began perceptibly to flag. However, she got up one more steep bit, only to miss the edge of the path in a banked place. We fell together some eighteen feet down the hill-side into a yard-deep drift of frozen snow. After the fall she rose to her feet whimpering and stood still, in a tremble.

When he-camels so baulked, they would die on their spot, after days; and I feared that now I had found the limit of effort in she-camels. I plunged to my neck in front of her, and tried to tow her out, vainly. Then I spent a long time hitting her behind. I mounted, and she sat down, I jumped off, heaved her up, and wondered if, perhaps, it was that the drift was too thick. So I carved her a beautiful little road, a foot wide, three deep, and eighteen paces long, using my bare feet and hands as tools. The snow was so frozen on the surface that it took all my weight, first to break it down, and then to scoop it out. The crust was sharp, and cut my wrists and ankles till they bled freely, and the roadside became lined with pink crystals, looking like pale, very pale, water-melon flesh.

Afterwards I went back to Wodheiha, patiently standing there, and climbed into the saddle. She started easily. We went running at it, and such was her speed that the rush carried her right over the shallow stuff, back to the proper road. Up this we went cautiously, with me afoot, sounding the path in front with my stick, or digging new passes when the drifts were deep. In three hours we were on the summit, and found it wind-swept on the western side. So we left the track, and scrambled unsteadily along the very broken crest, looking down across the chess-board houses of Dana village, into sunny Arabah, fresh and green thousands of feet below.

When the ridge served no more we did further heavy work, and at last Wodheiha baulked again. It was getting serious, for the evening was near; suddenly I realized the loneliness, and that if the night found us yet beyond help on this hill-top, Wodheiha would die, and she was a very noble beast. There was also the solid weight of gold, and I felt not sure how far, even in Arabia, I could safely put six thousand sovereigns by the roadside with a signet as mark of ownership, and leave them for a night. So I took her back a hundred yards along our beaten track, mounted, and charged her at the bank. She responded. We burst through and over the northern lip which looked down on the Senussi village of Rasheidiya.

This face of the hill, sheltered from the wind and open to the sun all afternoon, had thawed. Underneath the superficial snow lay wet and muddy ground; and when Wodheiha ran upon this at speed her feet

R

went from under her and she sprawled, with her four feet locked. So on her tail, with me yet in the saddle, we went sliding round and down a hundred feet. Perhaps it hurt the tail (there were stones under the snow) for on the level she sprang up unsteadily, grunting, and lashed it about like a scorpion's. Then she began to run at ten miles an hour down the greasy path towards Rasheidiya, sliding and plunging wildly: with me, in terror of a fall and broken bones, clinging to the horns of the saddle.

A crowd of Arabs, Zeid's men, weather-bound here on their way to Feysal, ran out when they heard her trumpeting approach, and shouted with joy at so distinguished an entry to the village. I asked them the news; they told me all was well. Then I remounted, for the last eight miles into Tafileh, where I gave Zeid his letters and some money, and went gladly to bed . . . flea-proof for another night.

CHAPTER XC

MORNING found me nearly snow-blind, but glad and vigorous. I cast about for something to fill the inactive days before the other gold arrived. The final judgement was to make a personal examination of the approaches to Kerak, and the ground over which we would later advance to Jordan. I asked Zeid to take from Motlog the coming twenty-four thousand pounds, and spend what was necessary for current expenses until my return.

Zeid told me there was another Englishman in Tafileh. The news astonished me, and I went off to meet Lieutenant Kirkbride, a young Arabic-speaking staff officer, sent by Deedes, to report intelligence possibilities on the Arab Front. It was the beginning of a connection profitable to us, and creditable to Kirkbride; a taciturn, enduring fellow, only a boy in years, but ruthless in action, who messed for eight months with the Arab officers, their silent companion.

The cold had passed off and movement, even on the heights, was practicable. We crossed Wadi Hesa, and rode as far as the edge of the Jordan Valley, whose depths were noisy with Allenby's advance. They said the Turks yet held Jericho. Thence we turned back to Tafileh, after a reconnaissance very assuring for our future. Each step of our road to join the British was possible: most of them easy. The weather was so fine that we might reasonably begin at once: and could hope to finish in a month.

Zeid heard me coldly. I saw Motlog next him, and greeted him sarcastically, asking what was his tally of the gold: then I began to repeat my programme of what we might fairly do. Zeid stopped me: 'But that will need a lot of money'. I said, 'Not at all': our funds in hand would cover it, and more. Zeid replied that he had nothing; and when I gaped at him, muttered rather shamefacedly that he had spent all I brought. I thought he was joking: but he went on to say that so much had been due to Dhiab, sheikh of Tafileh; so much to the villagers; so much to the Jazi Howeitat; so much to the Beni Sakhr.

Only for a defensive was such expenditure conceivable. The peoples named were elements centring in Tafileh, men whose blood feuds made them impossible for use north of Wadi Hesa. Admittedly, the Sherifs, as they advanced, enrolled all the men of every district at a monthly wage: but it was perfectly understood that the wage was fictitious, to be paid only if they had been called on for active service. Feysul had more than forty thousand on his Akaba books: while his whole subsidy from England would not pay seventeen thousand. The wages of the rest were nominally due and often asked for: but not a lawful liability. However, Zeid said that he had paid them.

I was aghast; for this meant the complete ruin of my plans and hopes, the collapse of our effort to keep faith with Allenby. Zeid stuck to his word that the money was all gone. Afterwards I went off to learn the truth from Nasir, who was in bed with fever. He despondently said that everything was wrong – Zeid too young and shy to counter his dishonest, cowardly counsellors.

All night I thought over what could be done, but found a blank; and when morning came could only send word to Zeid that, if he would not return the money, I must go away. He sent me back his supposed account of the spent money. While we were packing, Joyce and Marshall arrived. They had ridden from Guweira to give me a pleasant surprise. I told them why it had happened that I was going back to Allenby to put my further employment in his hands. Joyce made a vain appeal to Zeid, and promised to explain to Feisal.

He would close down my affairs and disperse my bodyguard. So I was able, with only four men, to set off, late that very afternoon, for Beersheba, the quickest way to British Headquarters. The coming of spring made the first part of the ride along the edge of the Araba scarp surpassingly beautiful, and my farewell mood showed me its beauties, keenly. The ravines were clothed below with trees: but near to us, by the top, their precipitous flanks, as seen from above, were a patchwork of close lawns, which tipped toward downright faces of bare rock of many colours. Some of the colours were mineral, in the rock itself: but others were accidental, due to water from the melting snow falling over the cliff-edge, either in drifts of dusty spray, or diamond-strings down hanging tresses of green fern.

At Buseira, the little village on a hull of rock over the abyss, they insisted that we halt to eat. I was willing, because if we fed our camels here with a little barley we might ride all night and reach Beersheba on the morrow: but to avoid delay I refused to enter their houses, and instead ate in the little cemetery, off a tomb, into whose joints were cemented plaits of hair, the sacrificed head-ornaments of mourners. Afterwards we went down the zigzags of the great pass into the hot bottom of Wadi Dhahal, over which the cliffs and the hills so drew together that hardly did the stars shine into its pitchy blackness. We halted a moment while our camels stilled the nervous trembling of their forelegs after the strain of the terrible descent. Then we plashed, fetlock deep, down the swift stream, under a long arch of rustling bamboos, which met so nearly over our heads that their fans brushed our faces. The strange echoes of the vaulted passage frightened our camels into a trot.

Soon we were out of it, and out of the horns of the valley, scouring across the open Araba. We reached the central bed, and found that we were off the track — not wonderful, for we were steering only on my three-year-old memories of Newcombe's map. A half-hour was wasted in finding a ramp for the camels, up the earth cliff.

At last we found one, and threaded the windings of the marly labyrinth beyond — a strange place, sterile with salt, like a rough sea suddenly stilled, with all its tossing waves transformed into hard, fibrous earth, very grey under to-night's half-moon. Afterwards we aimed westward till the tall branched tree of Husb outlined itself against the sky, and we heard the murmurings of the great spring which flowed out from the roots. Our camels drank a little. They had come down five thousand feet from the Tafileh hills, and had to climb up three thousand now to Palestine.

In the little foot-hills before Wadi Murra, suddenly, we saw a fire of large logs, freshly piled, and still at white heat. No one was visible, proof that the kindlers were a war party: yet it was not kindled in nomad fashion. The liveliness showed that they were still near it: the size that they were many: so prudence made us hurry on. Actually it was the camp-fire of a British section of Ford cars, under the two famous Macs, looking for a car-road from Sinai to Akaba. They were hidden in the shadows, covering us with their Lewis guns.

We climbed the pass as day broke. There was a little rain, balmy after the extreme of Tafileh. Rags of thinnest cloud stood unreasonably motionless in the hills, as we rode over the comfortable plain, to Beersheba, about noon: a good performance, down and up hills for nearly eighty miles.

They told us Jericho was just taken. I went through to Allenby's headquarters. Hogarth was there on the platform. To him I confessed that I had made a mess of things: and had come to beg Allenby to find me some smaller part elsewhere. I had put all myself into the Arab business, and had come to wreck because of my sick judgement; the occasion being Zeid, own brother to Feisal, and a little man I really liked. I now had no tricks left worth a meal in the Arab market-place, and wanted the security of custom: to be conveyed; to pillow myself on duty and obedience: irresponsibly.

I complained that since landing in Arabia I had had options and requests, never an order: that I was tired to death of free-will, and of many things beside free-will. For a year and a half I had been in motion, riding a thousand miles each month upon camels: with added nervous hours in crazy aeroplanes, or rushing across country in powerful cars. In my last five actions I had been hit, and my body so dreaded further pain that now I had to force myself under fire. Generally I had been hungry: lately always cold: and frost and dirt had poisoned my hurts into a festering mass of sores.

However, these worries would have taken their due petty place, in my despite of the body, and of my soiled body in particular, but for the rankling fraudulence which had to be my mind's habit: that pretence to lead the national uprising of another race, the daily posturing in alien dress, preaching in alien speech: with behind it a sense that the 'promises' on which the Arabs worked were worth what their armed strength would be when the moment of fulfilment came. We had deluded ourselves that perhaps peace might find the Arabs able, unhelped and untaught, to defend themselves with paper tools. Meanwhile we glozed our fraud by conducting their necessary war purely and cheaply. But now this gloss had gone from me. Chargeable against my conceit were the causeless, ineffectual deaths of Hesa. My will had gone and I feared to be alone, lest the winds of circumstance, or power, or lust, blow my empty soul away.

CHAPTER XCI

DIPLOMATICALLY, Hogarth replied not a word, but took me to breakfast with Clayton. There I gathered that Smuts had come from the War Cabinet to Palestine, with news which had changed our relative situation. For days they had been trying to get me to the Conferences, and finally had sent out aeroplanes to find Tafileh; but the pilots had dropped their messages near Shobek, among Arabs too weather-daunted to move.

Clayton said that in the new conditions there could be no question of letting me off. The East was only now going to begin. Allenby told me that the War Cabinet were leaning heavily on him to repair the stalemate of the West. He was to take at least Damascus; and, if possible, Aleppo, as soon as he could. Turkey was to be put out of the war once and for all. His difficulty lay with his eastern flank, the right, which to-day rested on Jordan. He had called me to consider if the Arabs could relieve him of its burden.

There was no escape for me. I must take up again my mantle of fraud in the East. With my certain contempt for half-measures I took it up quickly and wrapped myself in it completely. It might be fraud or it might be farce: no one should say that I could not play it. So I did not even mention the reasons which had brought me across; but pointed out that this was the Jordan scheme seen from the British angle. Allenby assented, and asked if we could still do it. I said: not at present, unless new factors were first discounted.

The first was Maan. We should have to take it before we could afford a second sphere. If more transport gave a longer range to the units of the Arab Regular Army, they could take position some miles north of Maan and cut the railway permanently, so forcing the Maan garrison to come out and fight them; and in the field the Arabs would easily defeat the Turks. We would require seven hundred baggage camels; more guns and machine-guns; and lastly, assurance against flank attack from Amman, while we dealt with Maan.

On this basis a scheme was worked out. Allenby ordered down to

Akaba two units of the Camel Transport Corps, an organization of Egyptians under British officers, which had proved highly successful in the Beersheba campaign. It was a great gift, for its carrying capacity ensured that we should now be able to keep our four thousand regulars eighty miles in advance of their base. The guns and machine-guns were also promised. As for shielding us against attack from Amman, Allenby said that was easily arranged. He intended, for his own flank's security, shortly to take Salt, beyond Jordan, and hold it with an Indian Brigade. A Corps Conference was due next day, and I was to stay for it.

At this Conference it was determined that the Arab Army move instantly to the Maan Plateau, to take Maan. That the British cross the Jordan, occupy Salt, and destroy south of Amman as much of the railway as possible; especially the great tunnel. It was debated what share the Amman Arabs should take in the British operation. Bols thought we should join in the advance. I opposed this, since the later retirement to Salt would cause rumour and reaction, and it would be easier if we did not enter till this had spent itself.

Chetwode, who was to direct the advance, asked how his men were to distinguish friendly from hostile Arabs, since their tendency was a prejudice against all wearing skirts. I was sitting skirted in their midst and replied, naturally, that skirt-wearers disliked men in uniform. The laugh clinched the question, and it was agreed that we support the British retention of Salt only after they came to rest there. As soon as Maan fell, the Arab Regulars would move up and draw supplies from Jericho. The seven hundred camels would come along, still giving them eighty miles' radius of action. This would be enough to let them work above Amman in Allenby's grand attack along the line from the Mediterranean to the Dead Sea, the second phase of the operation, directed to the capture of Damascus.

My business was finished. I went to Cairo for two days, and then was flown to Akaba, to make my new terms with Feisal. I told him I thought they had treated me badly, in diverting without my knowledge money of the special account which, by agreement, I had drawn solely for the Dead Sea campaign. Consequently, I had left Zeid, it being impossible for a flouted adviser to carry on.

Allenby had sent me back. But my return did not mean that the damage was repaired. A great opportunity had been missed, and a valuable advance thrown away. The Turks would retake Tafileh in a week's time without difficulty.

Feisal was distressed lest the loss of Tafileh do his reputation harm; and shocked by my little interest in its fate. To comfort him, I pointed out that it now meant nothing to us. The two interests were the extremes of his area, Amman and Maan. Tafileh was not worth losing a man over; indeed, if the Turks moved there, they would weaken either Maan or Amman, and make our real work easier.

He was a little reconciled by this, but sent urgent warnings to Zeid of the coming danger: without avail, for six days later the Turks retook Tafileh. Meanwhile, Feisal re-arranged the basis of his army funds. I gave him the good news that Allenby, as thanks for the Dead Sea and Aba el Lissan, had put three hundred thousand pounds into my independent credit, and given us a train of seven hundred pack-camels complete with personnel and equipment.

This raised great joy in all the army, for the baggage columns would enable us to prove the value in the field of the Arab regular troops on whose training and organization Joyce, Jaafar, and so many Arab and English officers had worked for months. We arranged rough time-tables and schemes: then I shipped busily back to Egypt.

R*

BOOK VIII

THE RUIN OF HIGH HOPE

Chapters XCII to XCVII

IN *conjunction with Allenby we laid a triple plan to join hands across Jordan, to capture Maan, and to cut off Medina, in one operation. This was too proud and neither of us fulfilled his part. So the Arabs exchanged the care of the placid Medina Railway for the greater burden of investing, in Maan, a Turk force as big as their available Regular Army.*

To help in this duty Allenby increased our transport, that we might have longer range and more mobility. Maan was impregnable for us, so we concentrated on cutting its northern railway and diverting the Turkish effort to relieve its garrison from the Amman side.

Clearly no decision lay in such tactics: but the German advance in Flanders at this moment took from Allenby his British units; and consequently his advantage over the Turks. He notified us that he was unable to attack.

A stalemate, as we were, throughout 1918 was an intolerable prospect. We schemed to strengthen the Arab Army for autumn operations near Deraa and in the Beni Sakhr country. If this drew off one division from the enemy in Palestine it would make possible a British ancillary attack, one of whose ends would be our junction in the lower Jordan valley, by Jericho. After a month's preparation this plan was dropped, because of its risk, and because a better offered.

IN Cairo, where I spent four days, our affairs were now far from haphazard. Allenby's smile had given us Staff. We had supply officers, a shipping expert, an ordnance expert, an intelligence branch: under Alan Dawnay, brother of the maker of the Beersheba plan, who had now gone to France. Dawnay was Allenby's greatest gift to us — greater than thousands of baggage camels. As a professional officer, he had the class-touch: so that even the reddest hearer recognized an authentic redness. His was an understanding mind, feeling instinctively the special qualities of rebellion: at the same time, his war-training enriched his treatment of this antithetic subject. He married war and rebellion in himself; as, of old in Yenbo, it had been my dream every regular officer would. Yet, in three years' practice, only Dawnay succeeded.

He could not take complete, direct command, because he did not know Arabic; and because of his Flanders-broken health. He had the gift, rare among Englishmen, of making the best of a good thing. He was exceptionally educated, for an Army officer, and imaginative. His perfect manner made him friends with all races and classes. From his teaching we began to learn the technique of fighting in matters we had been content to settle by rude and wasteful rules of thumb. His sense of fitness remodelled our standing.

The Arab Movement had lived as a wild-man show, with its means as small as its duties and prospects. Henceforward Allenby counted it as a sensible part of his scheme; and the responsibility upon us of doing better than he wished, knowing that forfeit for our failure would necessarily be part-paid in his soldiers' lives, removed it terrifyingly further from the sphere of joyous adventure.

With Joyce we laid our triple plan to support Allenby's first stroke. In our centre the Arab regulars, under Jaafar, would occupy the line a march north of Maan. Joyce with our armoured cars would slip down to Mudowwara, and destroy the railway — permanently this time, for now we were ready to cut off Medina. In the north, Merzuk, with myself, would join Allenby when he fell back to Salt about March the thirtieth. Such a date gave me leisure: and I settled to go to Shobek, with Zeid and Nasir.

It was springtime: very pleasant after the biting winter, whose excesses seemed dream-like, in the new freshness and strength of nature: for there was strength in this hill-top season, when a chill sharpness at sundown corrected the languid noons.

All life was alive with us: even the insects. In our first night I had laid my cashmere head-cloth on the ground under my head as pad: and at dawn, when I took it up again, twenty-eight lice were tangled in its snowy texture. Afterwards we slept on our saddle-covers, the tanned fleece hooked last of all over the saddle-load to make a slippy and sweat-proof seat for the rider. Even so, we were not left alone. The camel-ticks, which had drunk themselves (with blood from our tethered camels) into tight slaty-blue cushions, thumbnail wide, and thick, used to creep under us, hugging the leathern underside of the sheep-skins: and if we rolled on them in the night, our weight burst them to brown mats of blood and dust.

While we were in this comfortable air, with milk plentiful about us, news came from Azrak, of Ali ibn el Hussein and the Indians still on faithful watch. One Indian had died of cold, and also Daud, my Ageyli boy, the friend of Farraj. Farraj himself told us.

These two had been friends from childhood, in eternal gaiety: working together, sleeping together, sharing every scrape and profit with the openness and honesty of perfect love. So I was not astonished to see Farraj look dark and hard of face, leaden-eyed and old, when he came to tell me that his fellow was dead; and from that day till his service ended he made no more laughter for us. He took punctilious care, greater even than before, of my camel, of the coffee, of my clothes and saddles, and fell to praying his three regular prayings every day. The others offered themselves to comfort him, but instead he wandered restlessly, grey and silent, very much alone.

When looked at from this torrid East, our British conception of woman seemed to partake of the northern climate which had also contracted our faith. In the Mediterranean, woman's influence and supposed purpose were made cogent by an understanding in which she was accorded the physical world in simplicity, unchallenged, like the poor in spirit. Yet this same agreement, by denying equality of sex, made love, companionship and friendliness impossible between man and woman. Woman became a machine for muscular exercise, while man's psychic side could be slaked only amongst his peers. Whence arose these partnerships of man and man, to supply human nature with more than the contact of flesh with flesh.

We Westerners of this complex age, monks in our bodies' cells, who searched for something to fill us beyond speech and sense, were, by the mere effort of the search, shut from it for ever. Yet it came to children like these unthinking Ageyl, content to receive without return, even from one another. We racked ourselves with inherited remorse for the flesh-indulgence of our gross birth, striving to pay for it through a lifetime of misery; meeting happiness, life's overdraft, by a compensating hell, and striking a ledger-balance of good or evil against a day of judgement.

Meanwhile at Aba el Lissan things went not well with our scheme to destroy the Maan garrison by posting the Arab Army across the railway in the north, and forcing them to open battle, as Allenby attacked their base and supports at Amman. Feisal and Jaafar liked the scheme, but their officers clamoured for direct attack on Maan. Joyce pointed out their weakness in artillery and machine-guns, their untried men, the greater strategical wisdom of the railway scheme: it was of no effect. Maulud, hot for immediate assault, wrote memoranda to Feisal upon the danger of English interference with Arab liberty. At such a moment Joyce fell ill of pneumonia, and left for Suez. Dawnay came up to reason with the malcontents. He was our best card, with his proved military reputation, exquisite field-boots, and air of well-dressed science; but he came too late, for the Arab officers now felt their honour to be engaged.

We agreed that we must give them their heads on the point, though we were really all-powerful, with the money, the supplies, and now the transport, in our hands. However, if the people were slattern, why, then, they must have a slatternly government: and particularly must we go slow with that self-governing democracy, the Arab Army, in which service was as voluntary as enlistment. Between us we were familiar with the Turkish, the Egyptian and the British Armies: and championed our respective task-masters. Joyce alleged the parade-magnificence of his Egyptians — formal men, who loved mechanical movement and surpassed British troops in physique, in smartness, in perfection of drill. I maintained the frugality of the Turks, that shambling, ragged army of serfs. The British Army we all were acquainted with in a fashion; and as we contrasted services we found variety of obedience according to the degree of ordered force which served each as sanction.

In Egypt soldiers belonged to their service without check of public opinion. Consequently they had a peace-incentive to perfection of formal conduct. In Turkey the men were, in theory, equally the officers': body and soul: but their lot was mitigated by the possibility of escape. In England the voluntary recruit served as utterly as any Turk, except that the growth of civil decency had taken away from authority the resource of inflicting direct physical pain: but in practice, upon our less obtuse population, the effects of pack-drill or fatigues fell little short of an Oriental system.

In the regular Arab Army there was no power of punishment whatever: this vital difference showed itself in all our troops. They had no formality of discipline; there was no subordination. Service was active; attack always imminent: and like the Army of Italy, men recognized the duty of defeating the enemy. For the rest they were not soldiers, but pilgrims, intent always to go the little farther.

I was not discontented with this state of things, for it had seemed to me that discipline, or at least formal discipline, was a virtue of peace: a character or stamp by which to mark off soldiers from complete men, and obliterate the humanity of the individual. It resolved itself easiest into the restrictive, the making men not do this or that: and so could be fostered by a rule severe enough to make them despair of disobedience. It was a process of the mass, an element of the impersonal crowd, inapplicable to one man, since it involved obedience, a duality of will. It was not to impress upon men that their will must actively second the officer's, for then there would have been, as in the Arab Army and among irregulars, that momentary pause for thought transmission, or digestion; for the nerves to resolve the relaying private will into active consequence. On the contrary, each regular Army sedulously rooted out this significant pause from its companies on parade. The drill-instructors tried to make obedience an instinct, a mental reflex, following as instantly on the command as though the motor power of the individual wills had been invested together in the system.

This was well, so far as it increased quickness: but it made no provision for casualties, beyond the weak assumption that each subordinate had his will-motor not atrophied, but reserved in perfect order, ready at the instant to take over his late superior's office; the efficiency of direction passing smoothly down the great hierarchy till vested in the senior of the two surviving privates.

It had the further weakness, seeing men's jealousy, of putting power in the hands of arbitrary old age, with its petulant activity: additionally corrupted by long habit of control, an indulgence which ruined its victim, by causing the death of his subjunctive mood. Also, it was an idiosyncrasy with me to distrust instinct, which had its roots in our animality. Reason seemed to give men something deliberately more precious than fear or pain: and this made me discount the value of peace smartness as a war-education.

For with war a subtle change happened to the soldier. Discipline was modified, supported, even swallowed by an eagerness of the man to fight. This eagerness it was which brought victory in the moral sense, and often in the physical sense, of the combat. War was made up of crises of intense effort. For psychological reasons commanders wished for the least duration of this maximum effort: not because the men would not try to give it — usually they would go on till they dropped — but because each such effort weakened their remaining force. Eagerness of the kind was nervous, and, when present in high power, it tore apart flesh and spirit.

To rouse the excitement of war for the creation of a military spirit in peace-time would be dangerous, like the too-early doping of an athlete. Consequently discipline, with its concomitant 'smartness' (a suspect word implying superficial restraint and pain), was invented to take its place. The Arab Army, born and brought up in the fighting line, had never known a peace-habit, and was not faced with problems of maintenance till armistice-time: then it failed signally.

CHAPTER XCIII

AFTER Joyce and Dawnay had gone, I rode off from Aba el Lissan, with Mirzuk. Our starting day promised to crown the spring-freshness of this lofty tableland. A week before there had been a furious blizzard, and some of the whiteness of the snow seemed to have passed into the light. The ground was vivid with new grass; and the sunlight, which slanted across us, pale like straw, mellowed the fluttering wind.

With us journeyed two thousand Sirhan camels, carrying our ammunition and food. For the convoy's sake we marched easily, to reach the railway after dark. A few of us rode forward, to search the line by daylight, and be sure of peace during the hours these scattered numbers would consume in crossing.

My bodyguard was with me, and Mirzuk had his Ageyl, with two famous racing camels. The gaiety of the air and season caught them. Soon they were challenging to races, threatening one another, or skirmishing. My imperfect camel-riding (and my mood) forbade me to thrust among the lads, who swung more to the north, while I worked on, ridding my mind of the lees of camp-clamour and intrigue. The abstraction of the desert landscape cleansed me, and rendered my mind vacant with its superfluous greatness: a greatness achieved not by the addition of thought to its emptiness, but by its subtraction. In the weakness of earth's life was mirrored the strength of heaven, so vast, so beautiful, so strong.

Near sunset the line became visible, curving spaciously across the disclosed land, among low tufts of grass and bushes. Seeing everything was peaceful I pushed on, meaning to halt beyond and watch the others over. There was always a little thrill in touching the rails which were the target of so many of our efforts.

As I rode up the bank my camel's feet scrambled in the loose ballast, and out of the long shadow of a culvert to my left, where, no doubt, he had slept all day, rose a Turkish soldier. He glanced wildly at me and at the pistol in my hand, and then with sadness at his rifle against the abutment, yards beyond. He was a young man; stout, but sulky-looking. I stared at him, and said, softly, 'God is merciful'. He knew the sound and sense of the Arabic phrase, and raised his eyes like a flash to mine, while his heavy sleep-ridden face began slowly to change into incredulous joy.

However, he said not a word. I pressed my camel's hairy shoulder with my foot, she picked her delicate stride across the metals and down the further slope, and the little Turk was man enough not to shoot me in the back, as I rode away, feeling warm towards him, as ever towards a life one has saved. At a safe distance I glanced back. He put thumb to nose, and twinkled his fingers at me.

We lit a coffee-fire as beacon for the rest, and waited till their dark lines passed by. Next day we marched to Wadi el Jinz; to flood-pools, shallow eyes of water set in wrinkles of the clay, their rims lashed about with scrubby stems of brushwood. The water was grey, like the marly valley bed, but sweet. There we rested for the night, since the Zaagi had shot a bustard, and Xenophon did rightly call its white meat good. While we feasted the camels feasted. By the bounty of spring they were knee-deep in succulent green-stuff.

A fourth easy march took us to the Atara, our goal, where our allies, Mifleh, Fahad and Adhub, were camped. Fahad was still stricken, but Mifleh, with honeyed words, came out to welcome us, his face eaten up by greed, and his voice wheezy with it.

Our plan, thanks to Allenby's lion-share, promised simply. We would, when ready, cross the line to Themed, the main Beni Sakhr watering. Thence under cover of a screen of their cavalry we would move to Madeba, and fit it as our headquarters, while Allenby put the Jericho-Salt road in condition. We ought to link up with the British comfortably without firing a shot.

Meanwhile we had only to wait in the Atatir, which to our joy were really green, with every hollow a standing pool, and the valley beds of tall grass prinked with flowers. The chalky ridges, sterile with salt, framed the water-channels delightfully. From their tallest point we could look north and south, and see how the rain, running down, had painted the valleys across the white in broad stripes of green, sharp and firm like brush-strokes. Everything was growing, and daily the picture was fuller and brighter till the desert became like a rank water-meadow. Playful packs of winds came crossing and tumbling over one another, their wide, brief gusts surging through the grass, to lay it momentarily in swathes of dark and light satin, like young corn after the roller. On the hill we sat and shivered before these sweeping shadows, expecting a heavy blast — and there would come into our faces a warm and per-fumed breath, very gentle, which passed away behind us as a silver-grey light down the plain of green. Our fastidious camels grazed an hour or so, and then lay down to digest, bringing up stomach-load after stomach-load of butter-smelling green cud, and chewing weightily.

At last news came that the English had taken Amman. In half an hour we were making for Themed, across the deserted line. Later messages told us that the English were falling back, and though we had forewarned the Arabs of it, yet they were troubled. A further messen-ger reported how the English had just fled from Salt. This was plainly contrary to Allenby's intention, and I swore straight out that it was not true. A man galloped in to say that the English had broken only a few rails south of Amman, after two days of vain assaults against the town. I grew seriously disturbed in the conflict of rumour, and sent Adhub, who might be trusted not to lose his head, to Salt with a letter for Chetwode or Shea, asking for a note on the real situation. For the intervening hours we tramped restlessly over the fields of young barley, our minds working out plan after plan with feverish activity.

Very late at night Adhub's racing horse-hooves echoed across the valley and he came in to tell us that Jemal Pasha was now in Salt, victorious, hanging those local Arabs who had welcomed the English. The Turks were still chasing Allenby far down the Jordan Valley. It was thought that Jerusalem would be recovered. I knew enough of my countrymen to reject that possibility; but clearly things were very wrong. We slipped off, bemused, to the Atatir again.

This reverse, being unawares, hurt me the more. Allenby's plan had seemed modest, and that we should so fall down before the Arabs was deplorable. They had never trusted us to do the great things which I foretold; and now their independent thoughts set out to enjoy the springtide here. They were abetted by some gipsy families from the north with the materials of their tinkering trade on donkeys. The Zebn tribesmen greeted them with a humour I little understood -- till I saw that, beside their legitimate profits of handicraft, the women were open to other advances.

Particularly they were easy to the Ageyl; and for a while they prospered exceedingly, since our men were eager and very generous. I also made use of them. It seemed a pity to be at a loose end so near to Amman, and not bother to look at it. So Farraj and I hired three of the merry little women, wrapped ourselves up like them, and strolled through the village. The visit was successful, though my final determination was that the place should be left alone. We had one evil moment, by the bridge, when we were returning. Some Turkish soldiers crossed our party, and taking us all five for what we looked, grew much too friendly. We showed a coyness, and good turn of speed for gipsy women, and escaped intact. For the future I decided to resume my habit of wearing ordinary British soldiers' rig in enemy camps. It was too brazen to be suspect.

After this I determined to order the Indians from Azrak back to Feisal, and to return myself. We started on one of those clean dawns which woke up the senses with the sun, while the intellect, tired after the thinking of the night, was yet abed. For an hour or two on such a morning the sounds, scents and colours of the world struck man individually and directly, not filtered through or made typical by thought; they seemed to exist sufficiently by themselves, and the lack of design and of carefulness in creation no longer irritated.

We marched southward along the railway, expecting to cross the slower-moving Indians from Azrak; our little party on prize camels swooping from one point of vantage to another, on the look-out. The still day encouraged us to speed over all the flint-strewn ridges, ignoring the multitude of desert paths which led only to the abandoned camps of last year, or of the last thousand or ten thousand years: for a road, once trodden into such flint and limestone, marked the face of the desert for so long as the desert lasted.

By Faraifra we saw a little patrol of eight Turks marching up the line. My men, fresh after the holiday in the Atatir, begged me to ride on them. I thought it too trifling, but when they chafed, agreed. The younger ones instantly rushed forward at a gallop. I ordered the rest across the line, to drive the enemy away from their shelter behind a culvert. The Zaagi, a hundred yards to my right, seeing what was wanted, swerved aside at once. Mohsin followed him a moment later, with his section; whilst Abdulla and I pushed forward steadily on our side, to take the enemy on both flanks together.

Farraj, riding in front of everyone, would not listen to our cries nor notice the warning shots fired past his head. He looked round at our manœuvre, but himself continued to canter madly towards the bridge. which he reached before the Zaagi and his party had crossed the line. The Turks held their fire, and we supposed them gone down the further side of the embankment into safety; but as Farraj drew rein beneath the archway, there was a shot, and he seemed to fall or leap out of the saddle, and disappeared. A while after, the Zaagi got into position on the bank and his party fired twenty or thirty ragged shots, as though the enemy was still there.

I was very anxious about Farraj. His camel stood unharmed by the bridge, alone. He might be hit, or might be following the enemy. I could not believe that he had deliberately ridden up to them in the open and halted; yet it looked like it. I sent Feheyd to the Zaagi and told him to rush along the far side as soon as possible, whilst we went at a fast trot straight in to the bridge.

We reached it together, and found there one dead Turk, and Farraj terribly wounded through the body, lying by the arch just as he had fallen from his camel. He looked unconscious; but, when we dismounted, greeted us, and then fell silent, sunken in that loneliness which came to hurt men who believed death near. We tore his clothes away and looked uselessly at the wound. The bullet had smashed right through him, and his spine seemed injured. The Arabs said at once that he had only a few hours to live.

We tried to move him, for he was helpless, though he showed no pain. We tried to stop the wide, slow bleeding, which made poppy-splashes in the grass; but it seemed impossible, and after a while he told us to let him alone, as he was dying, and happy to die, since he had no care of life. Indeed, for long he had been so, and men very tired and sorry often fell in love with death, with that triumphal weakness coming home after strength has been vanquished in a last battle.

While we fussed about him Abd el Latif shouted an alarm. He could see about fifty Turks working up the line towards us, and soon after a motor trolley was heard coming from the north. We were only sixteen men, and had an impossible position. I said we must retire at once, carrying Farraj with us. They tried to lift him, first in his cloak, afterwards in a blanket; but consciousness was coming back, and he screamed so pitifully that we had not the heart to hurt him more.

We could not leave him where he was, to the Turks, because we had seen them burn alive our hapless wounded. For this reason we were all agreed, before action, to finish off one another, if badly hurt: but I had never realized that it might fall to me to kill Farraj.

I knelt down beside him, holding my pistol near the ground by his head, so that he should not see my purpose; but he must have guessed it, for he opened his eyes, and clutched me with his harsh, scaly hand, the tiny hand of these unripe Nejd fellows. I waited a moment, and he said, 'Daud will be angry with you', the old smile coming back so strangely to this grey shrinking face. I replied, 'Salute him from me'. He returned the formal answer, 'God will give you peace', and at last wearily closed his eyes.

The Turkish trolley was now very close, swaying down the line towards us like a dung-beetle: and its machine-gun bullets stung the air about our heads as we fled back into the ridges. Mohsin led Farraj's camel, on which were his sheepskin and trappings, still with the shape of his body in them just as he had fallen by the bridge. Near dark we halted; and the Zaagi came whispering to me that all were wrangling as to who should ride the splendid animal next day. He wanted her for himself; but I was bitter that these perfected dead had again robbed my poverty: and to cheapen the great loss with a little one I shot the poor beast with my second bullet.

Then the sun set on us. Through the breathless noon in the valleys of Kerak the prisoned air had brooded stagnantly without relief, while the heat sucked the perfume from the flowers. With darkness the world moved once more, and a breath from the west crept out over the desert. We were miles from the grass and flowers, but suddenly we felt them all about us, as waves of this scented air drew past us with a sticky sweetness. However, quickly it faded, and the night-wind, damp and wholesome, followed. Abdulla brought me supper, rice and camel-meat (Farraj's camel). Afterwards we slept.

IN the morning, near Wadi el Jinz, we met the Indians, halted by a solitary tree. It was like old times, like our gentle and memorable ride to the bridges the year before, to be going again across country with Hassan Shah, hearing the Vickers guns still clinking in the carriers, and helping the troopers re-tie their slipping loads, or saddles. They seemed just as unhandy with camels as at first; so not till dusk did we cross the railway.

There I left the Indians, because I felt restless, and movement fast in the night might cure my mind. So we pressed forward all the chill darkness, riding for Odroh. When we topped its rise we noticed gleams of fire to our left: bright flashes went up constantly, it might be from about Jerdun. We drew rein and heard the low boom of explosions: a steady flame appeared, grew greater and divided into two. Perhaps the station was burning. We rode quick, to ask Mastur.

However, his place was deserted, with only a jackal on the old camping-ground. I decided to push ahead to Feisal. We trotted our fastest, as the sun grew higher in the heavens. The road was bestial with locusts — though from a little distance they looked beautiful, silvering the air with the shimmer of their wings. Summer had come upon us unawares; my seventh consecutive summer in this East.

As we approached, we heard firing in front, on Semna, the crescent mound which covered Maan. Parties of troops walked gently up its face to halt below the crest. Evidently we had taken the Semna, so we rode towards the new position. On the flat, this side of it, we met a camel with litters. The man leading it said, 'Maulud Pasha', pointing to his load. I ran up, crying, 'Is Maulud hit?' for he was one of the best officers in the army, a man also most honest towards us; not, indeed that admiration could anyhow have been refused so sturdy and uncompromising a patriot. The old man replied out of his litter in a weak voice, saying, 'Yes, indeed, Lurens Bey, I am hurt: but, thanks be to God, it is nothing. We have taken Semna.' I replied that I was going there. Maulud craned himself feverishly over the edge of the litter, hardly able to see or speak (his thigh-bone was splintered above the knee), showing me point after point, for organizing the hill-side defensively.

We arrived as the Turks were beginning to throw half-hearted shells at it. Nuri Said was commanding in Maulud's place. He stood coolly on the hill-top. Most men talked faster under fire, and acted a betraying ease and joviality. Nuri grew calmer, and Zeid bored.

I asked where Jaafar was. Nuri said that at midnight he was due to have attacked Jerdun. I told him of the night-flares, which must have marked his success. While we were glad together his messengers arrived reporting prisoners and machine-guns; also the station and three thousand rails destroyed. So splendid an effort would settle the northern line for weeks. Then Nuri told me that the preceding dawn he had rushed Ghadir el Haj station and wrecked it, with five bridges and a thousand rails. So the southern line was also settled.

Late in the afternoon it grew deadly quiet. Both sides stopped their aimless shelling. They said that Feisal had moved to Uheida. We crossed the little flooded stream, by a temporary hospital where Maulud lay. Mahmud, the red-bearded, defiant doctor, thought that he would recover without amputation. Feisal was on the hill-top, on the very edge, black against the sun, whose light threw a queer haze about his slender figure, and suffused his head with gold, through the floss-silk of his head-cloth. I made my camel kneel. Feisal stretched out his hands crying, 'Please God, good?' I replied, 'The praise and the victory be to God'. And he swept me into his tent that we might exchange the news.

Feisal had heard from Dawnay more than I knew of the British failure before Amman; of the bad weather and confusion, and how Allenby had telephoned to Shea, and made one of his lightning decisions to cut the loss; a wise decision, though it hurt us sorely. Joyce was in hospital, but mending well; and Dawnay lay ready at Guweira to start for Mudowwara with all the cars.

Feisal asked me about Semna and Jaafar, and I told him what I knew, and Nuri's opinion, and the prospect. Nuri had complained that the Abu Tayi had done nothing for him all day. Auda denied it; and I recalled the story of our first taking the plateau, and the gibe by which

I had shamed them into the charge at Aba el Lissan. The tale was new to Feisal. Its raking-up hurt old Auda deeply. He swore vehemently that he had done his best to-day, only conditions were not favourable for tribal work: and, when I withstood him further, he went out of the tent, very bitter.

Maynard and I spent the next days watching operations. The Abu Tayi captured two outposts east of the station, while Saleh ibn Shefia took a breastwork with a machine-gun and twenty prisoners. These gains gave us liberty of movement round Maan; and on the third day Jaafar massed his artillery on the southern ridge, while Nuri Said led a storming party into the sheds of the railway station. As he reached their cover the French guns ceased fire. We were wandering in a Ford car, trying to keep up with the successive advances, when Nuri, perfectly dressed and gloved, smoking his briar pipe, met us and sent us back to Captain Pisani, artillery commander, with an urgent appeal for support. We found Pisani wringing his hands in despair, every round expended. He said he had implored Nuri not to attack at this moment of his penury.

There was nothing to do, but see our men volleyed out of the railway station again. The road was littered with crumpled khaki figures, and the eyes of the wounded, gone rich with pain, stared accusingly at us. The control had gone from their broken bodies and their torn flesh shook them helplessly. We could see everything and think dispassionately, but it was soundless: our hearing had been taken away by the knowledge that we had failed.

Afterwards we understood that we had never expected such excellent spirit from our infantry, who fought cheerfully under machine-gun fire, and made clever use of ground. So little leading was required that only three officers were lost. Maan showed us that the Arabs were good enough without British stiffening. This made us more free to plan: so the failure was not unredeemed.

On the morning of April the eighteenth, Jaafar wisely decided that he could not afford more loss, and drew back to the Semna positions while the troops rested. Being an old college friend of the Turkish Commandant, he sent him a white-flagged letter, inviting surrender. The reply said that they would love it, but had orders to hold out to the last cartridge. Jaafar offered a respite, in which they could fire off their reserves: but the Turks hesitated till Jemal Pasha was able to collect troops from Amman, re-occupy Jerdun, and pass a pack-convoy of food and ammunition into the beleaguered town. The railway remained broken for weeks.

Forthwith I took car to join Dawnay. I was uneasy at a regular fighting his first guerilla battle with that most involved and intricate weapon, the armoured car. Also Dawnay was no Arabist, and neither Peake, his camel-expert, nor Marshall, his doctor, was fluent. His troops were mixed, British, Egyptian and Bedouin. The last two were antipathetic. So I drove into his camp above Tell Shahm after midnight, and offered myself, delicately, as an interpreter.

Fortunately he received me well, and took me round his lines. A wonderful show. The cars were parked geometrically here; armoured cars there; sentries and pickets were out, with machine-guns ready. Even the Arabs were in a tactical place behind a hill, in support, but out of sight and hearing: by some magic Sherif Hazaa and himself had kept them where they were put. My tongue coiled into my cheek with the wish to say that the only thing lacking was an enemy.

His conversation as he unfolded his plan deepened my admiration to unplumbed depths. He had prepared operation orders; orthodox-sounding things with zero times and a sequence of movements. Each unit had its appointed duty. We would attack the 'plain post' at dawn (armoured cars) from the vantage of the hillock on which Joyce and myself had sat and laughed ruefully the last abortive time. The cars, with closed cut-out, would 'take station' before daylight, and carry the trenches by surprise. Tenders 1 and 3 would then demolish bridges A and B on the operations' plan (scale 1/250,000) at zero 1.30 hours while the cars moved to Rock Post, and with the support of Hazaa and the Arabs rushed it (zero 2.15).

Hornby and the explosives, in Talbots No. 40531 and 41226, would move after them, and demolish bridges D, E and F while the force lunched. After lunch, when the low sun permitted sight through the mirage, at zero 8 hours to be exact, the united mass would attack South Post; the Egyptians from the East, the Arabs from the North, covered by long range machine-gun fire from the cars, and by Brodie's ten-pounder guns, sited on Observation Hill. The post would fall and the force transport itself to the station of Tell Shahm, which would be shelled by Brodie from the North-West, bombed by aeroplanes flying from the mud-flats of Rum (at zero 10 hours) and approached by armoured cars from the west. The Arabs would follow the cars, while Peake with his Camel Corps descended from South Post. 'The station will be taken at zero 11.30' said the scheme, breaking into humour at the last. But there it failed, for the Turks, ignorantly and in haste, surrendered ten minutes too soon, and made the only blot on a bloodless day.

In a liquid voice I inquired if Hazaa understood. I was informed that as he had no watch to synchronize (by the way, would I please put mine right now?) he would make his first move when the cars turned northward and time his later actions by express order. I crept away and hid myself for an hour's sleep.

At dawn we saw the cars roll silently on top of the sleeping sandy trenches, and the astonished Turks walk out with their hands up. It was like picking a ripe peach. Hornby dashed up in his two Rolls tenders, put a hundredweight of gun-cotton under bridge A and blew it up convincingly. The roar nearly lifted Dawnay and myself out of our third tender, in which we sat grandly overseeing all: and we ran in, to show Hornby the cheaper way of the drainage holes as minechambers. Subsequent bridges came down for ten slabs apiece.

While we were at bridge B the cars concentrated their machine-guns on the parapet of 'Rock Post', a circle of thick stone walls (very visible from their long early shadows) on a knoll too steep for wheels. Hazaa was ready, willing and excited, and the Turks so frightened by the splashing and splattering of the four machine-guns that the Arabs took them almost in their stride. That was peach the second.

Then it was interval for the others, but activity for Hornby, and for myself, now assistant-engineer. We ran down the line in our Rolls-Royces, carrying two tons of gun-cotton; bridges and rails roared up wherever fancy dictated. The crews of the cars covered us; and sometimes covered themselves, under their cars, when fragments came sailing musically through the smoky air. One twenty-pound flint clanged plumb on a turret-head and made a harmless dint. At intervals everybody took photographs of the happy bursts. It was fighting de luxe, and demolition de luxe: we enjoyed ourselves. After the peripatetic lunch-hour we went off to see the fall of 'south post'. It fell to its minute, but not properly. Hazaa and his Amran were too wound up to advance soberly in alternate rushes like Peake and the Egyptians. Instead they thought it was a steeplechase, and did a camel-charge up the mound over breastwork and trenches. The war-weary Turks gave it up in disgust.

Then came the central act of the day, the assault upon the station. Peake drew down towards it from the north, moving his men by repeated exposure of himself; hardly, for they were not fierce for honour. Brodie opened on it with his usual nicety, while the aeroplanes circled round in their cold-blooded way, to drop whistling bombs into its trenches. The armoured cars went forward snuffling smoke, and through this haze a file of Turks waving white things rose out of their main trench in a dejected fashion.

We cranked up our Rolls tenders; the Arabs leaped on to their camels; Peake's now-bold men broke into a run, and the force converged wildly upon the station. Our car won; and I gained the station bell, a dignified piece of Damascus brass-work. The next man took the ticket punch and the third the office stamp, while the bewildered Turks stared at us, with a growing indignation that their importance should be merely secondary.

A minute later, with a howl, the Beduin were upon the maddest looting of their history. Two hundred rifles, eighty thousand rounds of ammunition, many bombs, much food and clothing were in the station, and everybody smashed and profited. An unlucky camel increased the confusion by firing one of the many Turkish trip-mines as it entered the yard. The explosion blew it arse over tip, and caused a panic. They thought Brodie was opening up again.

In the pause the Egyptian officer found an unbroken storehouse, and put a guard of soldiers over it, because they were short of food. Hazaa's wolves, not yet sated, did not recognize the Egyptians' right to share equally. Shooting began: but by mediation we obtained that the Egyptians pick first what rations they needed: afterwards there followed a general scramble, which burst the store-room walls.

The profit of Shahm was so great that eight out of every ten of the Arabs were contented with it. In the morning only Hazaa and a handful of men remained with us for further operations. Dawnay's programme said Ramleh station; but his orders were inchoate, since the position had not been examined. So we sent down Wade in his armoured car, with a second car in support. He drove on, cautiously, stage by stage, in dead silence. At last, without a shot fired, he entered the station yard, carefully, for fear of the mines, whose trip and trigger wires diapered the ground.

The station was closed up. He put half a belt through the door and shutters, and, getting no reply, slipped out of his car, searched the building, and found it empty of men, though full enough of desirable goods to make Hazaa and the faithful remnant prize their virtue aloud. We spent the day destroying miles more of the unoccupied line, till we judged that we had done damage to occupy the largest possible repair party for a fortnight.

The third day was to be Mudowwara, but we had no great hope or force left. The Arabs were gone, Peake's men too little warlike. However, Mudowwara might panic like Ramleh, so we slept the night by our latest capture. The unwearied Dawnay set out sentries, who, emulous of their smart commanding officer, did a Buckingham Palace stunt up and down beside our would-be sleeping heads, till I got up, and instructed them in the arts of desert-watching.

In the morning we set off to look at Mudowwara, driving like kings splendidly in our roaring cars over the smooth plains of sand and flint, with the low sun pale behind us in the east. The light hid us till we were close in and saw that a long train stood in the station. Reinforcement or evacuation? A moment afterwards they let fly at us with four guns, of which two were active and accurate little Austrian mountain howitzers. At seven thousand yards they did admirable shooting, while we made off in undignified haste to some distant hollows. Thence we made a wide circuit to where, with Zaal, we had mined our first train. We blew up the long bridge, under which the Turkish patrol had slept out that tense midday. Afterwards we returned to Ramleh, and persevered in destroying line and bridges, to make our break permanent, a demolition too serious for Fakhri ever to restore: while Feisal sent

Mohammed el Dheilan against the yet intact stations between our break and Maan. Dawnay joined up with them, geographically, below the escarpment, a day later; and so this eighty miles from Maan to Mudowwara, with its seven stations, fell wholly into our hands. The active defence of Medina ended with this operation.

A new officer, Young, came from Mesopotamia to reinforce our staff. He was a regular of exceptional quality, with long and wide experience of war, and perfect fluency in Arabic. His intended role was to double mine, with the tribes, that our activity against the enemy might be broader, and better directed. To let him play himself in to our fresh conditions, I handed him over the possibility of combining Zeid, Nasir and Mirzuk into an eighty-mile long interruption of the railway from Maan northward, while I went down to Akaba, and took ship for Suez, to discuss futures with Allenby.

CHAPTER XCV

DAWNAY met me, and we talked over our brief before going up to Allenby's camp. There General Bols smiled happily at us, and said, 'Well, we're in Salt all right'. To our amazed stares he went on that the chiefs of the Beni Sakhr had come into Jericho one morning, to offer the immediate co-operation of their twenty thousand tribesmen at Themed; and in his bath next day he had thought out a scheme, and fixed it all right.

I asked who the chief of the Beni Sakhr was, and he said 'Fahad': triumphing in his efficient inroad into what had been my province. It sounded madder and madder. I knew that Fahad could not raise four hundred men; and, that at the moment there was not a tent on Themed: they had moved south, to Young.

We hurried to the office for the real story, and learned that it was, unfortunately, as Bols had said. The British cavalry had gone impromptu up the hills of Moab on some airy promise of the Zebn sheikhs; greedy fellows who had ridden into Jerusalem only to taste Allenby's bounty but had there been taken at their mouth-value.

In this season there was no third partner at G.H.Q. Guy Dawnay, brother of our gladiator, he who had made the Jerusalem plan, had gone to Haig's staff: Bartholomew, who was to work out the autumn drive upon Damascus, was still with Chetwode. So the executive of Allenby's work in these months was unequal to the conception.

For, of course, this raid miscarried, while I was still in Jerusalem, solacing myself against the inadequacy of Bols with Storrs, now the urbane and artful Governor of the place. The Beni Sakhr were supine in their tents or away with Young. General Chauvel, without the help of one of them, saw the Turks re-open the Jordan fords behind his back and seize the road by which he had advanced. We escaped heavy disaster only because Allenby's instinct for a situation showed him his danger just in time. Yet we suffered painfully. The check taught the British to be more patient with Feisal's difficulties; convinced the Turks that the Amman sector was their danger point; and made the Beni Sakhr feel

539

that the English were past understanding: not great fighting men, perhaps, but ready on the spur of the moment to be odd. So, in part, it redeemed the Amman failure by its deliberate repetition of what had looked accidental. At the same time it ruined the hopes which Feisal had entertained of acting independently with the Beni Sakhr. This cautious and very wealthy tribe asked for dependable allies.

Our movement, clean-cut while alone with a simple enemy, was now bogged in its partner's contingencies. We had to take our tune from Allenby, and he was not happy. The German offensive in France was stripping him of troops. He would retain Jerusalem, but could not afford a casualty, much less an attack, for months. The War Office promised him Indian divisions from Mesopotamia, and Indian drafts. With these he would rebuild his army on the Indian model; perhaps, after the summer he might be again in fighting trim: but for the moment we must both just hold on.

This he told me on May the fifth, the date chosen under the Smuts arrangement for the heave northward of the whole army as prelude to the fall of Damascus and Aleppo. As first phase of his arrangement we had undertaken the liability of Maan: and Allenby's pause stuck us with this siege of a superior force. In addition, the Turks from Amman might now have leisure to sweep us off Aba el Lissan, back to Akaba. In so nasty a situation the common habit of joint operations — cursing the other partner — weighed strongly upon me. However, Allenby's staunchness was aiming to relieve us. He was threatening the enemy by a vast bridge-head across Jordan, as if he were about to cross a third time. So he would keep Amman tender. To strengthen us on our plateau he offered what technical equipment we needed.

We took the opportunity to ask for repeated air-raids on the Hejaz Railway. General Salmond was called in, and proved as generous, in word and deed, as the Commander-in-Chief. The Royal Air Force kept up a dull, troublesome pressure on Amman from now till the fall of Turkey. Much of the inactivity of the enemy in our lean season was due to the disorganization of their railway by bombing. At tea-time Allenby mentioned the Imperial Camel Brigade in Sinai, regretting that in the new stringency he must abolish it and use its men as mounted

reinforcements. I asked: 'What are you going to do with their camels?'
He laughed, and said, 'Ask "Q".'

Obediently, I went across the dusty garden, broke in upon the
Quartermaster-General, Sir Walter Campbell — very Scotch — and
repeated my question. He answered firmly that they were earmarked
as divisional transport for the second of the new Indian divisions. I
explained that I wanted two thousand of them. His first reply was
irrelevant: his second conveyed that I might go on wanting. I argued,
but he seemed unable to see my side at all. Of course, it was of the
nature of a 'Q' to be costive.

I returned to Allenby and said aloud, before his party, that there
were for disposal two thousand, two hundred riding-camels, and
thirteen hundred baggage camels. All were provisionally allotted to
transport; but of course, riding-camels were riding-camels. The staff
whistled, and looked wise; as though they, too, doubted whether
riding-camels could carry baggage. A technicality, even a sham one,
might be helpful. Every British officer understood animals, as a point
of honour. So I was not astonished when Sir Walter Campbell was
asked to dine with the Commander-in-Chief that night.

We sat on the right hand and on the left, and with the soup Allenby
began to talk about camels. Sir Walter broke out that the providential
dispersing of the camel brigade brought the transport of the ——th
Division up to strength; a godsend, for the Orient had been vainly
ransacked for camels. He over-acted. Allenby, a reader of Milton, had
an acute sense of style: and the line was a weak one. He cared nothing
for strengths, the fetish of administrative branches.

He looked at me with a twinkle, 'And what do you want them for?'
I replied hotly, 'To put a thousand men into Deraa any day you please'.
He smiled and shook his head at Sir Walter Campbell, saying sadly,
'Q, you lose'. The goat became giddy and the sheep sheepish. It was
an immense, a regal gift; the gift of unlimited mobility. The Arabs
could now win their war when and where they liked.

Next morning I was off to join Feisal in his cool eyrie at Aba el
Lissan. We discussed histories, tribes, migration, sentiments, the spring
rains, pasture, at length. Finally, I remarked that Allenby had given us
two thousand camels. Feisal gasped and caught my knee, saying, 'How?'

s

I told him all the story. He leaped up and kissed me; then he clapped his hands loudly. Hejris' black shape appeared at the tent-door. 'Hurry', cried Feisal, 'call them.' Hejris asked whom. 'Oh, Fahad, Abdulla el Feir, Auda, Motlog, Zaal . . .' 'And not Mirzuk?' queried Hejris mildly. Feisal shouted at him for a fool, and the black ran off; while I said, 'It is nearly finished. Soon you can let me go'. He protested, saying that I must remain with them always, and not just till Damascus, as I had promised in Um Lejj. I, who wanted so to get away.

Feet came pattering to the tent-door, and paused, while the chiefs recovered their grave faces and set straight their head-cloths for the entry. One by one they sat down stilly on the rugs, each saying unconcernedly, 'Please God, good?' To each Feisal replied, 'Praise God!' and they stared in wonder at his dancing eyes.

When the last had rustled in, Feisal told them that God had sent the means of victory — two thousand riding-camels. Our war was to march unchecked to freedom, its triumphant end. They murmured in astonishment; doing their best, as great men, to be calm; eyeing me to guess my share in the event. I said, 'The bounty of Allenby . . .' Zaal cut in swiftly for them all, 'God keep his life and yours'. I replied, 'We have been made victorious', stood up, with a 'by your leave' to Feisal, and slipped away to tell Joyce. Behind my back they burst out into wild words of their coming wilder deeds: childish, perhaps, but it would be a pretty war in which each man did not feel that he was winning it.

Joyce also was gladdened and made smooth by the news of the two thousand camels. We dreamed of the stroke to which they should be put: of their march from Beersheba to Akaba: and where for two months we could find grazing for this vast multitude of animals; they must be broken from barley if they were to be of use to us.

These were not pressing thoughts. We had, meanwhile, the need to maintain ourselves all summer on the plateau, besieging Maan, and keeping the railways cut. The task was difficult.

First, about supply. I had just thrown the existing arrangements out of gear. The Egyptian Camel Transport companies had been carrying steadily between Akaba and Aba el Lissan, but carrying less and marching less than our least sanguine estimate. We urged them to increase weights and speeds, but found ourselves up against cast-iron corps regulations, framed to keep down the figures of animal wastage. By increasing them slightly, we could double the carrying capacity of the column; consequently, I had offered to take over the animals and send back the Egyptian camel-men.

The British, being short of labour, jumped at my idea; almost too quickly. We had a terrible scramble to improvise drivers upon the moment. Goslett, single-handed, had hitherto done supplies, transport, ordnance, paymaster, base commandant. The extra work was cruelty to him. So Dawnay found Scott, a perfect Irishman, for base commandant. He had good temper, capacity, spirit. Akaba breathed quietly. Ordnance we gave to Bright, sergeant or sergeant-major: and Young took over transport and quartermaster work.

Young had overstrained himself, riding furiously between Naimat, Hejaia and Beni Sakhr, between Nasir and Mirzuk and Feisal, striving to combine and move them in one piece. Incidentally he had furiously overstrained the Arabs. In transport duties his drive and ability would be better employed. Using his full power, he grappled with the chaos. He had no stores for his columns, no saddles, no clerks, no veterinaries, no drugs and few drivers, so that to run a harmonious and orderly train was impossible; but Young very nearly did it, in his curious ungrateful way. Thanks to him, the supply problem of the Arab regulars on the plateau was solved.

All this time the face of our Revolt was growing. Feisal, veiled in his tent, maintained incessantly the teaching and preaching of his Arab movement. Akaba boomed: even our field-work was going well. The Arab regulars had just had their third success against Jerdun, the battered station which they made it almost a habit to take and lose. Our armoured cars happened on a Turkish sortie from Maan and smashed it in such style that the opportunity never recurred. Zeid, in command of half the army posted north of Uheida, was showing great vigour. His gaiety of spirit appealed more to the professional officers than did Feisal's poetry and lean earnestness; so this happy association of the two brothers gave every sort of man a sympathy with one or other of the leaders of the revolt.

Yet there were clouds in the north. At Amman was a forcible

Turkish concentration of troops earmarked for Maan when supply conditions would let them move. This supply reserve was being put in by rail from Damascus, as well as the bombing attacks of the Royal Air Force from Palestine permitted.

To make head against them, Nasir, our best guerilla general, had been appointed, in advance of Zeid, to do something great against the railway. He had camped in Wadi Hesa, with Hornby, full of explosives and Peake's trained section of Egyptian Army Camel Corps to help in demolition. Time, till Allenby recovered, was what we had to fight for, and Nasir would very much help our desire if he secured us a month's breathing space by playing the intangible ghost at the Turkish Army. If he failed we must expect the relief of Maan and an onslaught of the reinvigorated enemy upon Aba el Lissan.

NASIR attacked Hesa station in his old fashion, cutting the line to north and south the night before, and opening a sharp bombardment of the buildings when it was light enough to see. Rasim was the gunner and the gun our Krupp antiquity of Medina, Wejh and Tafileh. When the Turks weakened, the Arabs charged into the station, Beni Sakhr and Howeitat vying for the lead.

We had, of course, no killed; as was ever the way with such tactics. Hornby and Peake reduced the place to a heap of ruins. They blew in the well, the tanks, engines, pumps, buildings, three bridges, rolling stock, and about four miles of rail. Next day Nasir moved north, and destroyed Faraifra station. Peake and Hornby continued work that day and the day following. Altogether it sounded like our biggest demolition. I determined to go up and see for myself.

A dozen of my men marched with me. Below the Rasheidiya ridge we came to the lone tree, Shejerat el Tayar. My Hauranis drew rein under its thorny branches, on which were impaled many tatters of wayfarers' offered clothes. Mohammed said, 'Upon you, O Mustafa'. Reluctantly Mustafa let himself down from his saddle and piece by piece took off his clothes, till nearly naked, when he lay down arching himself over the tumbled cairn. The other men dismounted, picked each a thorn, and in solemn file drove them (hard and sharp as brass) deep into his flesh and left them standing there. The Ageyl stared open-mouthed at the ceremony, but before it ended swung themselves monkey-like down, grinning lewdly, and stabbed in their thorns where they would be most painful. Mustafa shivered quietly till he heard Mohammed say, 'Get up', using the feminine inflexion. He sadly pulled out the thorns, dressed, and remounted. Abdulla knew no reason for the punishment: and the Hauranis' manner showed that they did not wish me to ask them. We reached Hesa to find Nasir, with six hundred men, concealed under cliffs and bushes, afraid of enemy aircraft, which had killed many. One bomb had fallen into a pool while eleven camels had been drinking, and had thrown them all, dead, in a ring about the water-side among torn flowers of oleander. We wrote to Air-Vice-Marshal Salmond for a revengeful counter-stroke.

The railway was still in Nasir's hand, and whenever they had explosives Hornby and Peake went down to it. They had blown in a cutting, and were developing a new rail-demolition, turning over each section by main force, as it was cut. From Sultani in the north to Jurf in the south, the damage extended. Fourteen miles. Nasir fully understood the importance of maintaining his activity, and there seemed a fair hope of his lasting. He had found a comfortable and bomb-proof cave between two limestone reefs, which articulated like teeth, broke out from the green hill-side. The heat and flies in the valley were not yet formidable. It was running with water: fertile with pasture. Behind lay Tafileh; and if Nasir were hard pressed he had only to send a message, and the mounted peasantry of the villages, on their rough ponies jangling with shrill bells, would come pouring over the range to his support.

The day of our arrival the Turks sent a force of camel corps, cavalry and infantry, down to re-occupy Faraifra as a first counter-stroke. Nasir at once was up and at them. While his machine-guns kept down the Turks' heads, the Abu Tayi charged up to within a hundred yards of the crumbling wall which was the only defence, and cut out all the camels and some horses. To expose riding-animals to the sight of Beduins was a sure way to lose them.

Afterwards I was down with Auda, near the fork of the valley, when there came the throbbing and moaning overhead of Mercedes engines. Nature stilled itself before the master noise; even the birds and insects hushed. We crawled between fallen boulders, and heard the first bomb drop lower in the valley where Peake's camp lay hidden in a twelve-foot oleander thicket. The machines were flying towards us, for the next bombs were nearer; and the last fell just in front, with a shattering, dusty roar, by our captured camels.

When the smoke cleared, two of them were kicking in agony on the ground. A faceless man, spraying blood from a fringe of red flesh about his neck, stumbled screaming towards our rocks. He crashed blindly over one and another, tripping and scrambling, with arms outstretched, maddened by pain. In a moment he lay quiet, and we who had scattered from him ventured near: but he was dead.

I went back to Nasir, safe in his cave with Nawaf el Faiz, brother of Mithgal, head of the Beni Sakhr. Nawaf, a shifty man, was so full and careful of his pride that he would stoop to any private meanness to preserve it publicly: but then he was mad, like all the Faiz clan; uncertain like them; and voluble, with flickering eyes.

Our acquaintance of before the war had been renewed secretly a year before, when three of us crept in after sunset to their rich family tents near Ziza. Fawaz, the senior Faiz, was a notable Arab, a committeeman of the Damascus group, prominent in the party of independence. He received me with fair words and hospitality, fed us richly, and brought out, after we had talked, his richest bed-quilts.

I had slept an hour or two when a charged voice whispered through a smoke-smelling beard into my ear. It was Nawaf, the brother, to say that, behind the friendly seeming, Fawaz had sent horsemen to Ziza and soon the troops would be here to take me. We were certainly caught. My Arabs crouched in their place, meaning to fight like cornered animals, and kill at least some of the enemy before they themselves died. Such tactics displeased me. When combats came to the physical, bare hand against hand, I was finished. The disgust of being touched revolted me more than the thought of death and defeat: perhaps because one such terrible struggle in my youth had given me an enduring fear of contact: or because I so reverenced my wits and despised my body that I would not be beholden to the second for the life of the first.

I whispered to Nawaf for counsel. He crawled back through the tent-curtain; we followed dragging my few things in their light saddle-pouch. Behind the next tent, his own, sat the camels, knee-haltered and saddled. We mounted circumspectly. Nawaf led out his mare, and guided us, loaded rifle across his thigh, to the railway and beyond it into the desert. There he gave us the star-direction of our supposed goal in Bair. A few days later Sheikh Fawaz was dead.

I EXPLAINED to Feisal that Nasir's cutting of the line would endure another month; and, after the Turks had got rid of him, it would be yet a third month before they attacked us in Aba el Lissan. By then our new camels should be fit for use in an offensive of our own. I suggested that we ask his father, King Hussein, to transfer to Akaba the regular units at present with Ali and Abdulla. Their reinforcement would raise us to ten thousand strong, in uniformed men.

We would divide them into three parts. The immobile would constitute a retaining force to hold Maan quiet. A thousand, on our new camels, would attack the Deraa-Damascus sector. The balance would form a second expedition, of two or three thousand infantry, to move into the Beni Sakhr country and connect with Allenby at Jericho. The long-distance mounted raid, by taking Deraa or Damascus would compel the Turks to withdraw from Palestine one division, or even two, to restore their communications. By so weakening the enemy, we would give Allenby the power to advance his line, at any rate to Nablus. The fall of Nablus would cut the lateral communication which made the Turks strong in Moab; and they would be compelled to fall back on Amman, yielding us quiet possession of the Jordan bottom. Practically I was proposing that we use up the Hauran Arabs to let us reach Jericho, half-way to our Damascus goal. Feisal fell in with the proposal, and gave me letters to his father advising it. Unhappily the old man was, nowadays, little inclined to take his advice, out of green-eyed hatred for this son who was doing too well and was being disproportionately helped by the British. For dealing with the King I relied on joint-action by Wingate and Allenby, his paymasters. I decided to go up to Egypt personally, to press them to write him letters of the necessary stiffness. In Cairo, Dawnay agreed both to the transfer of the southern regulars, and to the independent offensive. We went to Wingate, argued it, and convinced him that the ideas were good. He wrote letters to King Hussein strongly advising the reinforcement of Feisal. I pressed him to make clear to the King that the continuance of a war-subsidy would depend on his giving effect to our advice: but he refused to be stringent, and couched the letter in terms of politeness, which would be lost on the hard and suspicious old man in Mecca.

Yet the effort promised so much for us that we went up to Allenby, to beg his help with the King. At G.H.Q., we felt a remarkable difference in the air. The place was, as always, throbbing with energy and hope, but now logic and co-ordination were manifest in an uncommon degree. Allenby had a curious blindness of judgement in choosing men, due largely to his positive greatness, which made good qualities in his subordinates seem superfluous; but Chetwode, not content, had interposed again, setting up Bartholomew, his own Chief of Staff, in the third place of the hierarchy. Bartholomew, not made, like Dawnay, with many foreign sides to his imagination, was yet more intricate, yet more polished as a soldier, more careful and conscientious, and seemed a friendly team-leader.

We unrolled before him our scheme to start the ball rolling in the autumn, hoping by our pushes to make it possible for him to come in later vigorously to our support. He listened smiling, and said that we were three days too late. Their new army was arriving to time from Mesopotamia and India; prodigious advances in grouping and training were being made. On June the fifteenth it had been the considered opinion of a private conference that the army would be capable of a general and sustained offensive in September.

The sky was, indeed, opening over us; and we went in to Allenby, who said outright that late in September he would make a grand attack to fulfil the Smuts' plan even to Damascus and Aleppo. Our role would be as laid down in the spring; we must make the Deraa raid on the two thousand new camels. Times and details would be fixed as the weeks went on, and as Bartholomew's calculations took shape.

Our hopes of victory had been too often dashed for me to take this as assured. So, for second string, I got Allenby's blessing upon the transfer of Ali's and Abdulla's khaki-clad contingents; and set off, fortified, to Jeddah, where I had no more success than I expected. The

s*

King had got wind of my purpose and took refuge, on the pretext of Ramadhan, in Mecca, his inaccessible capital. We talked over the telephone, King Hussein sheltering himself behind the incompetence of the operators in the Mecca exchange, whenever the subject turned dangerous. My thronged mind was not in the mood for farce, so I rang off, put Feisal's, Wingate's and Allenby's letters back unopened into my bag and returned to Cairo in the next ship.

BOOK IX

BALANCING FOR A LAST EFFORT

Chapters XCVIII to CVI

ALLENBY, *in rapid embodiment of reliefs from India and Mesopotamia, so surpassed hope that he was able to plan an Autumn offensive. The near balance of the forces on each side meant that victory would depend on his subtly deceiving the Turks that their entire danger yet lay beyond the Jordan.*

We might help, by lying quiet for six weeks, feigning a feebleness which should tempt the Turks to attack.

The Arabs were then to lead off at the critical moment by cutting the railway communications of Palestine.

Such bluff within bluff called for most accurate timing, since the balance would have been wrecked either by a premature Turkish retreat in Palestine, or by their premature attack against the Arabs beyond Jordan. We borrowed from Allenby some Imperial Camel Corps to lend extra colour to our supposed critical situation; while preparations for Deraa went on with no more check than an untimely show of pique from King Hussein.

ON July the eleventh Dawnay and I were again talking to Allenby and Bartholomew, and of their generosity and confidence, seeing the undress working of a general's mind. It was an experience: technical, reassuring, and very valuable to me, who was mildly a general, too, in my own odd show. Bols was on leave while the plans were working out. Sir Walter Campbell also was absent; Bartholomew and Evans, their deputies, plotted to re-arrange the army transport, regardless of formations, with such elasticity that any pursuit could be sustained.

Allenby's confidence was like a wall. Before the attack he went to see his troops massed in secrecy, waiting the signal, and told them he was sure, with their good help, of thirty thousand prisoners; this, when the whole game turned on a chance! Bartholomew was most anxious. He said it would be desperate work to have the whole army re-formed by September, and, even if they were ready (actually some brigades existed as such for the first time when they went over), we must not assume that the attack would follow as planned. It could be delivered only in the coastal sector, opposite Ramleh, the railhead, where only could a necessary reserve of stores be gathered. This seemed so obvious that he could not dream of the Turks staying blind, though momently their dispositions ignored it.

Allenby's plan was to collect the bulk of his infantry and all his cavalry under the orange and olive groves of Ramlegh just before September the nineteenth. Simultaneously he hoped to make in the Jordan Valley such demonstrations as should persuade the Turks of a concentration there in progress. The two raids to Salt had fixed the Turks' eyes exclusively beyond Jordan. Every move there, whether of British or Arabs, was accompanied by counter-precautions on the Turks' part, showing how fearful they were. In the coast sector, the area of real danger, the enemy had absurdly few men. Success hung on maintaining them in this fatal mis-appreciation.

After the Meinertzhagen success, deceptions, which for the ordinary

general were just witty hors d'œuvres before battle, became for
Allenby a main point of strategy. Bartholomew would accordingly
erect (near Jericho) all condemned tents in Egypt; would transfer
veterinary hospitals and sick lines there; would put dummy camps,
dummy horses and dummy troops wherever there was plausible
room; would throw more bridges across the river; would collect and
open against enemy country all captured guns; and on the right days
would ensure the movement of non-combatant bodies along the dusty
roads, to give the impression of eleventh-hour concentrations for an
assault. At the same time the Royal Air Force was going to fill the air
with husbanded formations of the latest fighting machines. The pre-
ponderance of these would deprive the enemy for days of the advantage
of air reconnaissance.

Bartholomew wished us to supplement his efforts with all vigour and
ingenuity, from our side of Amman. Yet he warned us that, even with
this, success would hang on a thread, since the Turks could save themselves and their army, and give us our concentration to do over again,
by simply retiring their coast sector seven or eight miles. The British
Army would then be like a fish flapping on dry land, with its railways,
its heavy artillery, its dumps. its stores, its camps all misplaced; and
without olive groves in which to hide its concentration next time. So,
while he guaranteed that the British were doing their utmost, he
implored us not to engage the Arabs, on his behalf, in a position from
which they could not escape.

The noble prospect sent Dawnay and myself back to Cairo in great
fettle and cogitation. News from Akaba had raised again the question
of defending the plateau against the Turks, who had just turned Nasir
out of Hesa and were contemplating a stroke against Aba el Lissan
about the end of August, when our Deraa detachment should start.
Unless we could delay the Turks another fortnight, their threat might
cripple us. A new factor was urgently required.

At this juncture Dawnay was inspired to think of the surviving
battalion of the Imperial Camel Corps. Perhaps G.H.Q. might lend it
us to confuse the Turks' reckoning. We telephoned Bartholomew, who
understood, and backed our request to Bols in Alexandria, and to
Allenby. After an active telegraphing, we got our way. Colonel

Buxton, with three hundred men, was lent to us for a month on two conditions: first, that we should forthwith furnish their scheme of operations; second, that they should have no casualties. Bartholomew felt it necessary to apologize for the last magnificent, heart-warming condition, which he thought unsoldierly!

Dawnay and I sat down with a map and measured that Buxton should march from the Canal to Akaba; thence, by Rum, to carry Mudowwara by night-attack; thence by Bair, to destroy the bridge and tunnel near Amman; and back to Palestine on August the thirtieth. Their activity would give us a peaceful month, in which our two thousand new camels could learn to graze, while carrying the extra dumps of forage and food which Buxton's force would expect.

As we worked out these schemes, there came from Akaba one more elaborate, worked out graphically by Young for Joyce, on our June understanding for independent Arab operations in Hauran. They had figured out the food, ammunition, forage, and transport for two thousand men of all ranks, from Aba el Lissan to Deraa. They had taken into consideration all our resources and worked out schedules by which dumps would be completed and the attack begun in November.

Even had Allenby not pulled his army together this scheme would have broken down intrinsically. It depended on the immediate reinforcement of the Arab Army at Aba el Lissan, which King Hussein had refused; also November was too near to winter with its muddy impassable roads in the Hauran.

Weather and strengths might be matters of opinion: but Allenby meant to attack on September the nineteenth, and wanted us to lead off not more than four nor less than two days before he did. His words to me were that three men and a boy with pistols in front of Deraa on September the sixteenth would fill his conception; would be better than thousands a week before or a week after. The truth was, he cared nothing for our fighting power, and did not reckon us part of his tactical strength. Our purpose, to him, was moral, psychological, diathetic; to keep the enemy command intent upon the trans-Jordan front. In my English capacity I shared this view, but on my Arab side both agitation and battle seemed equally important, the one to serve the joint success, the other to establish Arab self-respect, without which victory would not be wholesome.

So, unhesitatingly, we laid the Young scheme aside and turned to build up our own. To reach Deraa from Aba el Lissan would take a fortnight: the cutting of the three railways and withdrawal to reform in the desert, another week. Our raiders must carry their maintenance for three weeks. The picture of what this meant was in my head — we had been doing it for two years — and so at once I gave Dawnay my estimate that our two thousand camels, in a single journey, without advanced depots or supplementary supply columns, would suffice five hundred regular mounted infantry, the battery of French quick-firing .65 mountain guns, proportionate machine-guns, two armoured cars, sappers, camel-scouts, and two aeroplanes until we had fulfilled our mission. This seemed like a liberal reading of Allenby's three men and a boy. We told Bartholomew, and received G.H.Q. blessing.

Young and Joyce were not best pleased when I returned to say that the great schedule had been torn up. I did not call their plans top-heavy and too late: I threw the onus of change on Allenby's recovery. My new proposal — for which in advance I had pledged their performance — was an intricate dovetailing in the next crowded month and a half, of a 'spoiling' raid by the British Camel Corps and the main raid to surprise the Turks by Deraa.

Joyce felt that I had made a mistake. To introduce foreigners would unman the Arabs; and to let them go a month later would be even worse. Young returned a stubborn, combative 'impossible' to my idea. The Camel Corps would engross the baggage camels, which otherwise might have enabled the Deraa force to reach its goal. By trying to do two greedy things I should end in doing neither. I argued my case and we had a battle.

In the first place I tackled Joyce concerning the Imperial Camel Corps. They would arrive one morning at Akaba — no Arab suspecting them — and would vanish equally suddenly towards Rumm. From Mudowwara to Kissir bridge they would march in the desert, far from the sight of the Arab Army, and from the hearing of the villages. In the resultant vagueness the enemy intelligence would conclude that the whole of the defunct camel brigade was now on Feisal's front. Such an accession of shock-strength to Feisal would make the Turks very tender of the safety of their railway: while Buxton's appearance at Kissir, apparently on preliminary reconnaissance, would put credence into the wildest tales of our intention shortly to attack Amman. Joyce, disarmed by these reasonings, now backed me with his favourable opinion.

For Young's transport troubles I had little sympathy. He, a new comer, said my problems were insoluble: but I had done such things casually, without half his ability and concentration; and knew they were not even difficult. For the Camel Corps, we left him to grapple with weights and time-tables, since the British Army was his profession; and though he would not promise anything (except that it could not be done), done of course it was, and two or three days before the necessary time. The Deraa raid was a different proposition, and point by point I disputed his conception of its nature and equipment.

I crossed out forage, the heaviest item, after Bair. Young became ironic upon the patient endurance of camels: but this year the pasture was grand in the Azrak Deraa region. From the men's food I cut off provision for the second attack, and the return journey. Young supposed aloud that the men would fight well hungry. I explained that we would live on the country. Young thought it a poor country to live on. I called it very good.

He said that the ten days' march home after the attacks would be a long fast: but I had no intention of coming back to Akaba. Then might he ask if it was defeat or victory which was in my mind? I pointed out how each man had a camel under him, and if we killed only six camels a day the whole force would feed abundantly. Yet this did not solace him. I went on to cut down his petrol, cars, ammunition, and everything else to the exact point, without margin, which would meet what we planned. In riposte he became aggressively regular. I prosed forth on my hoary theorem that we lived by our raggedness and beat the Turk by our uncertainty. Young's scheme was faulty, because precise.

Instead, we would march a camel column of one thousand men to Azrak where their concentration must be complete on September the thirteenth. On the sixteenth we would envelop Deraa, and cut its railways. Two days later we would fall back east of the Hejaz Railway and wait events with Allenby. As reserve against accident we would purchase barley in Jebel Druse, and store it at Azrak.

Nuri Shaalan would accompany us with a contingent of Rualla: also the Serdiyeh; the Serahin; and Haurani peasants of the 'Hollow Land', under Talal el Hareidhin. Young thought it a deplorable adventure. Joyce, who had loved our dog-fight conference, was game to try, though doubting I was ambitious. However, it was sure that both would do their best, since the thing was already settled; and Dawnay had helped the organizing side by getting us from G.H.Q. the loan of Stirling, a skilled staff officer, tactful and wise. Stirling's passion for horses was a passport to intimacy with Feisal and the chiefs.

Among the Arab officers were distributed some British military decorations, tokens of their gallantry about Maan. These marks of Allenby's esteem heartened the Arab Army. Nuri Pasha Said offered to command the Deraa expedition, for which his courage, authority and coolness marked him as the ideal leader. He began to pick for it the best four hundred men in the army.

Pisani, the French commandant, fortified by a Military Cross, and in urgent pursuit of a D.S.O., took bodily possession of the four Schneider guns which Cousse had sent down to us after Bremond left; and spent agonized hours with Young, trying to put the scheduled ammunition, and mule-forage, with his men and his own private kitchen on to one-half the requisite camels. The camps buzzed with eagerness and preparation, and all promised well.

Our own family rifts were distressing, but inevitable. The Arab affair had now outgrown our rough and ready help-organization. But the next was probably the last act, and by a little patience we might make our present resources serve. The troubles were only between ourselves, and thanks to the magnificent unselfishness of Joyce, we preserved enough of team-spirit to prevent a complete breakdown, however high-handed I appeared: and I had a reserve of confidence to carry the whole thing, if need be, on my shoulders. They used to think me boastful when I said so: but my confidence was not so much ability to do a thing perfectly, as a preference for botching it somehow rather than letting it go altogether by default.

CHAPTER XCIX

IT was now the end of July, and by the end of August the Deraa expedition must be on the road. In the meantime Buxton's Camel Corps had to be guided through their programme, Nuri Shaalan warned, the armoured cars taught their road to Azrak, and landing-grounds found for aeroplanes. A busy month. Nuri Shaalan, the furthest, was tackled first. He was called to meet Feisal at Jefer about August the seventh. Buxton's force seemed the second need. I told Feisal, under seal, of their coming. To ensure their having no casualties, they must strike Mudowwara with absolute surprise. I would guide them myself to Rumm, in the first critical march through the fag-ends of Howeitat about Akaba.

Accordingly I went down to Akaba, where Buxton let me explain to each company their march, and the impatient nature of the Allies whom they, unasked, had come to help; begging them to turn the other cheek if there was a row; partly because they were better educated than the Arabs, and therefore less prejudiced; partly because they were very few. After such solemnities came the ride up the oppressive gorge of Itm, under the red cliffs of Nejed and over the breast-like curves of Imran — that slow preparation for Rumm's greatness — till we passed through the gap before the rock Khuzail, and into the inner shrine of the springs, with its worship-compelling coolness. There the landscape refused to be accessory, but took the skies, and we chattering humans became dust at its feet.

In Rumm the men had their first experience of watering in equality with Arabs, and found it troublesome. However, they were wonderfully mild, and Buxton was an old Sudan official, speaking Arabic, and understanding nomadic ways; very patient, good-humoured, sympathetic. Hazaa was helpful in admonishing the Arabs, and Stirling and Marshall, who accompanied the column were familiars of the Beni Atiyeh. Thanks to their diplomacy, and to the care of the British rank and file, nothing untoward happened.

I stayed at Rumm for their first day, dumb at the unreality of these healthy-looking fellows, like stiff-bodied school boys in their shirt-sleeves and shorts, as they wandered, anonymous and irresponsible, about the cliffs which had been my private resort. Three years of Sinai had burned the colour from their tanned faces, in which the blue eyes flickered weakly against the dark possessed gaze of the Beduin. For the rest they were a broad-faced, low-browed people, blunt-featured beside the fine-drawn Arabs whom generations of in-breeding had sharpened to a radiance ages older than the primitive, blotched, honest Englishmen. Continental soldiers looked lumpish beside our lean-bred fellows: but against my supple Nejdis the British in their turn looked lumpish.

Later I rode for Akaba, through the high-walled Itm, alone now with six silent, unquestioning guards, who followed after me like shadows, harmonious and submerged in their natural sand and bush and hill; and a home-sickness came over me, stressing vividly my outcast life among these Arabs, while I exploited their highest ideals and made their love of freedom one more tool to help England win.

It was evening, and on the straight bar of Sinai ahead the low sun was falling, its globe extravagantly brilliant in my eyes, because I was dead-tired of my life, longing as seldom before for the moody skies of England. This sunset was fierce, stimulant, barbaric; reviving the colours of the desert like a draught — as indeed it did each evening, in a new miracle of strength and heat — while my longings were for weakness, chills and grey mistiness, that the world might not be so crystalline clear, so definitely right and wrong.

We English, who lived years abroad among strangers, went always dressed in the pride of our remembered country, that strange entity which had no part with the inhabitants, for those who loved England most, often liked Englishmen least. Here, in Arabia, in the war's need, I was trading my honesty for her sustenance, inevitably.

In Akaba the rest of my bodyguard were assembled, prepared for victory, for I had promised the Hauran men that they should pass this great feast in their freed villages: and its date was near. So for the last time we mustered on the windy beach by the sea's edge, the sun on its brilliant waves glinting in rivalry with my flashing and changing men.

They were sixty. Seldom had the Zaagi brought so many of his troop together, and as we rode into the brown hills for Guweira he was busy sorting them in Ageyl fashion, centre and wings, with poets and singers on the right and left. So our ride was musical. It hurt him I would not have a banner, like a prince.

I was on my Ghazala, the old grandmother camel, now again magnificently fit. Her foal had lately died, and Abdulla, who rode next me, had skinned the little carcase, and carried the dry pelt behind his saddle, like a crupper piece. We started well, thanks to the Zaagi's chanting, but after an hour Ghazala lifted her head high, and began to pace uneasily, picking up her feet like a sword-dancer.

I tried to urge her; but Abdulla dashed alongside me, swept his cloak about him, and sprang from his saddle, calf's skin in hand. He lighted with a splash of gravel in front of Ghazala, who had come to a standstill, gently moaning. On the ground before her he spread the little hide, and drew her head down to it. She stopped crying, shuffled its dryness thrice with her lips; then again lifted her head and, with a whimper, strode forward. Several times in the day this happened; but afterwards she seemed to forget.

At Guweira, Siddons had an aeroplane waiting. Nuri Shaalan and Feisal wanted me at once in Jefer. The air was thin and bumpy, so that we hardly scraped over the crest of Shtar. I sat wondering if we would crash, almost hoping it. I felt sure Nuri was about to claim fulfilment of our dishonourable half-bargain, whose execution seemed more impure than its thought. Death in the air would be a clean escape; yet I scarcely hoped it, not from fear, for I was too tired to be much afraid: nor from scruple, for our lives seemed to me absolutely our own, to keep or give away: but from habit, for lately I had risked myself only when it seemed profitable to our cause.

I was busy compartmenting-up my mind, finding instinct and reason as ever at strong war. Instinct said 'Die', but reason said that was only to cut the mind's tether, and loose it into freedom: better to seek some mental death, some slow wasting of the brain to sink it below these puzzlements. An accident was meaner than deliberate fault. If I did not hesitate to risk my life, why fuss to dirty it? Yet life and honour seemed in different categories, not able to be sold one for another; and for honour, had I not lost that a year ago when I assured the Arabs that England kept her plighted word?

Or was honour like the Sybil's leaves, the more that was lost the more precious the little left? Its part equal to the whole? My self-secrecy had left me no arbiter of responsibility. The debauch of physical work yet ended in a craving for more, while the everlasting doubt, the questioning, bound up my mind in a giddy spiral and left me never space for thought.

So we came at last, alive, to Jefer, where met us Feisal and Nuri in the smoothest spirits, with no mention of my price. It seemed incredible that this old man had freely joined our youth. For he was very old; livid, and worn, with a grey sorrow and remorse about him and a bitter smile the only mobility of his face. Upon his coarse eyelashes the eyelids sagged down in tired folds, through which, from the overhead sun, a red light glittered into his eye-sockets and made them look like fiery pits in which the man was slowly burning. Only the dead black of his dyed hair, only the dead skin of the face, with its net of lines, betrayed his seventy years.

There was ceremonial talk about this little-spoken leader, for with him were the head men of his tribe, famous sheikhs so bodied out with silks of their own wearing, or of Feisal's gift, that they rustled like women while moving in slow state like oxen. First of them was Faris: like Hamlet, not forgiving Nuri his murdered father, Sottam: a lean man with drooping moustache, and white, unnatural face, who met the hidden censure of the world with a soft manner and luscious deprecating voice. '*Yifham*' he squeaked of me in astonishment 'He understands our Arabic'. Trad and Sultan were there, round-eyed, grave, and direct-spoken; honourable figures of men and great leaders of cavalry. Also Mijhem, the rebellious, had been brought in by Feisal and reconciled with his unwilling uncle, who seemed only half to tolerate his small-featured bleak presence beside him, though Mijhem's manner was eagerly friendly.

Mijhem was a great leader too, Trad's rival in the conduct of raids, but weak and cruel at heart. He sat next Khalid, Trad's brother, another healthy, cheerful rider, like Trad in face, but not so full a man. Durzi ibn Dughmi swelled in and welcomed me, reminding me ungratefully of his greediness at Nebk: a one-eyed, sinister, hook-nosed man; heavy, menacing and mean, but brave. There was the Khaffaji, the spoilt child of Nuri's age, who looked for equality of friendliness from me, because of his father, and not for any promise in himself: he was young enough to be glad of the looming adventure of war and proud of his new bristling weapons.

Bender, the laughing boy, fellow in years and play with the Khaffaji tripped me before them all by begging for a place in my bodyguard. He had heard from my Rahail, his foster-brother, of their immoderate griefs and joys, and servitude called to him with its unwholesome glamour. I fenced, and when he pleaded further, turned it by muttering that I was not a King to have Shaalan servants. Nuri's sombre look met mine for a moment, in approval.

Beside me sat Rahail, peacocking his lusty self in strident clothes. Under cover of the conversation he whispered me the name of each chief. They had not to ask who I was, for my clothes and appearance were peculiar in the desert. It was notoriety to be the only cleanshaven one, and I doubled it by wearing always the suspect pure silk, of the whitest (at least outside), with a gold and crimson Meccan head-rope, and gold dagger. By so dressing I staked a claim which Feisal's public consideration of me confirmed.

Many times in such councils had Feisal won over and set aflame new tribes, many times had the work fallen to me; but never until to-day had we been actively together in one company, reinforcing and relaying one another, from our opposite poles: and the work went like child's play; the Rualla melted in our double heat. We could move them with a touch and a word. There was tenseness, a holding of breath, the glitter of belief in their thin eyes so fixed on us.

Feisal brought nationality to their minds in a phrase, which set them thinking of Arab history and language; then he dropped into silence for a moment: for with these illiterate masters of the tongue words were lively, and they liked to savour each, unmingled, on the palate. Another phrase showed them the spirit of Feisal, their fellow and leader, sacrificing everything for the national freedom; and then silence again, while they imagined him day and night in his tent, teaching, preaching, ordering and making friends: and they felt something of the idea behind this pictured man sitting there iconically, drained of desires, ambitions, weakness, faults; so rich a personality enslaved by an abstraction, made one-eyed, one armed, with the one sense and purpose, to live or die in its service.

Of course it was a picture-man; not flesh and blood, but nevertheless true, for his individuality had yielded its third dimension to the idea, had surrendered the world's wealth and artifices. Feisal was hidden in his tent, veiled to remain our leader: while in reality he was nationality's best servant, its tool, not its owner. Yet in the tented twilight nothing seemed more noble.

He went on to conjure up for them the trammelled enemy on the eternal defensive, whose best end was to have done no more than the necessary. While we abstinents swam calmly and coolly in the friendly silence of the desert, till pleased to come ashore.

Our conversation was cunningly directed to light trains of their buried thoughts; that the excitement might be their own and the conclusions native, not inserted by us. Soon we felt them kindle: we leaned back, watching them move and speak, and vivify each other with mutual heat, till the air was vibrant, and in stammered phrases they experienced the first heave and thrust of notions which ran up beyond their sight. They turned to hurry us, themselves the begetters, and we laggard strangers: strove to make us comprehend the full intensity of their belief; forgot us; flashed out the means and end of our desire. A new tribe was added to our comity: though Nuri's plain 'Yes' at the end carried more than all had said.

In our preaching there was nothing merely nervous. We did our best to exclude the senses, that our support might be slow, durable, unsentimental. We wanted no rice-converts. Persistently we did refuse to let our abundant and famous gold bring over those not spiritually convinced. The money was a confirmation; mortar, not building stone. To have bought men would have put our movement on the base of interest; whereas our followers must be ready to go all the way without other mixture in their motives than human frailty. Even I, the stranger, the godless fraud inspiring an alien nationality, felt a delivery from the hatred and eternal questioning of self in my imitation of their bondage to the idea; and this despite the lack of instinct in my own performance.

For naturally I could not long deceive myself; but my part was worked out so flippantly that none but Joyce, Nesib and Mohammed el Dheilan seemed to know I was acting. With man-instinctive, anything believed by two or three had a miraculous sanction to which individual ease and life might honestly be sacrificed. To man-rational, wars of nationality were as much a cheat as religious wars, and nothing was worth fighting for: nor could fighting, the act of fighting, hold any need of intrinsic virtue. Life was so deliberately private that no circumstances could justify one man in laying violent hands upon another's: though a man's own death was his last free will, a saving grace and measure of intolerable pain.

We made the Arabs strain on tip-toe to reach our creed, for it led to works, a dangerous country where men might take the deed for the will. My fault, my blindness of leadership (eager to find a quick means to conversion) allowed them this finite image of our end, which properly existed only in unending effort towards unattainable imagined light. Our crowd seeking light in things were like pathetic dogs snuffling round the shank of a lamp-post. It was only myself who valeted the abstract, whose duty took him beyond the shrine.

The irony was in my loving objects before life or ideas; the incongruity in my answering the infectious call of action, which laid weight on the diversity of things. It was a hard task for me to straddle feeling and action. I had had one craving all my life — for the power of self-expression in some imaginative form — but had been too diffuse ever to acquire a technique. At last accident, with perverted humour, in casting me as a man of action had given me place in the Arab Revolt, a theme ready and epic to a direct eye and hand, thus offering me an outlet in literature, the technique-less art. Whereupon I became excited only over mechanism. The epic mode was alien to me, as to my generation. Memory gave me no clue to the heroic, so that I could not feel such men as Auda in myself. He seemed fantastic as the hills of Rumm, old as Mallory.

Among the Arabs I was the disillusioned, the sceptic, who envied their cheap belief. The unperceived sham looked so well-fitting and becoming a dress for shoddy man. The ignorant, the superficial, the deceived were the happy among us. By our swindle they were glorified. We paid for them our self-respect, and they gained the deepest feeling of their lives. The more we condemned and despised ourselves, the more we could cynically take pride in them, our creatures. It was so easy to overcredit others: so impossible to write down their motives to the level of our own uncharitable truth. They were our dupes, wholeheartedly fighting the enemy. They blew before our intentions like chaff, being not chaff, but the bravest, simplest and merriest of men. *Credo quia sum?* But did not the being believed by many make for a distorted righteousness? The mounting together of the devoted hopes of years from near-sighted multitudes, might endow even an unwilling idol with Godhead, and strengthen It whenever men prayed silently to Him.

CHAPTER C

UPON this text my mind went weaving across its dusty space, amid the sunbeam thoughts and their dancing motes of idea. Then I saw that this preferring the Unknown to the God was a scapegoat idea, which lulled only to a false peace. To endure by order, or because it was a duty — that was easy. The soldier suffered only involuntary knocks; whereas our will had to play the ganger till the workmen fainted, to keep in a safe place and thrust others into danger. It might have been heroic to have offered up my own life for a cause in which I could not believe: but it was a theft of souls to make others die in sincerity for my graven image. Because they accepted our message as truth, they were ready to be killed for it; a condition which made their acts more proper than glorious, a logical bastard fortitude, suitable to a profit and loss balance of conduct. To invent a message, and then with open eye to perish for its self-made image — that was greater.

The whole business of the movement seemed to be expressible only in terms of death and life. Generally we were conscious of our flesh because it hurt us. Joy came sharper from our long habitude of pain; but our resources in suffering seemed greater than our capacity for gladness. Lethargy played its part here. Both emotions were in our gift, for our pain was full of eddies, confusing its purity.

A reef on which many came to a shipwreck of estimation was the vanity that our endurance might win redemption, perhaps for all a race. Such false investiture bred a hot though transient satisfaction, in that we felt we had assumed another's pain or experience, his personality. It was triumph, and a mood of enlargement; we had avoided our sultry selves, conquered our geometrical completeness, snatched a momentary 'change of mind'.

Yet in reality we had borne the vicarious for our own sakes, or at least because it was pointed for our benefit: and could escape from this knowledge only by a make-belief in sense as well as in motive.

The self-immolated victim took for his own the rare gift of sacrifice;

and no pride and few pleasures in the world were so joyful, so rich as this choosing voluntarily another's evil to perfect the self. There was a hidden selfishness in it, as in all perfections. To each opportunity there could be only one vicar, and the snatching of it robbed the fellows of their due hurt. Their vicar rejoiced, while his brethren were wounded in their manhood. To accept humbly so rich a release was imperfection in them: their gladness at the saving of its cost was sinful in that it made them accessory, part-guilty of inflicting it upon their mediator. His purer part, for the mediator, might have been to stand among the crowd, to watch another win the cleanness of a redeemer's name. By the one road lay self-perfection, by the other self-immolation, and a making perfect of the neighbour. Hauptmann told us to take as generously as we gave: but rather we seemed like the cells of a bee-comb, of which one might change, or swell itself, only at the cost of all.

To endure for another in simplicity gave a sense of greatness. There was nothing loftier than a cross, from which to contemplate the world. The pride and exhilaration of it were beyond conceit. Yet each cross, occupied, robbed the late-comers of all but the poor part of copying: and the meanest of things were those done by example. The virtue of sacrifice lay within the victim's soul.

Honest redemption must have been free and child-minded. When the expiator was conscious of the under-motives and the after-glory of his act, both were wasted on him. So the introspective altruist appropriated a share worthless, indeed harmful, to himself, for had he remained passive, his cross might have been granted to an innocent. To rescue simple ones from such evil by paying for them his complicated self would be avaricious in the modern man. He, thought-riddled, could not share their belief in others' discharge through his agony, and they, looking on him without understanding, might feel the shame which was the manly disciple's lot: or might fail to feel it and incur the double punishment of ignorance.

Or was this shame, too, a self-abnegation, to be admitted and admired for its own sake? How was it right to let men die because they did not understand? Blindness and folly aping the way of right were punished more heavily than purposed evil, at least in the present consciousness and remorse of man alive. Complex men who knew how self-sacrifice uplifted the redeemer and cast down the bought, and who held back in his knowledge, might so let a foolish brother take the place of false nobility and its later awakened due of heavier sentence. There seemed no straight walking for us leaders in this crooked lane of conduct, ring within ring of unknown, shamefaced motives cancelling or double-charging their precedents.

Yet I cannot put down my acquiescence in the Arab fraud to weakness of character or native hypocrisy: though of course I must have had some tendency, some aptitude, for deceit, or I would not have deceived men so well, and persisted two years in bringing to success a deceit which others had framed and set afoot. I had had no concern with the Arab Revolt in the beginning. In the end I was responsible for its being an embarrassment to the inventors. Where exactly in the interim my guilt passed from accessory to principal, upon what headings I should be condemned, were not for me to say. Suffice it that since the march to Akaba I bitterly repented my entanglement in the movement, with a bitterness sufficient to corrode my inactive hours, but insufficient to make me cut myself clear of it. Hence the wobbling of my will, and endless, vapid complainings.

SIDDONS flew me back to Guweira that evening, and in the night at Akaba I told Dawnay, just arrived, that life was full, but slipping smoothly. Next morning we heard by aeroplane how Buxton's force had fared at Mudowwara. They decided to assault it before dawn mainly by means of bombers, in three parties, one to enter the station, the other two for the main redoubts.

Accordingly, before midnight white tapes were laid as guides to the zero point. The opening had been timed for a quarter to four but the way proved difficult to find, so that daylight was almost upon them before things began against the southern redoubt. After a number of bombs had burst in and about it, the men rushed up and took it easily — to find that the station party had achieved their end a moment before. These alarms roused the middle redoubt, but only for defeat. Its men surrendered twenty minutes later.

The northern redoubt, which had a gun, seemed better-hearted and splashed its shot freely into the station yard, and at our troops. Buxton, under cover of the southern redoubt, directed the fire of Brodie's guns which, with their usual deliberate accuracy, sent in shell after shell. Siddons came over in his machines and bombed it, while the Camel Corps from north and east and west subjected the breastworks to severe Lewis gun-fire. At seven in the morning the last of the enemy surrendered quietly. We had lost four killed and ten wounded. The Turks lost twenty-one killed, and one hundred and fifty prisoners, with two field-guns and three machine-guns.

Buxton at once set the Turks to getting steam on the pumping engine, so that he could water his camels, while men blew in the wells, and smashed the engine-pumps, with two thousand yards of rail. At dusk, charges at the foot of the great water-tower spattered it in single stones across the plain: Buxton a moment later called 'Walk-march!' to his men, and the four-hundred camels, rising like one and roaring like the day of judgement, started off for Jefer. Dawnay went up very brightly to Aba el Lissan, to greet Feisal. Allenby had sent him across to give Feisal a warning message. He was to beg him to do nothing rash, as the British push was a chance, and if it failed the Arabs would be on the wrong side of Jordan to be given help. Particularly, Allenby begged Feisal not to rush upon Damascus, but to hold his hand till events were surely favourable.

This very sound and proper caution had come on my account. Exasperated one night at G.H.Q., I had blurted out that to me 1918 seemed the last chance, and we would take Damascus, anyhow, whatever happened at Deraa or Ramleh; since it was better to have taken it and lost it, than never to have taken it at all.

Feisal smiled wisely at Dawnay's homily, and replied that he would try this autumn for Damascus though the heavens fell, and, if the British were not able to carry their share of the attack, he would save his own people by making separate peace with Turkey.

He had been long in touch with elements in Turkey, Jemal Pasha opening the correspondence. By instinct, when sober, Jemal was Islamic, and to him the revolt of Mecca was a judgement. He was ready to do almost anything to compose such a breach in the faith. His letters were, for this reason, illuminating. Feisal sent them to Mecca and Egypt, hoping that they would read into them what we did: but the points were taken literally, and we received injunction to reply that the sword was now our judge. This was magnificent; but in war so rich a diathetical opportunity could not be missed.

True, that accommodation with Jemal was not possible. He had lopped the tall heads of Syria, and we should deny our friends' blood if we admitted him to our peace: but by indicating this subtly in our reply we might widen the national-clerical rift in Turkey.

Our particular targets were the anti-German section of the General Staff, under Mustapha Kemal, who were too keen on the 'Turkishness' of their mission to deny the right of autonomy to the Arabic provinces of the Ottoman Empire. Accordingly, Feisal sent back tendencious answers; and the correspondence continued brilliantly. The Turkish soldiers began to complain of the pietists, who put relics before strategy. The Nationalists wrote that Feisal was only putting into premature and disastrous activity their own convictions upon the just, inevitable self-determination of Turkey.

Knowledge of the ferment affected Jemal's determination. At first we were offered autonomy for Hejaz. Then Syria was admitted to the benefit: then Mesopotamia. Feisal seemed still not content; so Jemal's deputy (while his master was in Constantinople) boldly added a Crown to the offered share of Hussein of Mecca. Lastly, they told us they saw logic in the claim of the Prophet's family to the spiritual leadership of Islam!

The comic side of the letters must not obscure their real help in dividing the Turkish Staff. Old-fashioned Moslems thought the Sherif an unpardonable sinner. Modernists thought him a sincere but impatient Nationalist misled by British promises. They had a desire to correct him rather by argument than by military defeat.

Their strongest card was the Sykes-Picot agreement, an old-style division of Turkey between England, France, and Russia, made public by the Soviets. Jemal read the more spiteful paragraphs at a banquet in Beyrout. For a while the disclosure hurt us; justly, for we and the French had thought to plaster over a split in policy by a formula vague enough for each to interpret in his divergent way.

Fortunately, I had early betrayed the treaty's existence to Feisal, and had convinced him that his escape was to help the British so much that after peace they would not be able, for shame, to shoot him down in its fulfilment: while, if the Arabs did as I intended, there would be no one-sided talk of shooting. I begged him to trust not in our promises, like his father, but in his own strong performance.

Conveniently, at this juncture the British Cabinet, in joyous style, gave with the left hand also. They promised to the Arabs, or rather to an unauthorized committee of seven Gothamites in Cairo, that the Arabs should keep, for their own, the territory they conquered from Turkey in the war. The glad news circulated over Syria.

To help the downcast Turks, and to show us that it could give as many promises as there were parties, the British finally countered document A to the Sherif, B to their Allies, C to the Arab Committee, by document D to Lord Rothschild, a new power, whose race was promised something equivocal in Palestine. Old Nuri Shaalam, wrinkling his wise nose, returned to me with his file of documents, asking in puzzlement which of them all he might believe. As before, I glibly repeated, 'The last in date', and the Emir's sense of the honour of his word made him see the humour. Ever after he did his best for our joint cause, only warning me, when he failed in a promise, that it had been superseded by a later intention!

However, Jemal went on hoping, he being an obstinate and ruffianly man. After Allenby's defeat at Salt, he sent down to us the Emir Mohammed Said, brother of the egregious Abd el Kadir. Mohammed Said, a low-browed degenerate with a bad mouth, was as devious as his brother, but less brave. He was very modest as he stood before Feisal and offered him Jemal's peace.

Feisal told him that he was come at an opportune moment. He could offer Jemal the loyal behaviour of the Arab Army, if Turkey evacuated Amman, and handed over its province to Arab keeping. The seely Algerian, thinking he had scored a huge success, rushed back to Damascus: where Jemal nearly hanged him for his pains.

Mustafa Kemal, alarmed, begged Feisal not to play into Jemal's hands, promising that when the Arabs were installed in their capital, the disaffected in Turkey would rally to them, and use their territory as a base from which to attack Enver and his German allies in Anatolia. Mustafa hoped that the adhesion of all Turkish forces east of the Taurus would enable him to march direct on Constantinople.

Events at the end made abortive these complicated negotiations, which were not disclosed to Egypt or to Mecca, because of the disappointing issue of our first confidence. I feared that the British might be shaken at Feisal's thus entertaining separate relations. Yet in fairness to the fighting Arabs, we could not close all avenues of accommodation with Turkey. If the European war failed, it was their only way out: and I had always the lurking fear that Great Britain might forestall Feisal and conclude its own separate peace, not with the Nationalist, but with the Conservative Turks.

The British Government had gone very far in this direction, without informing her smallest ally. Our information of the precise steps, and of the proposals (which would have been fatal to so many of the Arabs in arms on our side), came, not officially, to me, but privately. It was only one of the twenty times in which friends helped me more than did our Government: whose action and silence were at once an example, a spur and a silence to me to do the like.

T

CHAPTER CII

AFTER the peace-talk we could set again to clean work. Joyce and myself decided upon another of our joint car excursions, this time to Azrak, to break trail so far towards Deraa. Therefore we ran out to Jefer to meet the victorious Camel Corps, who came gliding, in splendid trim and formal appearance, across the shining flat just before sunset, officers and men delighted at their Mudowwara success, and their freedom from orders and restraint in the desert. Buxton said they were fit to go anywhere.

They would rest two nights and draw four days' rations from their store, duly set out near Auda's tent by Young's care. Accordingly, on the morrow, early, Joyce and I got into our tender, with the resourceful Rolls to drive us, and ran easily into Wadi Bair, at whose wells lay Alwain, Auda's kinsman, a smooth-cheeked, oppressed silent man; hiding, to possess himself in peace far from Auda.

We stopped only the few minutes to arrange with him the safety of Buxton's men; and then drove out, with a young and very wild Sherari to help us find our way. His camel-training would not equip him to road-pick for a five-ton armoured car: but his knowing the track might serve other cars coming up by themselves later.

The plateau of Erha was good going, its flint openings interspersed with beds of hard mud; and we devoured the fast miles into the shallow heads of Wadi Jinz, well grown with pasture.

There, numbers of grazing camels were being driven anxiously together by their ragged herdsmen of the Abu Tayi, who, riding bareheaded, rifles in hand, were singing a war-chant. When they heard our roaring exhausts they rushed towards us, with urgent shouts of mounted men seen lurking in the low grounds ahead. We put the cars in the direction and after a little flushed five camel-riders, who made off northwards at their best. We ran them down in ten minutes. They couched their camels gracefully and came to meet us as friends — the only role left them, since naked men could not quarrel with swifter men in armour. They were Jazi Howeitat, undoubted robbers, but now all kindness, crying loudly at the pleasure of meeting me here suddenly. I was a little short, and ordered them back to their tents at once. They went off, crestfallen, westwards.

We followed Um Kharug's east bank, finding the way firm, but slow, for there were gutters of tributaries to cross; and we had to lay brushwood fascines where the old beds of the flood-water were soft or full of sand. Towards the end of the day the valleys grew thick with tufted grass, grazing for our prospective caravans.

In the morning the northern air and fresh wind of this desert were so cool to us that we made a hot breakfast before we cranked up the cars and purred over the meeting of Um Kharug and Dhirwa, over the broad basin of Dhirwa itself, and past its imperceptible water-parting into the Jesha. These were shallow systems running into Sirhan, by Ammari, which I meant to visit; for if evil came to us at Azrak, our next refuge should be Ammari, if accessible to cars. Such battalions of 'ifs' skirmished about every new plan continually.

The night's rest had freshened Rolls and Sanderson, and they drove splendidly over the saffron ridge of the little Jesha into the great valley. In the afternoon we saw the chalk banks, and turned down their ashy slopes, into the Sirhan. just by the water-holes. This made our retreat always safe, for no enemy would be mobile enough to close both Azrak and Ammari at once to us.

So we refilled our radiators with the horrible water of the pool in which Farraj and Daud had played, and drew westward over the open ridges, until far enough from the wells to acquit raiding parties from the need to stumble on us in the dark. There Joyce and I sat down and watched a sunset, which grew from grey to pink, and to red; and then to a crimson so intolerably deep that we held our breath in trepidation for some stroke of flame or thunder to break its dizzy stillness. The men, meanwhile, cut open tinned meats, boiled tea, and laid them out with biscuits on a blanket for our supper table. Afterwards there were more blankets, in which we slept lusciously.

Next day we ran quickly across the delta of Ghadaf till we were out on the immense mud-flat which stretched for seven miles, southward and eastward from the marshes by the old castle of Azrak.

To-day the mirage blotted its limits for us with blurs of steely blue, which were the tamarisk bounds raised high in the air and smoothed by heat-vapour. I wanted the Mejaber springs, down whose tree-grown bed we might creep unperceived: so Rolls made his car leap forward in a palpitant rush across the great width. The earth fell away in front of us, and a plume like a dust-devil waved along our track behind.

At the end the brakes sang protestingly as we slowed into a young plantation of tamarisk, tall on heaps of wind-collected sand. We twisted through them on the hard, intervening soil, till tamarisk ceased, and damp sand, speckled with close thorn-bushes, took its place. The cars stopped behind the hummock of Ain el Assad, under cover of this high-lipped cup of reeds, between whose vivid stems the transparent water dripped like jewels.

We went gently up the knoll of graves over the great pools, and saw that the watering places were empty. A mirage hung over the open spaces: but here, where the ground was bushed, no heat-waves could collect, and the strong sunlight showed us the valley as crystal clear as its running waters, and deserted except by wild birds, and these herds of gazelles, which alarmed by the popple of our closed exhausts, were grouping timidly in preparation for flight.

Rolls drew his tender past the Roman fish-pond; we skirted the western lava-field, along the now hard, grass-grown swamp, to the blue walls of the silent fort, with its silken-sounding palms, behind whose stillness lay perhaps more fear than peace. I felt guilty at introducing the throbbing car, and its trim crew of khaki-clad northerners, into the remoteness of this most hidden legendary place: but my anticipation went astray, for it was the men who looked real and the background which became scene-painting. Their newness and certainty (the Definiteness of British troops in uniform) did Azrak greater honour than plain loneliness.

We stopped only a moment. Joyce and I climbed the western tower, and agreed upon the manifold advantages of Azrak as a working base; though, to my sorrow, there was no grazing here, so that we could not linger in it for the interval of our first and second raids. Then we crossed to the northern lobe of the mud-flat, a fit landing-ground for the aeroplanes which Siddons was adding to our flying column. Amongst other qualities was its visibility. Our machines flying two hundred miles to this, their new base, could not fail to see its electrum shield reflecting the sunlight.

We went back to Ain el Assad, where the armoured car was, and led it at a faster pace out to the open flint desert once again. It was mid-afternoon, and very hot, especially in the glowing metal of the steel-turreted car; but the broiling drivers kept at it, and before sunset we were on the dividing ridge between the Jesha valleys, to find a shorter and easier way than our coming.

Night caught us not far south of Ammari, and we camped on the top of the country, with a breeze, very precious after the blistering day, coming down to us scent-laden from the flowering slopes of Jebel Druse. It made us glad of the men's hot tea, and of the blankets with which we had softly padded the angles of the box-body.

The trip was one delight to me, since I had no responsibility but the road. Also there was the spice of the reflections of the Sherari boy, reflections naturally confided to me, since I alone wore his sort of clothes, and spoke his dialect. He, poor outcast, had never before been treated as a considerate thing, and was astonished at the manners of the English. Not once had he been struck or even threatened.

He said that each soldier carried himself apart like a family, and that he felt something of defence in their tight, insufficient clothes and laborious appearance. He was fluttering in skirts, head-cloth and cloak. They had only shirts and shorts, puttees and boots, and the breeze could take no hold on them. Indeed, they had worn these things so long day and night in heat and sweat busied about the dusty oily cars, that the cloth had set to their bodies, like bark to a tree.

Then they were all clean-shaven, and all dressed alike; and his eye, which most often distinguished man from man by clothes, here was baffled by an outward uniformity. To know them apart he must learn their individual, as though naked, shapes. Their food took no cooking, their drink was hot, they hardly spoke to one another; but then a word sent them into fits of incomprehensible crackling laughter, unworthy and inhuman. His belief was that they were my slaves, and that there was little rest or satisfaction in their lives, though to a Sherari it would have been luxury so to travel like the wind, sitting down; and a privilege to eat meat, tinned meat, daily.

In the morning we hurried along our ridge, to reach Bair in the afternoon. Unfortunately there were tyre-troubles. The armoured car was too heavy for the flints, and always she sank in a little, making heavy going on third speed. This heated up the covers. We endured a vexatious series of bursts, of stoppings to jack up and change wheel or tyre. The day was hot and we were hurried, so that the repeated levering and pumping wore thin our tempers. At noon we reached the great spinal ridge to Ras Muheiwir. I promised the sulky drivers it would be splendid going.

And it was. We all took new heart, even the tyres stood better, while we rushed along the winding ridge, swinging in long curves from east to west and back again, looking now to the left over the shallow valleys trending towards Sirhan, now to the right as far as the Hejaz Railway. Gleaming specks in the haze of distance were its white stations lit by the pouring sun.

In late afternoon we reached the end of the ridge, dipped into the hollow and roared at forty miles an hour up the breast of Hadi. Darkness was near as we cut across the furrows of Ausaji to Bair wells, where the valley was alive with fires; Buxton, Marshall and the Camel Corps were pitching camp, after two easy marches from El Jefer.

There was heartburning among them, for Bair had still only two wells, and both were beset. At one the Howeitat and Beni Sakhr were drawing for six hundred of their camels, thirsty from the pastures a day's journey to the south-east, and at the other was a mob of a thousand Druses and Syrian refugees, Damascus merchants and Armenians, on their way to Akaba. These unhandy travellers cluttered up our access to the water with their noisy struggles.

We sat down with Buxton in a council of war. Young had duly sent to Bair fourteen days' rations for man and beast. Of this there remained eight days for the men, ten for the animals. The camel-drivers of the supply column, driven forward only by Young's strong will, had left Jefer half-mutinous with fear of the desert. They had lost, stolen or sold the rest of Buxton's stores upon their way.

I suspected the complaining Armenians, but nothing could be recovered from them, and we had to adjust the plan to its new conditions. Buxton purged his column of every inessential, while I cut down the two armoured cars to one, and changed the route.

CHAPTER CIII

LAZILY and mildly I helped the Camel Corps in their long watering at the forty-foot wells, and enjoyed the kindness of Buxton and his three hundred fellows. The valley seemed alive with them; and the Howeitat, who had never imagined there were so many English in the world, could not have their fill of staring. I was proud of my kind, for their dapper possession and the orderly busyness of their self-appointed labour. Beside them the Arabs looked strangers in Arabia; also Buxton's talk was a joy, as he was understanding, well read and bold; though mostly he was engaged in preparing for the long forced march.

Accordingly, I spent hours apart by myself, taking stock of where I stood, mentally, on this my thirtieth birthday. It came to me queerly how, four years ago, I had meant to be a general and knighted, when thirty. Such temporal dignities (if I survived the next four weeks) were now in my grasp — only that my sense of the falsity of the Arab position had cured me of crude ambition: while it left me my craving for good repute among men.

This craving made me profoundly suspect my truthfulness to myself. Only too good an actor could so impress his favourable opinion. Here were the Arabs believing me, Allenby and Clayton trusting me, my bodyguard dying for me: and I began to wonder if all established reputations were founded, like mine, on fraud.

The praise-wages of my acting had now to be accepted. Any protestation of the truth from me was called modesty, self depreciation; and charming — for men were always fond to believe a romantic tale. It irritated me, this silly confusion of shyness, which was conduct, with modesty, which was a point of view. I was not modest, but ashamed of my awkwardness, of my physical envelope, and of my solitary unlikeness which made me no companion, but an acquaintance, complete, angular, uncomfortable, as a crystal.

With men I had a sense always of being out of depth. This led to elaboration — the vice of amateurs tentative in their arts. As my war was overthought, because I was not a soldier, so my activity was over-wrought, because I was not a man of action. They were intensely conscious efforts, with my detached self always eyeing the performance from the wings in criticism.

To be added to this attitude were the cross-strains of hunger, fatigue, heat or cold, and the beastliness of living among the Arabs. These made for abnormality. Instead of facts and figures, my note-books were full of states of mind, the reveries and self-questioning induced or educed by our situations, expressed in abstract words to the dotted rhythm of the camels' marching.

On this birthday in Bair, to satisfy my sense of sincerity, I began to dissect my beliefs and motives, groping about in my own pitchy darkness. This self-distrusting shyness held a mask, often a mask of indifference or flippancy, before my face, and puzzled me. My thoughts clawed, wondering, at this apparent peace, knowing that it was only a mask; because, despite my trying never to dwell on what was interesting, there were moments too strong for control when my appetite burst out and frightened me.

I was very conscious of the bundled powers and entities within me; it was their character which hid. There was my craving to be liked — so strong and nervous that never could I open myself friendly to another. The terror of failure in an effort so important made me shrink from trying; besides, there was the standard; for intimacy seemed shameful unless the other could make the perfect reply, in the same language, after the same method, for the same reasons.

There was a craving to be famous; and a horror of being known to like being known. Contempt for my passion for distinction made me refuse every offered honour. I cherished my independence almost as did a Beduin, but my impotence of vision showed me my shape best in painted pictures, and the oblique overheard remarks of others best taught me my created impression. The eagerness to overhear and over-see myself was my assault upon my own inviolate citadel.

The lower creation I avoided, as a reflection upon our failure to attain real intellectuality. If they forced themselves on me I hated them. To put my hand on a living thing was defilement; and it made me tremble if they touched me or took too quick an interest in me. This was an atomic repulsion, like the intact course of a snowflake. The opposite would have been my choice if my head had not been tyrannous. I had a longing for the absolutism of women and animals, and lamented myself most when I saw a soldier with a girl, or a man fondling a dog, because my wish was to be as superficial, as perfected; and my jailer held me back.

Always feelings and illusion were at war within me, reason strong enough to win, but not strong enough to annihilate the vanquished, or refrain from liking them better; and perhaps the truest knowledge of love might be to love what self despised. Yet I could only wish to: could see happiness in the supremacy of the material, and could not surrender to it: could try to put my mind to sleep that suggestion might blow through me freely; and remained bitterly awake.

I liked the things underneath me and took my pleasures and adventures downward. There seemed a certainty in degradation, a final safety. Man could rise to any height, but there was an animal level beneath which he could not fall. It was a satisfaction on which to rest. The force of things, years and an artificial dignity, denied it me more and more; but there endured the after-taste of liberty from one youthful submerged fortnight in Port Said, coaling steamers by day with other outcasts of three continents and curling up by night to sleep on the breakwater by De Lesseps, where the sea surged past.

True there lurked always that Will uneasily waiting to burst out. My brain was sudden and silent as a wild cat, my senses like mud clogging its feet, and my self (conscious always of itself and its shyness) telling the beast it was bad form to spring and vulgar to feed upon the kill. So meshed in nerves and hesitation, it could not be a thing to be afraid of; yet it was a real beast, and this book its mangy skin, dried, stuffed and set up squarely for men to stare at.

I quickly outgrew ideas. So I distrusted experts, who were often intelligences confined within high walls, knowing indeed every paving-stone of their prison courts: while I might know from what quarry the stones were hewn and what wages the mason earned. I gainsaid them out of carelessness, for I had found materials always apt to serve a purpose, and Will a sure guide to some one of the many roads leading from purpose to achievement. There was no flesh.

T*

Many things I had picked up, dallied with, regarded, and laid down; for the conviction of doing was not in me. Fiction seemed more solid than activity. Self-seeking ambitions visited me, but not to stay, since my critical self would make me fastidiously reject their fruits. Always I grew to dominate those things into which I had drifted, but in none of them did I voluntarily engage. Indeed, I saw myself a danger to ordinary men, with such capacity yawing rudderless at their disposal.

I followed and did not institute; indeed, had no desire even to follow. It was only weakness which delayed me from mind-suicide, some slow task to choke at length this furnace in my brain. I had developed ideas of other men, and helped them, but had never created a thing of my own, since I could not approve creation. When other men created, I would serve and patch to make it as good as might be; for, if it were sinful to create, it must be sin and shame added to have created one-eyed or halt.

Always in working I had tried to serve, for the scrutiny of leading was too prominent. Subjection to order achieved economy of thought, the painful, and was a cold-storage for character and Will, leading painlessly to the oblivion of activity. It was a part of my failure never to have found a chief to use me. All of them, through incapacity or timidity or liking, allowed me too free a hand; as if they could not see that voluntary slavery was the deep pride of a morbid spirit, and vicarious pain its gladdest decoration. Instead of this, they gave me licence, which I abused in insipid indulgence. Every orchard fit to rob must have a guardian, dogs, a high wall, barbed wire. Out upon joyless impunity!

Feisal was a brave, weak, ignorant spirit, trying to do work for which only a genius, a prophet or a great criminal, was fitted. I served him out of pity, a motive which degraded us both. Allenby came nearest to my longings for a master, but I had to avoid him, not daring to bow down for fear lest he show feet of clay with that friendly word which must shatter my allegiance. Yet, what an idol the man was to us, prismatic with the unmixed self-standing quality of greatness, instinct and compact with it.

There were qualities like courage which could not stand alone, but must be mixed with a good or bad medium to appear. Greatness in

Allenby showed itself other, in category: self-sufficient, a facet of character, not of intellect. It made superfluous in him ordinary qualities; intelligence, imagination, acuteness, industry, looked silly beside him. He was not to be judged by our standards, any more than the sharpness of bow of a liner was to be judged by the sharpness of razors. He dispensed with them by his inner power.

The hearing other people praised made me despair jealously of myself, for I took it at its face value; whereas, had they spoken ten times as well of me, I would have discounted it to nothing. I was a standing court martial on myself, inevitably, because to me the inner springs of action were bare with the knowledge of exploited chance. The creditable must have been thought out beforehand, foreseen, prepared, worked for. The self, knowing the detriment, was forced into depreciation by other's uncritical praise. It was a revenge of my trained historical faculty upon the evidence of public judgement, the lowest common denominator to those who knew, but from which there was no appeal because the world was wide.

When a thing was in my reach, I no longer wanted it; my delight lay in the desire. Everything which my mind could consistently wish for was attainable, as with all the ambitions of all sane men, and when a desire gained head, I used to strive until I had just to open my hand and take it. Then I would turn away, content that it had been within my strength. I sought only to assure myself, and cared not a jot to make the others know it.

There was a special attraction in beginnings, which drove me into everlasting endeavour to free my personality from accretions and project it on a fresh medium, that my curiosity to see its naked shadow might be fed. The invisible self appeared to be reflected clearest in the still water of another man's yet incurious mind. Considered judgements, which had in them of the past and the future, were worthless compared with the revealing first sight, the instinctive opening or closing of a man as he met the stranger.

Much of my doing was from this egoistic curiosity. When in fresh company, I would embark on little wanton problems of conduct, observing the impact of this or that approach on my hearers, treating fellow-men as so many targets for intellectual ingenuity: until I could hardly tell my own self where the leg-pulling began or ended. This pettiness helped to make me uncomfortable with other men, lest my whim drive me suddenly to collect them as trophies of marksmanship; also they were interested in so much which my self-consciousness rejected. They talked of food and illness, games and pleasures, with me, who felt that to recognize our possession of bodies was degradation enough, without enlarging upon their failings and attributes. I would feel shame for myself at seeing them wallow in the physical which could be only a glorification of man's cross. Indeed, the truth was I did not like the 'myself' I could see and hear.

CHAPTER CIV

I HAD reached this useful stage when there was a disturbance from the Toweiha tents. Shouting men ran towards me. I pulled myself together to appease a fight between the Arabs and the Camel Corps, but instead it was an appeal for help against a Shammar raid two hours since, away by the Snainirat. Eighty camels had been driven off. Not to seem wholly ungracious, I put on our spare camels the four or five of my men whose friends or relatives had suffered, and sent them off.

Buxton and his men started in the mid-afternoon while I delayed till evening, seeing my men load our six thousand pounds of gun-cotton on the thirty Egyptian pack-camels. My disgusted bodyguard were for this ride to lead or drive the explosives' train.

We had judged that Buxton would sleep just short of the Hadi, so we rode thither: but saw no camp-fire, nor was the track trodden. We looked over the crest of the ridge, into a bitter north wind coming off Hermon into our flustered faces. The slopes beyond were black and silent, and to us town-dwellers, accustomed to the reek of smoke, or sweat, or the ferment of soil freshly dug, there was something searching, disquieting, almost dangerous, in the steely desert wind. So we turned back a few paces, and hid under the lip of the ridge to sleep comfortably in its cloistered air.

In the morning we looked out across fifty miles of blank country, and wondered at this missing our companions: but Daher shouted suddenly from the Hadi side, seeing their column winding up from the south-east. They had early lost the track and camped till dawn. My men jested with humour against Sheikh Saleh, their guide, as one who could lose his road between the Thlaithukhwat and Bair: just like one might say between the Marble Arch and Oxford Circus.

However, it was a perfect morning, with the sun hot on our backs, and the wind fresh in our faces. The Camel Corps strode splendidly past the frosted tips of the three peaks into the green depths of Dhirwa. They looked different from the stiff, respectful companies which had reached Akaba, for Buxton's supple brain and friendly observation had taken in the experience of irregular fighting, and revised their training rules for the new needs.

He had changed their column formation, breaking its formal subdivision of two hard companies: he had changed the order of march, so that, instead of their old immaculate lines, they came clotted, in groups which split up or drew together without delay upon each variation of road or ground surface. He had reduced the loads and rehung them, thereby lengthening the camels' pace and daily mileage. He had cut into their infantry system of clockwork halts every so often (to let the camels stale!) and grooming was less honoured. In the old days, they had prinked their animals, cosseting them like Pekinese, and each halt had been lightened by a noisy flapping massage of the beasts' stripped humps with the saddle-blanket; whereas now the spare time was spent in grazing.

Consequently, our Imperial Camel Corps had become rapid, elastic, enduring, silent; except when they mounted by numbers, for then the three hundred he-camels would roar in concert, giving out a wave of sound audible miles across the night. Each march saw them more workmanlike, more at home on the animals, tougher, leaner, faster. They behaved like boys on holiday, and the easy mixing of officers and men made their atmosphere delightful.

My camels were brought up to walk in Arab fashion, that bent-kneed gait with much swinging of the fetlock, the stride a little longer and a little quicker than the normal. Buxton's camels strolled along at their native pace, unaffected by the men on their backs, who were kept from direct contact with them by iron-shod boots and by their wood and steel Manchester-made saddles.

Consequently, though I started each stage alongside Buxton in the van, I forged steadily in front with my five attendants; especially when I rode my Baha, the immensely tall, large-boned, upstanding beast, who got her name from the bleat-voice forced on her by a bullet through the chin. She was very finely bred, but bad-tempered, half a wild camel, and had never patience for an ordinary walk. Instead, with high nose and wind-stirred hair, she would jig along in an uneasy dance, hateful to my Ageyl for it strained their tender loins, but to me not un-amusing.

In this fashion we would gain three miles on the British, look for a plot of grass or juicy thorns, lie in the warm freshness of air, and let our beasts graze while we were overtaken; and a beautiful sight the Camel Corps would be as it came up.

Through the mirage of heat which flickered over the shining flint-stones of the ridge we would see, at first, only the knotted brown mass of the column, swaying in the haze. As it grew nearer the masses used to divide into little groups, which swung; parting and breaking into one another. At last, when close to us, we would distinguish the individual riders, like great water-birds breast-deep in the silver mirage, with Buxton's athletic, splendidly-mounted figure leading his sun-burnt, laughing, khaki men.

It was odd to see how diversely they rode. Some sat naturally, despite the clumsy saddle; some pushed out their hinder-parts, and leaned forward like Arab villagers; others lolled in the saddle as if they were Australians riding horses. My men, judging by the look, were inclined to scoff. I told them how from that three hundred I would pick forty fellows who would out-ride, out-fight and out-suffer any forty men in Feisal's army.

At noon, by Ras Muheiwer, we halted an hour or two, for though the heat to-day was less than in Egypt in August, Buxton did not wish to drive his men through it without a break. The camels were loosed out, while we lay and lunched and tried to sleep, defying the multitude of flies which had marched with us from Bair in colonies on our sweaty backs. Meanwhile, my bodyguard passed through, grumbling at their indignity of baggage driving, making believe never to have been so shamed before, and praying profanely that the world would not hear of my tyranny to them.

Their sorrow was doubled since the baggage animals were Somali camels, whose greatest speed was about three miles an hour. Buxton's force marched nearly four, myself more than five, so that the marches were for the Zaagi and his forty thieves a torment of slowness, modified only by baulking camels, or displaced loads.

We abused their clumsiness, calling them drovers and coolies, offering to buy their goods when they came to market; till perforce they laughed at their plight. After the first day they kept up with us by lengthening the march into the night (only a little, for these ophthalmia-stricken brutes were blind in the dark) and by stealing from the breakfast and midday halts. They brought their caravan through without losing one of all their charges; a fine performance for such gilded gentlemen; only possible because under their gilt they were the best camel-masters for hire in Arabia.

That night we slept in Ghadaf. The armoured car overtook us as we halted, its delighted Sherari guide grinning in triumph on the turret lid. An hour or two later the Zaagi arrived, reporting all up and well. He begged that Buxton should not kill, directly in the road, such camels as broke down on the march; for his men made each successive carcase excuse for a feast and a delay.

Abdulla was troubled to understand why the British shot their abandoned beasts. I pointed out how we Arabs shot one another if badly wounded in battle; but Abdulla retorted it was to save us from being so tortured that we might do ourselves shame. He believed there was hardly a man alive who would not choose a gradual death of weakness in the desert, rather than a sudden cutting off; indeed, in his judgement, the slowest death was the most merciful of all, since absence of hope would prevent the bitterness of a losing fight, and leave the man's nature untrammelled to compose itself and him into the mercy of God. Our English argument, that it was kinder to kill quickly anything except a man, he would not take seriously.

OUR morrow was like the day before, a steady grind of forty miles. Next day was the last before the bridge-effort. I took half of my men from the baggage train, and threw them forward on our line of march, to crown each hill-top. This was well done, but did not profit us, for in mid-morning, with Muaggar, our ambush, in full sight, we were marching strongly and hopefully when a Turkish aeroplane came from the south, flew the length of our column, and went down, before us, into Amman.

We plodded heavily into Muaggar by noon, and hid in the sub-structures of the Roman temple-platform. Our watchers took post on the crest, looking out over the harvested plains to the Hejaz Railway. Over these hill-slopes, as we stared through our glasses, the grey stones seemed to line out like flocks of grazing sheep.

We sent my peasants into the villages below us, to get news, and warn the people to keep within doors. They returned to say that chance was fighting against us. Round the winnowed corn upon the threshing floors stood Turkish soldiers, for the tax-gatherers were measuring the heaps under guard of sections of mounted infantry. Three such troops, forty men, lay for this night in the three villages nearest the great bridge -- villages through whose precincts we must necessarily go and come.

We held a hurried council. The aeroplane had or had not seen us. It would cause, at worst, the strengthening of the bridge-guard, but I had little fear of its effect. The Turks would believe we were the advance-guard of a third raid on Amman, and were more likely to concentrate than to detach troops. Buxton's men were great fighters, he had laid admirable plans. Success was certain.

The doubt was about the bridge's cost, or rather as to its value in British life, having regard to Bartholomew's prohibition of casualties.

The presence of these mule-riders meant that our retreat would not be unencumbered. The camel corps were to dismount nearly a mile from the bridge (their noisy camels!) and advance on foot. The noise of their assault, not to speak of the firing of three tons of gun-cotton against the bridge-piers, would wake up the district. The Turkish patrols in the villages might stumble on our camel-park — a disaster for us — or, at least, would hamper us in the broken ground, as we retired.

Buxton's men could not scatter like a swarm of birds, after the bridge explosion, to find their own way back to the Muaggar. In any night-fighting some would be cut off and lost. We should have to wait for them, possibly losing more in the business. The whole cost might be fifty men, and I put the worth of the bridge at less than five. Its destruction was so to frighten and disturb the Turks, that they would leave us alone till August the thirtieth when our long column set out for Azrak. To-day was the twentieth. The danger had seemed pressing in July, but was now nearly over.

Buxton agreed. We decided to cry off, and move back at once. At the moment more Turkish machines got up from Amman and quartered the rough hills northward from Muaggar, looking for us.

The men groaned in disappointment when they heard the change. They had set pride on this long raid, and were burning to tell incredulous Egypt that their programme had been literally fulfilled.

To gain what we could, I sent Saleh and the other chiefs down to spruce their people with tall rumours of our numbers, and our coming as the reconnaissance of Feisal's army, to carry Amman by assault in the new moon. This was the story the Turks feared to learn: the operation they imagined: the stroke they dreaded. They pushed cavalry cautiously into Muaggar, and found confirmation of the wild tales of the villagers, for the hill-top was littered with empty meat tins, and the valley slopes cut up by the deep tracks of enormous cars. Very many tracks there were! This alarm checked them, and, at a bloodless price for us, kept them hovering a week. The destruction of the bridge would have gained us a fortnight.

We waited till dusk was thick, and then rode off for Azrak, fifty miles away. We pretended that the raid was become a tour, and talked of Roman remains and of Ghassanide hunting-places. The Camel Corps had a practice, almost a habit, of night-journeys, so that their pace was as by day, and units never strayed nor lost touch. There was a brilliant moon and we marched till it was pale in the morning, passing the lone palace of Kharaneh about midnight, too careless to turn aside and see its strangeness. Part-blame for this lay on the moon, whose whiteness made our minds as frozen and shadowless as itself, so that we sat still in our saddles, just sitting still.

At first I feared lest we encounter Arab raiders, who might have attacked the Camel Corps in ignorance; so I put forward with my men some half-mile before the column. As we slipped on, gradually we became aware of night-birds, flying up from under our feet in numbers, black and large. They increased, till it seemed as though the earth was carpeted in birds, so thickly did they start up, but in dead silence, and dizzily, wheeling about us in circles, like feathers in a soundless whirl or wind. The weaving curves of their mad flight spun into my brain. Their number and quietness terrified my men, who unslung their rifles, and lashed bullet after bullet into the flutter. After two miles the night became empty again; and at last we lay down and slept in the fragrant wormwood, till the sun roused us out.

In the afternoon, tired, we came to Kusair el Amra, the little hunting lodge of Harith, the Shepherd King, a patron of poets; it stood beautifully against its background of bosky rustling trees. Buxton put headquarters in the cool dusk of its hall, and we lay there puzzling out the worn frescoes of the wall, with more laughter than moral profit. Of the men, some sheltered themselves in other rooms, most, with the camels, stretched themselves beneath the trees, for a slumberous afternoon and evening. The aeroplanes had not found us — could not find us here. To-morrow there was Azrak, and fresh water to replace this stuff of Bair which, with the passing days, was getting too tasty for our liking.

Also Azrak was a famous place, queen of these oases, more beautiful than Amruh, with its verdure and running springs. I had promised everyone a bathe; the Englishmen, not washed since Akaba, were longing towards it. Meanwhile, Amruh was wonderful. They asked me with astonishment who were these Kings of Ghassan with the unfamiliar halls and pictures. I could tell them vague tales of their poetry, and cruel wars: but it seemed so distant and tinselled an age.

Next day we walked gently to Azrak. When we were over the last ridge of lava-pebbles and saw the ring of the Mejabar graves, that most beautifully put of cemeteries, I trotted forward with my men, to be sure against accident in the place, and to feel again its remoteness before the others came. These soldiers seemed so secure that I dreaded lest Azrak lose its rareness and be drawn back to the tide of life which had left it a thousand years ago.

However, both fears were silly. Azrak was empty of Arabs, beautiful as ever, and even more beautiful a little later when its shining pools were brilliant with the white bodies of our men swimming, and the slow drift of the wind through its reeds was pointed by their gay shouts and splashing echoed off the water. We made a great pit, and buried our tons of gun-cotton, for the Deraa expedition in September; and then roamed about collecting the scarlet sweet-water-berry of the Saa bushes. 'Sherari grapes' my followers, indulgent to our caprice, called them.

We rested there two days, the refreshment of the pools being so great. Buxton rode with me to the fort, to examine the altar of Diocletian and Maximian, meaning to add a word in favour of King George the Fifth; but our stay was poisoned by the grey flies, and then ruined by a tragic accident. An Arab, shooting fish in the fort pool, dropped his rifle, which exploded and killed instantly Lieutenant Rowan, of the Scottish Horse. We buried him in the little Mejaber graveyard, whose spotless quiet had long been my envy.

On the third day we marched past Ammari, across Jesha to near the Thlaithukhwat, the old country whose almost imperceptible variations I had come to know. By the Hadi we felt at home, and made a night-march, the men's strident yells of 'Are we well fed? No'. 'Do we see life? Yes', thundering up the long slopes after me. When they tired of telling the truth I could hear the rattle of their accoutrements hitched over the wooden saddles — eleven or fifteen hitchings they had, each time they loaded up, in place of the Arab's all-embracing saddle-bag thrown on in one movement.

I was so bound up in their dark body and tail behind me, that I, too, lost my way between the Hadi and Bair. However, till dawn we steered by the stars (the men's next meal was in Bair, for yesterday their iron ration was exhausted), and day broke on us in a wooded valley which was certainly Wadi Bair; but for my life I could not tell if we were above or below the wells. I confessed my fault to Buxton and Marshall and we tettered for a while, till, by chance, Sagr ibn Shaalan, one of our old allies of the distant days of Wejh, rode down the track, and put us on the road. An hour later the Camel Corps had new rations and their old tents by the wells, and found that Salama, the provident Egyptian doctor, calculating their return to-day, had already filled the drinking cisterns with enough water to slake the half of their thirsty beasts.

I determined to go into Aba el Lissan with the armoured cars, for Buxton was now on proved ground among friends, and could do without my help. So we drove fast down the scarp to the Jefer flat, and skipped across it at sixty miles an hour, ourselves the leading car. We threw up such a dust-cloud that we lost our sister, and when we reached the south edge of the flat she was nowhere visible. Probably tyre trouble, so we sat down to wait, gazing back into the dappled waves of mirage which streamed over the ground. Their dark vapour, below the pale sky (which got more and more blue as it went higher), shifted a dozen times in the hour, giving us a false alarm of our coming friends; but at last, through the greyness, came spinning a black spot wagging a long trail of sun-shining dust.

This was Greenhill tearing after, at speed through the shrivelling air, which eddied about his burning metal turret, making it so hot that its naked steel seared the bare arms and knees of the crew whenever the huge car lurched in the soft heat-powdered ground, whose carpeted dust lay waiting for the low autumn wind to sweep it across the open in a blinding choking storm.

Our car stood tyre-deep, and, while we waited, the men slopped petrol on a hillock of dust and boiled tea for us — Army tea, as full of leaves as flood water, and yellow with tinned milk, but good for parched throats. While we drank the others drew alongside, and reported two bursts of Beldam tubes in the heat of their swoop at a mile a minute across the scorching plain. We gave them of our boiled tea, and laughing they knocked the dust off their faces with oily hands. They looked aged, with its greyness in their bleached eyebrows and eyelashes and in the pores of their faces, except where the sweat had washed dark-edged furrows through to the red skin.

They drank hurriedly (for the sun was falling, and we had yet fifty miles to go), throwing out the last dregs on the ground, where the drops ran apart like quicksilver upon the dusty surface till they were clotted and sank in speckled shot-holes over its drifted greyness. Then we drove through the ruined railway to Aba el Lissan, where Joyce, Dawnay and Young reported all going marvellously. In fact, preparations were complete, and they were breaking up, Joyce for Cairo to see a dentist, Dawnay for G.H.Q., to tell Allenby we were prosperous and obedient.

JOYCE'S ship had come up from Jidda, with the Meccan mail. Feisal opened his Kibla (King Hussein's Gazette) to find staring at him a Royal Proclamation, saying that fools were calling Jaafar Pasha the General Officer Commanding the Arab Northern Army, whereas there was no such rank, indeed no rank higher than captain in the Arab Army, wherein Sheikh Jaafar, like another, was doing his duty!

This has been published by King Hussein (after reading that Allenby had decorated Jaafar) without warning Feisal; to spite the northern town-Arabs, the Syrian and Mesopotamian officers, whom the King at once despised for their laxity and feared for their accomplishments. He knew that they were fighting, not to give him dominion, but to set free their own countries for their own governing, and the lust for power had grown uncontrollable in the old man.

Jaafar came in and proffered his resignation to Feisal. There followed him our divisional officers and their staffs, with the regimental and battalion commanders. I begged them to pay no heed to the humours of an old man of seventy, out of the world in Mecca, whose greatness they themselves had made; and Feisal refused to accept their resignations, pointing out that the commissions (since his father had not approved their service) were issued by himself, and he alone was discredited by the proclamation.

On this assumption he telegraphed to Mecca, and received a return telegram which called him traitor and outlaw. He replied laying down his command of the Akaba front. Hussein appointed Zeid to succeed him. Zeid promptly refused. Hussein's cipher messages became corrupt with rage, and the military life of Aba el Lissan came to a sudden stop. Dawnay, from Akaba, before the ship sailed, rang me up, and asked dolefully if all hope were over. I answered that things hung on chance, but perhaps we should get through.

Three courses lay before us. The first, to get pressure put on King Hussein to withdraw his statement. The second, to carry on, ignoring it. The third, to set up Feisal in formal independence of his father. There were advocates of each course, amongst the English, as amongst the Arabs. We wired to Allenby asking him to smooth out the incident. Hussein was obstinate and crafty, and it might take weeks to force him out of his obstacles to an apology. Normally, we could have afforded three weeks; but to-day we were in the unhappy position that after these days, if at all, our expedition to Deraa must start. We must find some means of carrying on the war, while Egypt sought for a solution.

My first duty was to send express to Nuri Shaalan that I could not meet him at the gathering of his tribes in Kaf, but would be in Azrak from the first day of the new moon, at his service. This was a sad expedient, for Nuri might take suspicion of my change and fail at the tryst; and without the Rualla half our efficiency and importance at Deraa on September the sixteenth would disappear. However, we had to risk this smaller loss, since without Feisal and the regulars and Pisani's guns there would be no expedition, and for the sake of reforming their tempers I must wait in Aba el Lissan.

My second duty was to start off the caravans for Azrak – the baggage, the food, the petrol, the ammunition. Young prepared these, rising, as ever, to any occasion not of his own seeking. He was his own first obstacle, but would have no man hinder him. Never could I forget the radiant face of Nuri Said, after a joint conference, encountering a group of Arab officers with the cheerful words, 'Never mind, you fellows; he talks to the English just as he does to us!' Now he saw that each echelon started – not, indeed, to time but only a day late – under its appointed officers, according to programme. It had been our principle to issue orders to the Arabs only through their own chiefs, so they had no precedent either for obedience or for disobedience: and off they went like lambs.

My third duty was to face a mutiny of the troops. They had heard false rumours about the crisis. Particularly, the gunners misunderstood, and one afternoon fell out with their officers, and rushed off to turn the guns on their tents. However, Rasim, the artillery commandant, had forestalled them by collecting the breech-blocks into a pyramid inside his tent. I took advantage of this comic moment to meet the men.

They were tense at first, but eventually out of curiosity they fell to talking with me, who to them had been only an eccentric name, as a half-Beduin Englishman.

I told them the coffee-cup storm which was raging among the high heads, and they laughed merrily. Their faces were turned towards Damascus, not Mecca, and they cared for nothing outside their army. Their fear was that Feisal had deserted, since for days he had not been out. I promised to bring him down instantly. When he, with Zeid, looking as usual, drove through the lines in the Vauxhall, which Bols had had painted specially green for him, their eyes convinced them of their error.

My fourth duty was to start off the troops for Azrak on the right day. To effect this, their confidence in the confidence of the officers had to be restored. Stirling's tact was called upon. Nuri Said was ambitious, as any soldier would have been, to make much of the opportunity before him, and readily agreed to move as far as Azrak, pending Hussein's apology. If this was unsatisfactory they could return, or throw off allegiance; if it was adequate, as I assured him it would be, the interim and unmerited services of the Northern Army should bring a blush to the old man's cheek.

The ranks responded to bluffer arguments. We made plain that such gross questions as food and pay depended entirely on the maintenance of organization. They yielded, and the separate columns, of mounted infantry, of machine-gunners, of Egyptian sappers, of Ghurkas, of Pisani's gunners, moved off in their courses, according to the routine of Stirling and Young, only two days late.

The last obligation was to restore Feisal's supremacy. To attempt anything serious between Deraa and Damascus without him would be vain. We could put in the attack on Deraa, which was what Allenby expected from us; but the capture of Damascus — which was what I expected from the Arabs, the reason why I had joined with them in the field, taken ten thousand pains, and spent my wit and strength — that depended on Feisal's being present with us in the fighting line, undistracted by military duties, but ready to take over and exploit the political value of what our bodies conquered for him. Eventually he offered to come up under my orders.

As for the apology from Mecca, Allenby and Wilson were doing their best, engrossing the cables. If they failed, my course would be to promise Feisal the direct support of the British Government, and drive him into Damascus as sovereign prince. It was possible: but I wanted to avoid it except as a last necessity. The Arabs hitherto in their revolt had made clean history, and I did not wish our adventure to come to the pitiable state of scission before the common victory and its peace.

King Hussein behaved truly to type, protesting fluently, with endless circumlocution, showing no understanding of the grave effect of his incursion into Northern Army affairs. To clear his mind we sent him plain statements which drew abusive but involved returns. His telegrams came through Egypt and by wireless to our operators in Akaba, and were sent up to me by car, for delivery to Feisal. The Arabic ciphers were simple, and I had undesirable passages mutilated by rearranging their figures into nonsense, before handing them in code to Feisal. By this easy expedient the temper of his entourage was not needlessly complicated.

The play went on for several days, Mecca never repeating a message notified corrupt, but telegraphing in its place a fresh version toned down at each re-editing from the previous harshness. Finally, there came a long message, the first half a lame apology and withdrawal of the mischievous proclamation, the second half a repetition of the offence in a new form. I suppressed the tail, and took the head marked 'very urgent' to Feisal's tent, where he sat in the full circle of his staff officers.

His secretary worked out the despatch, and handed the decipher to Feisal. My hints had roused expectation, and all eyes were on him as he read it. He was astonished, and gazed wonderingly at me, for the meek words were unlike his father's querulous obstinacy. Then he pulled himself together, read the apology aloud, and at the end said thrillingly, 'The telegraph has saved all our honour'.

A chorus of delight burst out, during which he bent aside to whisper in my ear, 'I mean the honour of nearly all of us'. It was done so delightfully that I laughed, and said demurely, 'I cannot understand what you mean'. He replied, 'I offered to serve for this last march under your orders: why was that not enough?' 'Because it would not go with your honour.' He murmured, 'You prefer mine always before your own', and then sprang energetically to his feet, saying, 'Now, Sirs, praise God and work'.

In three hours we had settled time-tables, and arranged for our successors here in Aba el Lissan, with their spheres and duties. I took my leave. Joyce had just returned to us from Egypt, and Feisal promised that he would come, with him and Marshall, to Azrak to join me on the twelfth at latest. All the camp was happy as I got into a Rolls tender and set off northward, hoping yet to rally the Rualla under Nuri Shaalan in time for our attack on Deraa.

BOOK X

THE HOUSE IS PERFECTED

Chapters CVII to CXXII

OUR *mobile column of aeroplanes, armoured cars, Arab regulars and Beduin collected at Azrak, to cut the three railways out of Deraa. The southern line we cut near Mafrak; the northern at Arar; the western by Mezerib. We circumnavigated Deraa, and rallied, despite air raids, in the desert.*

Next day Allenby attacked, and in a few hours had scattered the Turkish armies beyond recovery.

I flew to Palestine for aeroplane help, and got orders for a second phase of the thrust northward.

We moved behind Deraa to hasten its abandonment. General Barrow joined us; in his company we advanced to Kiswe, and there met the Australian Mounted Corps. Our united forces entered Damascus unopposed. Some confusion manifested itself in the city. We strove to allay it; Allenby arrived and smoothed out all difficulties. Afterwards he let me go.

CHAPTER CVII

IT was an inexpressible pleasure to have left the mists behind. We caught at each other with thankfulness as we drove along, Winterton, Nasir and myself. Lord Winterton was our last-found recruit; an experienced officer from Buxton's Camel Corps. Sherif Nasir, who had been the spear-point of the Arab Army since the first days of Medina, had been chosen by us for the field-work on this last occasion also. He deserved the honour of Damascus, for his had been the honours of Medina, of Wejh, of Akaba, and of Tafileh; and of many barren days beside.

A painstaking little Ford hung on in the dust, behind, as our splendid car drank up the familiar miles. Once I had been proud of riding from Azrak to Akaba in three days; but now we drove it in two, and slept well of nights after this mournful comfort of being borne at ease in Rolls-Royces, like the great ones of war.

We noted again how easy their lives were; the soft body and its unexhausted sinews helping the brain to concentrate upon an arm-chair work: whereas our brains and bodies lay down only for the stupor of an hour's sleep, in the flush of dawn and the flush of sunset, the two seasons of the day unwholesome for riding. Many a day we had been twenty-two out of the twenty-four hours in the saddle, each taking it in turn to lead through the darkness while the others let their heads nod forward over the pommel in nescience.

Not that it was more than a thin nescience: for even in the deepest of such sleep the foot went on pressing the camel's shoulder to keep it at the cross-country pace, and the rider awoke if the balance were lost ever so little at a false stride or turn. Then we had had rain, snow or sun beating upon us; little food, little water, and no security against either Turks or Arabs. Yet those forced months with the tribes had let me plan in a surety which seemed lunatic rashness to new comers, but actually was an exact knowledge of my materials.

Now the desert was not normal: indeed, it was shamefully popular. We were never out of sight of men; of tenuous camel columns of troops and tribesmen and baggage moving slowly northward over the interminable Jefer flat. Past this activity (of good omen for our punctual concentration at Azrak) we roared, my excellent driver, Green, once achieving sixty-seven miles an hour. The half-stifled Nasir who sat in the box-body could only wave his hand across a furlong to each friend we overtook.

At Bair we heard from the alarmed Beni Sakhr that the Turks, on the preceding day, had launched suddenly westward from Hesa into Tafileh. Mifleh thought I was mad, or most untimely merry, when I laughed outright at the news which four days sooner would have held up the Azrak expedition: but, now we were started, the enemy might take Aba el Lissan, Guweira, Akaba itself — and welcome! Our formidable talk of advance by Amman had pulled their leg nearly out of socket, and the innocents were out to counter our feint. Each man they sent south was a man, or rather ten men, lost.

In Azrak we found a few servants of Nuri Shaalan, and the Crossley car with a flying officer, an airman, some spares, and a canvas hangar for the two machines protecting our concentration. We spent our first night on their aerodrome and suffered for it. A reckless armoured-plated camel-fly, biting like a hornet, occupied our exposed parts till sunset. Then came a blessed relief as the itch grew milder in the evening cool — but the wind changed and hot showers of blinding salty dust swept us for three hours. We lay down and drew covers over our heads, but could not sleep. Each half-hour we had to throw off the sand which threatened to bury us. At midnight the wind ceased. We issued from our sweaty nests and restfully prepared to sleep — when, singing, a cloud of mosquitoes rolled over us: them we fought till dawn.

Consequently, at dawn we changed camp to the height of the Mejaber ridge, a mile west of the water and a hundred feet above the marshes, open to all winds that blew. We rested a while, then put up the hangar, and afterwards went off to bathe in the silver water. We undressed beside the sparkling pools whose pearl-white sides and floor reflected the sky with a moony radiance. 'Delicious!' I yelled as I splashed in and swam about. 'But why do you keep on bobbing under water?' asked Winterton a moment later. Then a camel-fly bit him behind, and he understood, and leapt in after me. We swam about desperately keeping our heads wet, to dissuade the grey swarms: but they were too bold with hunger to be afraid of water, and after five minutes we struggled out, and frantically into our clothes, the blood running from twenty of their dagger-bites.

Nasir stood and laughed at us: and later we journeyed together to the fort, to rest midday there. Ali ibn el Hussein's old corner tower, this only roof in the desert, was cool and peaceful. The wind stirred the palm-fronds outside to a frosty rustling: neglected palms, too northerly for their red date-crop to be good; but the stems were thick with low branches, and threw a pleasant shade. Under them, on his carpet, sat Nasir in the quietness. The grey smoke of his thrown-away cigarette undulated out on the warm air, flickering and fading through the sun-spots which shone between the leaves. 'I am happy', said he. We were all happy.

In the afternoon an armoured car came up, completing our necessary defence, though the risk of enemy was minute. Three tribes covered the country between us and the railway. There were only forty horse-men in Deraa, none in Amman: also, as yet the Turks had no news of us. One of their aeroplanes flew over on the morning of the ninth, made a perfunctory circle, and went off, probably without seeing us. Our camp, on its airy summit, gave us splendid observation of the Deraa and Amman roads. By day we twelve English, with Nasir and his slave, lazed, roaming, bathing at sunset, sight-seeing, thinking; and slept comfortably at night: or rather I did: enjoying the precious interval between the conquered friends of Aba el Lissan and the enemy of next month.

The preciousness would seem to have been partly in myself, for on this march to Damascus (and such it was already in our imagination) my normal balance had changed. I could feel the taut power of Arab excitement behind me. The climax of the preaching of years had come, and a united country was straining towards its historic capital. In confidence that this weapon, tempered by myself, was enough for the utmost of my purpose, I seemed to forget the English companions who stood outside my idea in the shadow of ordinary war. I failed to make them partners of my certainty.

Long after, I heard that Winterton rose each dawn and examined the horizon, lest my carelessness subject us to surprise: and at Umtaiye and Sheikh Saad the British for days thought we were a forlorn hope. Actually I knew (and surely said?) that we were as safe as anyone in the world at war. Because of the pride they had, I never saw their doubt of my plans.

These plans were a feint against Amman and a real cutting of the Deraa railways: further than this we hardly went, for it was ever my habit, while studying alternatives, to keep the stages in solution.

The public often gave credit to Generals because it had seen only the orders and the result: even Foch said (before he commanded troops) that Generals won battles: but no General ever truly thought so. The Syrian campaign of September 1918 was perhaps the most scientifically perfect in English history, one in which force did least and brain most. All the world, and especially those who served them, gave the credit of the victory to Allenby and Bartholomew: but those two would never see it in our light, knowing how their inchoate ideas were discovered in application, and how their men, often not knowing, wrought them.

By our establishment at Azrak the first part of our plan, the feint, was accomplished. We had sent our 'horsemen of St. George', gold sovereigns, by the thousand to the Beni Shakr, purchasing all the barley on their threshing floors: begging them not to mention it, but we would require it for our animals and for our British allies, in a fortnight. Dhiab of Tafileh — that jerky, incomplete hobbledehoy — gossiped the news instantly through to Kerak.

In addition, Feisal warned the Zebn to Bair, for service; and Hornby, now (perhaps a little prematurely) wearing Arab clothes, was active in preparations for a great assault on Madeba. His plan was to move about the nineteenth, when he heard that Allenby was started; his hope being to tie on to Jericho, so that if we failed by Deraa our force could return and reinforce his movement: which would then be, not a feint, but the old second string to our bow. However, the Turks knocked this rather crooked by their advance to Tafileh, and Hornby had to defend Shobek against them.

For our second part, the Deraa business, we had to plan an attack proper. As preliminary we determined to cut the line near Amman, thus preventing Amman's reinforcement of Deraa, and maintaining its conviction that our feint against it was real. It seemed to me that (with Egyptians to do the actual destruction) this preliminary could be undertaken by the Ghurkas, whose detachment would not distract our main body from the main purpose.

This main purpose was to cut the railways in the Hauran and keep them cut for at least a week; and there seemed to be three ways of doing it. The first was to march north of Deraa to the Damascus railway, as on my ride with Tallal in the winter, cut it; and then cross to the Yarmuk railway. The second was to march south of Deraa to the Yarmuk, as with Ali ibn el Hussein in November, 1917. The third was to rush straight at Deraa town.

The third scheme could be undertaken only if the Air Force would promise so heavy a daylight bombing of Deraa station that the effect would be tantamount to artillery bombardment, enabling us to risk an assault against it with our few men. Salmond hoped to do this; but it depended on how many heavy machines he received or assembled in time. Dawnay would fly over to us here with his last word on September the eleventh. Till then we would hold the schemes equal in our judgement.

Of our supports, my bodyguard were the first to arrive, prancing up Wadi Sirhan on September the ninth: happy, fatter than their fat camels, rested, and amused after their month of feasting with the Rualla. They reported Nuri nearly ready, and determined to join us. The contagion of the new tribe's first vigour had quickened in them a life and spirit which made us jolly.

On the tenth the two aeroplanes came through from Akaba. Murphy and Junor, the pilots, settled down to the horse-flies, which gambolled in the air about their juiciness. On the eleventh, the other armoured cars and Joyce drove in, with Stirling, but without Feisal. Marshall had remained to squire him up next day; and things were always safe to go well where Marshall, the capable soul, directed them with a cultivated humour, which was not so much riotous as persistent. Young, Peake, Scott-Higgins and the baggage arrived. Azrak became many-peopled and its lakes were again resonant with voices and the

U

plunge of brown and lean, brown and strong, copper-coloured, or white bodies into the transparent water.

On the eleventh the aeroplane from Palestine arrived. Unfortunately, Dawnay was again ill, and the staff officer who took his place (being raw) had suffered severely from the roughness of the air; and had left behind the notes he was to bring us. His rather concrete assurance, that regard upon his world of the finished Englishman, gave way before these shocks, and the final shock of our naked carelessness out there in the desert, without pickets or watching posts, signallers, sentries or telephones, or any apparent reserves, defence-line, refuges and bases.

So he forgot his most important news, how on September the sixth Allenby, with a new inspiration, had said to Bartholomew, 'Why bother about Messudieh? Let the cavalry go straight to Afuleh, and Nazareth': and so the whole plan had been changed, and an enormous indefinite advance substituted for the fixed objective. We got no notion of this; but by cross-questioning the pilot, whom Salmond had informed, we got a clear statement of the resources in bombing machines. They fell short of our minimum for Deraa; so we asked for just a hamper-bombing of it while we went round it by the north, to make sure of destroying the Damascus line.

The next day Feisal arrived with, behind him, the army of troops, Nuri Said the spick and span, Jemil the gunner, Pisani's coster-like Algerians, and the other items of our 'three men and a boy' effort. The grey flies had now two-thousand camels to fatten upon, and in their weariness gave up Junor and his half-drained mechanics.

In the afternoon Nuri Shaalan appeared, with Trad and Khalid, Faris, Durzi, and the Khaffaji. Auda abu Tayi arrived, with Mohammed el Dheilan; also Fahad and Adhub, the Zebn leaders, with ibn Bani, the chief of the Serahin, and ibn Genj of the Serdiyeh. Majid ibn Sultan, of the Adwan near Salt, rode across to learn the truth of our attack on Amman. Later in the evening there was a rattle of rifle fire in the north, and Talal el Hareidhin, my old companion, came ruffling at the gallop, with forty or fifty mounted peasants behind him. His sanguine face beamed with joy at our long-hoped-for arrival. Druses and town-Syrians, Isawiyeh and Hawarneh swelled the company. Even the barley for our return if the venture failed (a possibility we seldom entertained) began to arrive in a steady file of loads. Everyone was stout and in health. Except myself. The crowd had destroyed my pleasure in Azrak, and I went off down the valley to our remote Ain el Essad and lay there all day in my old lair among the tamarisk, where the wind in the dusty green branches played with such sounds as it made in English trees. It told me I was tired to death of these Arabs; petty incarnate Semites who attained heights and depths beyond our reach, though not beyond our sight. They realized our absolute in their unrestrained capacity for good and evil; and for two years I had profitably shammed to be their companion!

To-day it came to me with finality that my patience as regards the false position I had been led into was finished. A week, two weeks, three, and I would insist upon relief. My nerve had broken; and I would be lucky if the ruin of it could be hidden so long.

Joyce meanwhile shouldered the responsibility which my defection endangered. By his orders Peake, with the Egyptian Camel Corps, now a sapper party, Scott-Higgins, with his fighting Ghurkas, and two armoured cars as insurance, went off to cut the railway by Ifdein.

The scheme was for Scott-Higgins to rush a blockhouse after dark with his nimble Indians — nimble on foot that was to say, for they were like sacks, on camels. Peake was then to demolish until dawn. The cars would cover their retreat eastward in the morning, over the plain, upon which we, the main body, would be marching north from Azrak for Umtaiye, a great pit of rain-water fifteen miles below Deraa, and our advanced base. We gave them Rualla guides and saw them off, hopefully, for this important preliminary.

CHAPTER CVIII

JUST at dawn our column marched. Of them one thousand were the Aba el Lissan contingent: three hundred were Nuri Shaalan's nomad horse. He had also two thousand Rualla camel-riders: these we asked him to keep in Wadi Sirhan. It seemed not wise, before the supreme day, to launch so many disturbing Beduin among the villages of Hauran. The horsemen were sheikhs, or sheikhs' servants, men of substance, under control.

Affairs with Nuri and Feisal held me the whole day in Azrak: but Joyce had left me a tender, the Blue Mist, by which on the following morning I overtook the army, and found them breakfasting among the grass-filled roughness of the Giaan el Khunna. The camels, joying to be out of the barren circle of Azrak, were packing their stomachs hastily with this best of food.

Joyce had bad news. Peake had rejoined, reporting failure to reach the line, because of trouble with Arab encampments in the neighbourhood of his proposed demolition. We had set store on breaking the Amman railway, and the check was an offence. I left the car, took a load of gun-cotton, and mounted my camel, to push in advance of the force. The others made a detour to avoid harsh tongues of lava which ran down westwards towards the railway; but we, Ageyl and others of the well-mounted, cut straight across by a thieves' path to the open plain about the ruined Um el Jemal.

I was thinking hard about the Amman demolition, puzzled as to what expedient would be quickest and best; and the puzzle of these ruins added to my care. There seemed evidence of bluntness of mind in these Roman frontier cities, Um el Jemal, Um el Surab, Umtaiye. Such incongruous buildings, in what was then and now a desert cockpit, accused their builders of insensitiveness; almost of a vulgar assertion of man's right (Roman right) to live unchanged in all his estate. Italianate buildings – only to be paid for by taxing more docile provinces – on these fringes of the world disclosed a prosaic blindness to the transience of politics. A house which so survived the purpose of its builder was a pride too trivial to confer honour upon the mind responsible for its conception.

Um el Jemal seemed aggressive and impudent, and the railway beyond it so tiresomely intact, that they blinded me to an air-battle between Murphy in our Bristol Fighter and an enemy two-seater. The Bristol was badly shot about before the Turk went down in flames. Our army were delighted spectators, but Murphy, finding the damage too great for his few materials at Azrak, went for repair to Palestine in the morning. So our tiny Air Force was reduced to the B.E.12, a type so out of date that it was impossible for fighting, and little use for reconnaissance. This we discovered on the day: meanwhile we were as glad as the army at our man's win.

Umtaiye was reached, just before sunset. The troops were five or six miles behind, so as soon as our beasts had had a drink we struck off to the railway, four miles downhill to the westward, thinking to do a snatch-demolition. The dusk let us get close without alarm, and, to our joy, we found that the going was possible for armoured cars: while just before us were two good bridges.

These points decided me to return in the morning, with cars and more gun-cotton, to abolish the larger, four-arched bridge. Its destruction would give the Turks some days' hard mending, and set us free of Amman all the time of our first Deraa raid; thus the purpose of Peake's frustrated demolition would be filled. It was a happy discovery, and we rode back, quartering the ground while the darkness gathered, to pick the best car road.

As we climbed the last ridge, a high unbroken watershed which hid Umtaiye completely from the railway and its possible watchmen, the fresh north-east wind blew into our faces the warm smell and dust of ten thousand feet; and from the crest the ruins appeared so startlingly unlike themselves three hours before that we pulled up to gasp. The hollow ground was festively spangled with a galaxy of little evening fires, fresh-lighted, still twinkling with the flame reflections in their smoke. About them men were making bread or coffee, while others drove their noisy camels to and from the water.

I rode to the dark camp, the British one, and sat there with Joyce and Winterton and Young, telling them of what we must do first thing in the morning. Beside us lay and smoked the British soldiers, quietly risking themselves on this expedition, because we ordered it. It was a thing typical, as instinct with our national character as that babbling laughing turmoil over there was Arab. In their crises the one race drew in, the other spread.

In the morning, while the army breakfasted, and thawed the dawn-chill from its muscles in the sun, we explained to the Arab leaders in council the fitness of the line for a car-raid; and it was determined that two armoured cars should run down to the bridge and attack it, while the main body continued their march to Tell Arar on the Damascus Railway, four miles north of Deraa. They would take post there, possessing the line, at dawn to-morrow, September the seventeenth; and we with the cars would have finished this bridge and rejoined them before that.

About two in the afternoon, as we drove towards the railway, we had the great sight of a swarm of our bombing planes droning steadily up towards Deraa on their first raid. The place had hitherto been carefully reserved from air attack; so the damage among the unaccustomed, unprotected, unarmed garrison was heavy. The morale of the men suffered as much as the railway traffic: and till our onslaught from the north forced them to see us, all their efforts went into digging bomb-proof shelters.

We lurched across plots of grass, between bars and fields of rough stone, in our two tenders and two armoured cars; but arrived all well behind a last ridge, just this side of our target. On the rise south of the bridge stood a stone blockhouse.

We settled to leave the tenders here, under cover. I transferred myself, with one hundred and fifty pounds of gun-cotton, fused and ready, to one armoured car; intending to drive passively down the valley towards the bridge, till its arches, sheltering us from the fire of the post, enabled me to lay and light the demolition charges. Meanwhile the other, the active fighting car, would engage the blockhouse at short range to cover my operation.

The two cars set out simultaneously. When they saw us the astonished garrison of seven or eight Turks got out of their trenches, and, rifles in hand, advanced upon us in open order: moved either by panic, by misunderstanding, or by an inhuman unmixed courage.

In a few minutes the second car came into action against them: while four other Turks appeared beside the bridge and shot at us. Our machine-gunners ranged, and fired a short burst. One man fell, another was hit: the rest ran a little way, thought better of it, and returned, making friendly signs. We took their rifles, and sent them up valley to the tenders, whose drivers were watching us keenly from their ridge. The blockhouse surrendered at the same moment. We were very content to have taken the bridge, and its section of track, in five minutes without loss.

Joyce rushed down in his tender with more gun-cotton, and hastily we set about the bridge, a pleasant little work, eighty feet long and fifteen feet high, honoured with a shining slab of white marble, bearing the name and titles of Sultan Abd el Hamid. In the drainage holes of the spandrils six small charges were inserted zigzag, and with their explosion all the arches were scientifically shattered; the demolition being a fine example of that finest sort which left the skeleton of its bridge intact indeed, but tottering, so that the repairing enemy had a first labour to destroy the wreck, before they could attempt to rebuild.

When we had finished, enemy patrols were near enough to give us fair excuse for quitting. The few prisoners, whom we valued for Intelligence reasons, were given place on our loads; and we bumped off. Unfortunately we bumped too carelessly in our satisfaction, and at the first watercourse there was a crash beneath my tender. One side of its box-body tipped downward till the weight came on the tyre at the back wheel, and we stuck.

The front bracket of the near back spring had crystallized through by the chassis, in a sheer break which nothing but a workshop could mend. We gazed in despair, for we were only three hundred yards from the railway, and stood to lose the car, when the enemy came along in ten minutes. A Rolls in the desert was above rubies: and though we had been driving in these for eighteen months, not upon the polished roads of their makers' intention, but across country of the vilest, at speed, day or night, carrying a ton of goods and four or five men up, yet this was our first structural accident in the team of nine.

Rolls, the driver, our strongest and most resourceful man, the ready mechanic, whose skill and advice largely kept our cars in running order, was nearly in tears over the mishap. The knot of us, officers and men, English, Arabs and Turks, crowded round him and watched his face anxiously. As he realized that he, a private, commanded in this emergency, even the stubble on his jaw seemed to harden in sullen determination. At last he said there was just one chance. We might jack up the fallen end of the spring, and wedge it by baulks upon the running board in nearly its old position. With the help of ropes the thin angle-irons of the running boards might carry the additional weight.

We had on each car a length of scantling to place between the double tyres if ever the car stuck in sand or mud. Three blocks of this would make the needful height. We had no saw, but drove bullets through it cross-wise till we could snap it off. The Turks heard us firing, and halted cautiously. Joyce heard us and ran back to help. Into his car we piled our load, jacked up the spring and the chassis, lashed in the wooden baulks, let her down on them (they bore splendidly), cranked up, and drove off. Rolls eased her to walking speed at every stone and ditch, while we, prisoners and all, ran beside with cries of encouragement, clearing the track.

In camp we stitched the blocks with captured telegraph wire, and bound them together and to the chassis, and the spring to the chassis; till it looked as strong as possible, and we put back the load. So enduring was the running board that we did the ordinary work with the car for the next three weeks, and took her so into Damascus at the end. Great was Rolls, and great was Royce! They were worth hundreds of men to us in these deserts.

This darning the car delayed us for hours, and at its end we slept in Umtaiye, confident that, by starting before dawn, we should not be much late in meeting Nuri Said on the Damascus line to-morrow: and we could tell him that, for a week, the Amman line was sealed, by loss of a main bridge. This was the side of quickest reinforcement for Deraa, and its death made our rear safe. Even we had helped poor Zeid behind there in Aba el Lissan: for the Turks massed in Tafileh would hold up that attack till their communications were again open. Our last campaign was beginning auspiciously.

DULY, before dawn, we drove upon the track of Stirling's cars, eager to be with them before their fight. Unfortunately the going was not helpful. At first we had a bad descent, and then difficult flats of jagged dolerite, across which we crawled painfully. Later we ran over ploughed slopes. The soil was heavy for the cars, for with summer drought this red earth cracked a yard deep and two or three inches wide. The five-ton armoured cars were reduced to first speed, and nearly stuck.

We overtook the Arab Army about eight in the morning, on the crest of the slope to the railway, as it was deploying to attack the little bridge-guarding redoubt between us and the mound of Tell Arar whose head overlooked the country-side to Deraa.

Rualla horsemen, led by Trad, dashed down the long slope and over the liquorice-grown bed of the watercourse to the line. Young bounced after them in his Ford. From the ridge we thought the railway taken without a shot, but while we gazed, suddenly from the neglected Turkish post came a vicious spitting fire, and our braves, who had been standing in splendid attitudes on the coveted line (wondering privately what on earth to do next) disappeared.

Nuri Said moved down Pisani's guns and fired a few shots. Then the Rualla and troops rushed the redoubt easily, with only one killed. So the southern ten miles of the Damascus line was freely ours by nine in the morning. It was the only railway to Palestine and Hejaz and I could hardly realize our fortune; hardly believe that our word to Allenby was fulfilled so simply and so soon.

The Arabs streamed down from the ridge in rivers of men, and swarmed upon the round head of Tell Arar, to look over their plain, whose rimmed flatness the early sun speciously relieved, by yet throwing more shadow than light. Our soldiers could see Deraa, Mezerib and Ghazale, the three key-stations, with their naked eyes.

I was seeing further than this: northward to Damascus, the Turkish base, their only link with Constantinople and Germany, now cut off:

southward to Amman and Maan and Medina, all cut off: westward to Liman von Sandars isolated in Nazareth: to Nablus: to the Jordan Valley. To-day was September the sixteenth, the promised day, forty-eight hours before Allenby would throw forward his full power. In forty-eight hours the Turks might decide to change their dispositions to meet our new danger; but they could not change them before Allenby struck. Bartholomew had said, 'Tell me if he will be in his Auja line the day before we start, and I will tell you if we will win'. Well, he was; so we would win. The question was by how much.

I wanted the whole line destroyed in a moment: but things seemed to have stopped. The army had done its share: Nuri Said was posting machine-guns about the Arar mound to keep back any sortie from Deraa: but why was there no demolition going on? I rushed down, to find Peake's Egyptians making breakfast. It was Drake's game of bowls, and I fell dumb with admiration.

However, in an hour they were mustered for their rhythmic demolition by numbers; and already the French gunners, who also carried gun-cotton, had descended with intention upon the near bridge. They were not very good, but at the second try did it some hurt.

From the head of Tell Arar, before the mirage had begun to dance, we examined Deraa carefully through my strong glass, wanting to see what the Turks had in store for us this day. The first discovery was disturbing. Their aerodrome was alive with gangs pulling machine after machine into the open. I could count eight or nine lined up. Otherwise things were as we expected. Some few infantry were doubling out into the defence position, and their guns were being fired towards us: but we were four miles off. Locomotives were getting up steam: but the trains were unarmoured. Behind us, towards Damascus, the country lay still as a map. From Mezerib on our right, there was no movement. We held the initiative.

Our hope was to fire six hundred charges, tulip-fashion, putting out of commission six kilometres of rail. Tulips had been invented by Peake and myself for this occasion. Thirty ounces of gun-cotton were planted beneath the centre of the central sleeper of each ten-metre section of the track. The sleepers were steel, and their box-shape left an air-chamber which the gas expansion filled, to blow the middle of the sleeper upward. If the charge was properly laid, the metal did not snap, but humped itself, bud-like, two feet in the air. The lift of it pulled the rails three inches up: the drag of it pulled them six inches together; and, as the chairs gripped the bottom flanges, warped them inward seriously. The triple distortion put them beyond repair. Three or five sleepers would be likewise ruined, and a trench driven across the earthwork: all this with one charge, fired by a fuse, so short that the first, blowing off while the third was being lighted, cast its debris safely overhead.

Six hundred such charges would take the Turks a fair week to mend. This would be a generous reading of Allenby's 'three men and a boy with pistols'. I turned to go back to the troops, and at that moment two things happened. Peake fired his first charge, like a poplar-tree of black smoke, with a low following report; and the first Turkish machine got up and came for us. Nuri Said and I fitted admirably under an outcrop of rock, fissured into deep natural trenches, on the hill's southern face. There we waited coolly for the bomb: but it was only a reconnaissance machine, a Pfalz, which studied us, and returned to Deraa with its news.

Bad news it must have been, for three two-seaters, and four scouts and an old yellow-bellied Albatros got up in quick succession, and circled over us, dropping bombs, or diving at us with machine-gun fire. Nuri put his Hotchkiss gunners in the rock cracks, and rattled back at them. Pisani cocked up his four mountain guns, and let fly some optimistic shrapnel. This disturbed the enemy, who circled off, and came back much higher. Their aim became uncertain.

We scattered out the troops and camels, while the irregulars scattered themselves. To open into the thinnest target was our only hope of safety, as the plain had not overhead cover for a rabbit; and our hearts misgave us when we saw what thousands of men we had, dotted out below. It was strange to stand on the hill-top looking at these two rolling square miles, liberally spread with men and animals, and bursting out irregularly with lazy silent bulbs of smoke where bombs dropped (seemingly quite apart from their thunder) or with sprays of dust where machine-gun groups lashed down.

Things looked and sounded hot, but the Egyptians went on working as methodically as they had eaten. Four parties dug in tulips, while Peake and one of his officers lit each series as it was laid. The two slabs of gun-cotton in a tulip-charge were not enough to make a showy explosion, and the aeroplanes seemed not to see what was going on: at least they did not wash them particularly with bombs; and as the demolition proceeded, the party drew gradually out of the danger-area into the quiet landscape to the north. We traced their progress by the degradation of the telegraph. In virgin parts its poles stood trimly, drilled by the taut wire: but behind Peake they leaned and tottered anyhow, or fell.

Nuri Said, Joyce and myself met in council, and pondered how to get at the Yarmuk section of the Palestine line to top off our cutting of the Damascus and Hejaz Railways. In view of the reported opposition there we must take nearly all our men, which seemed hardly wise under such constant air observation. For one thing, the bombs might hurt us badly on the march across the open plain; and, for another, Peake's demolition party would be at the mercy of Deraa if the Turks plucked up the courage to sally. For the moment they were fearful: but time might make them brave.

While we hesitated, things were marvellously solved. Junor, the pilot of the B.E.12 machine, now alone at Azrak, had heard from the disabled Murphy of the enemy machines about Deraa, and in his own mind decided to take the Bristol Fighter's place, and carry out the air programme. So when things were at their thickest with us he suddenly sailed into the circus.

We watched with mixed feelings, for his hopelessly old-fashioned machine made him cold meat for any one of the enemy scouts or two-seaters: but at first he astonished them, as he rattled in with his two guns. They scattered for a careful look at this unexpected opponent. He flew westward across the line, and they went after in pursuit, with that amiable weakness of aircraft for a hostile machine, however important the ground target.

We were left in perfect peace. Nuri caught at the lull to collect three hundred and fifty regulars, with two of Pisani's guns; and hurried them over the saddle behind Tell Arar, on the first stage of their march to Mezerib. If the aeroplanes gave us a half-hour's law, they would probably notice neither the lessened numbers by the mound, nor the scattered groups making along every slope and hollow across the stubble westward. This cultivated land had a quilt-work appearance from the air: also the ground was tall with maize stalks, and thistles grew saddle-high about it in great fields.

We sent the peasantry after the soldiers, and half an hour later I was calling up my bodyguard that we might get to Mezerib before the others, when again we heard the drone of engines; and, to our astonishment, Junor reappeared, still alive, though attended on three sides by enemy machines, spitting bullets. He was twisting and slipping splendidly, firing back. Their very numbers hindered them but of course the affair could have only one ending.

In the faint hope that he might get down intact we rushed towards the railway where was a strip of ground, not too boulder-strewn. Everyone helped to clear it at speed, while Junor was being driven lower. He threw us a message to say his petrol was finished. We worked feverishly for five minutes, and then put out a landing-signal. He dived at it, but as he did so the wind flawed and blew across at a sharp angle. The cleared strip was too little in any case. He took ground beautifully, but the wind puffed across once more. His under-carriage went, and the plane turned over in the rough.

We rushed up to rescue, but Junor was out, with no more hurt than a cut on the chin. He took off his Lewis gun, and the Vickers, and the drums of tracer ammunition for them. We threw everything into Young's Ford, and fled, as one of the Turkish two-seaters dived viciously and dropped a bomb by the wreck.

Junor five minutes later was asking for another job. Joyce gave him a Ford for himself, and he ran boldly down the line till near Deraa, and blew a gap in the rails there, before the Turks saw him. They found such zeal excessive, and opened on him with their guns: but he rattled away again in his Ford, unhurt for the third time.

CHAPTER CX

MY bodyguard waited in two long lines on the hill-side. Joyce was staying at Tell Arar as covering force, with a hundred of Nuri Said's men, the Rualla, the Ghurkas and the cars; while we slipped across to break the Palestine Railway. My party would look like Beduins, so I determined to move openly to Mezerib by the quickest course, for we were very late.

Unfortunately we drew enemy attention. An aeroplane crawled over us, dropping bombs: one, two, three, misses: the fourth into our midst. Two of my men went down. Their camels, in bleeding masses, struggled on the ground. The men had not a scratch, and leaped up behind two of their friends. Another machine floated past us, its engine cut off. Two more bombs, and a shock which spun my camel round, and knocked me half out of the saddle with a burning numbness in my right elbow. I felt I was hard hit, and began to cry for the pity of it: to be put out just when another day's control would have meant a vast success. The blood was running down my arm: perhaps if I did not look at it I might carry on as if I were unhurt.

My camel swung to a spatter of machine-gun bullets. I clutched at the pommel, and found my damaged arm there and efficient. I had judged it blown off. My left hand threw the cloak aside and explored for the wound — to feel only a very hot little splinter of metal, too light to do real harm after driving through the massed folds of my cloak. The trifle showed how much my nerve was on edge. Curiously enough it was the first time I had been hit from the air.

We opened out and rode greatly, knowing the ground by heart; checking only to tell the young peasants we met that the work was now at Mezerib. The field-paths were full of these fellows, pouring out afoot from every village to help us. They were very willing: but our eyes had rested so long on the brown leanness of desert men that these gay village lads with their flushed faces, clustering hair, and plump pale arms and legs seemed like girls. They had kilted up their gowns above the knee for fast work: and the more active raced beside us through the fields, chaffing back my veterans.

As we reached Mezerib, Durzi ibn Dughmi met us, with news that Nuri Said's soldiers were only two miles back. We watered our camels, and drank deeply ourselves, for it had been a long, hot day, and was not ended. Then from behind the old fort we looked over the lake, and saw movement in the French railway station.

Some of the white-legged fellows told us that the Turks held it in force. However the approaches were too tempting. Abdulla led our charge, for my days of adventure were ended, with the sluggard excuse that my skin must be kept for a justifying emergency. Otherwise I wanted to enter Damascus. This job was too easy. Abdulla found grain: also flour; and some little booty of weapons, horses, ornaments. These excited my hangers-on. New adherents came running across the grass, like flies to honey. Tallal arrived at his constant gallop. We passed the stream, and walked together up the far bank knee-deep in weeds till we saw the Turkish station three hundred yards in front. We might capture this before attacking the great bridge below Tell el Shehab. Tallal advanced carelessly. Turks showed themselves to right and left. 'It's all right,' said he, 'I know the stationmaster': but when we were two hundred yards away, twenty rifles fired a shocking volley at us. We dropped unhurt into the weeds (nearly all of them thistles), and crawled gingerly back, Tallal swearing.

My men heard him, or the shots, and came streaming up from the river: but we returned them, fearing a machine-gun in the station buildings. Nuri Said was due. He arrived with Nasir, and we considered the business. Nuri pointed out that delay at Mezerib might lose us the bridge, a greater objective. I agreed, but thought this bird in hand might suffice, since Peake's main line demolition would stand for a week, and the week's end bring a new situation.

So Pisani unfolded his willing guns and smashed in a few rounds of point-blank high explosive. Under their cover, with our twenty machine-guns making a roof overhead, Nuri walked forward, gloved and sworded, to receive the surrender of the forty soldiers left alive.

Upon this most rich station hundreds of Haurani peasants hurled themselves in frenzy, plundering. Men, women and children fought like dogs over every object. Doors and windows, door-frames and window-frames, even steps of the stairs, were carried off. One hopeful blew in the safe and found postage stamps inside. Others smashed open the long range of waggons in the siding, to find all manner of goods. Tons were carried off. Yet more were strewn in wreckage on the ground.

Young and I cut the telegraph, here an important network of trunk and local lines, indeed the Palestine army's main link with their home-land. It was pleasant to imagine Liman von Sandars' fresh curse, in Nazareth, as each severed wire tanged back from the clippers. We did them slowly, with ceremony, to draw out the indignation. The Turks' hopeless lack of initiative made their army a 'directed' one, so that by destroying the telegraphs we went far towards turning them into a leaderless mob. After the telegraph we blew in the points, and planted tulips: not very many, but enough to annoy. While we worked a light engine came down the line from Deraa on patrol. The bang and dust-clouds of our tulips perturbed it. It withdrew discreetly. Later an aeroplane visited us.

Among the captured rolling stock, on platform trucks, were two lorries crammed with delicacies for some German canteen. The Arabs, distrusting tins and bottles, had spoiled nearly everything: but we got some soups and meat, and later Nuri Said gave us bottled asparagus. He had found an Arab prizing open the case and had cried 'pigs' bones' at him in horror when the contents came to light. The peasant spat and dropped it, and Nuri quickly stuffed all he could into his saddle-bags.

The lorries had huge petrol tanks. Beyond them were some trucks of firewood. We set the whole afire at sunset, when the plundering was finished, and the troops and tribesmen had fallen back to the soft grass by the outlet from the lake.

The splendid blaze spreading along the line of waggons illuminated our evening meal. The wood burned with a solid glare, and the fiery tongues and bursts of the petrol went towering up, higher than the water-tanks. We let the men make bread and sup and rest, before a night-attempt on the Shehab bridge, which lay three miles to the westward. We had meant to attack at dark, but the wish for food stopped us, and then we had swarms of visitors, for our beacon-light advertised us over half Hauran.

Visitors were our eyes, and had to be welcomed. My business was to see every one with news, and let him talk himself out to me, afterwards arranging and combining the truth of these points into a complete picture in my mind. Complete, because it gave me certainty of judgement: but it was not conscious nor logical, for my informants were so many that they informed me to distraction, and my single mind bent under all its claims.

Men came pouring down from the north on horse, on camel, and on foot, hundreds and hundreds of them in a terrible grandeur of enthusiasm, thinking this was the final occupation of the country, and that Nasir would seal his victory by taking Deraa in the night. Even the magistrates of Deraa came to open us their town. By acceding we should hold the water supply of the railway station, which must inevitably yield: yet later, if the ruin of the Turkish army came but slowly, we might be forced out again, and lose the plainsmen between Deraa and Damascus, in whose hands our final victory lay. A nice calculation, if hardly a fresh one, but on the whole the arguments were still against taking Deraa. Again we had to put off our friends with excuses within their comprehension.

S LOW work; and when at last we were ready a new visitor appeared, the boy-chief of Tell el Shehab. His village was the key to the bridge. He described the position; the large guard; how it was placed. Obviously the problem was harder than we had believed, if his tale was true. We doubted it, for his just-dead father had been hostile, and the son sounded too suddenly devoted to our cause. However, he finished by suggesting that he return after an hour with the officer commanding the garrison, a friend of his. We sent him off to bring his Turk, telling our waiting men to lie down for another brief rest.

Soon the boy was back with a captain, an Armenian, anxious to harm his government in any way he could. Also he was very nervous. We had hard work to assure him of our enlightenment. His subalterns, he said, were loyal Turks, and some of the non-commissioned officers. He proposed we move close to the village, and lie there secretly, while three or four of our lustiest men hid in his room. He would call his subordinates one by one to see him; and, as each entered, our ambush might pinion him.

This sounded in the proper descent from books of adventure, and we agreed enthusiastically. It was nine at night. At eleven precisely we would line up round the village and wait for the Sheikh to show our strong men to the Commandant's house. The two conspirators departed, content, while we woke up our army, asleep with the sleep of exhaustion beside their loaded camels. It was pitchy dark.

My bodyguard prepared bridge-cutting charges of gelatine. I filled my pockets with detonators. Nasir sent men to each section of the Camel Corps to tell them of the coming adventure, that they might work themselves up to the height of it: and to ensure their mounting quietly, without the disaster of a roaring camel. They played up. In a long double line our force crept down a winding path, beside an irrigation ditch, on the crest of the dividing ridge. If there was treachery before us, this bare road would be a death-trap, without issue to right or left, narrow, tortuous, and slippery with the ditch-water. So Nasir and I went first with our men, their trained ears attentive to every sound, their eyes keeping constant guard. In front of us was the waterfall, whose burdening roar had given its character to that unforgettable night with Ali ibn el Hussein when we had attempted this bridge from the other wall of the ravine. Only to-night we were nearer, so that the noise flooded up oppressively and filled our ears.

We crept very slowly and carefully now, soundless on our bare feet, while behind us the heavier soldiery snaked along, holding their breath. They also were soundless, for camels moved always stilly at night, and we had packed the equipment not to tap, the saddles not to creak. Their quietness made the dark darker, and deepened the menace of those whispering valleys either side. Waves of dank air from the river met us, chilly in our faces; and then Rahail came down swiftly from the left and caught my arm, pointing to a slow column of white smoke rising from the valley.

We ran to the edge of the descent, and peered over: but the depth was grey with mist risen off the water, and we saw only dimness and this pale vapour spiring from the level fog bank. Somewhere down there was the railway, and we stopped the march, afraid lest this be the suspected trap. Three of us went foot by foot down the slippery hill-side till we could hear voices. Then suddenly the smoke broke and shifted, with the panting of an opened throttle, and afterwards the squealing of brakes as an engine came again to a standstill. There must be a long train waiting beneath; reassured, we marched again to the very spur below the village.

We extended in line across its neck, and waited five minutes, ten minutes. They passed slowly. The murk night before moonrise was hushing in its solidity, and would have compelled patience on our restless fellows, without the added warnings of the dogs, and the intermittent ringing challenge of sentries about the bridge. At length we let the men slip quietly from their camels to the ground, and sat wondering at the delay, and the Turks' watchfulness, and the meaning of that silent train standing below us in the valley. Our woollen cloaks got stiff and heavy with the mist, and we shivered.

After a long while a lighter speck came through the dark. It was the boy sheikh, holding his brown cloak open to show us his white shirt like a flag. He whispered that his plan had failed. A train (this one in the ravine), had just arrived with a German colonel and the German and Turk reserves from Afuleh, sent up by Liman von Sandars, to rescue panic-stricken Deraa.

They had put the little Armenian under arrest for being absent from his post. There were machine-guns galore, and sentries patrolling the approaches with ceaseless energy. In fact, there was a strong picket on the path, not a hundred yards from where we sat: the oddity of our joint state made me laugh, though quietly.

Nuri Said offered to take the place by main force. We had bombs enough, and pistol flares; numbers and preparedness would be on our side. It was a fair chance: but I was at the game of reckoning the value of the objective in terms of life, and as usual finding it too dear. Of course, most things done in war were too dear, and we should have followed good example by going in and going through with it. But I was secretly and disclaimedly proud of the planning of our campaigns: so I told Nuri that I voted against it. We had to-day twice cut the Damascus-Palestine railway; and the bringing here of the Afuleh garrison was a third benefit to Allenby. Our bond had been most heavily honoured.

Nuri, after a moment's thought, agreed. We said good-night to the lad who had honestly tried to do so much for us. We passed down the lines, whispering to each man to lead back in silence. Then we sat in a group with our rifles (mine Enver's gold-inscribed Lee-Enfield trophy from the Dardanelles, given by him to Feisal years ago) waiting till our men should be beyond the danger zone.

Oddly enough this was the hardest moment of the night. Now the work was over we could scarcely resist the temptation to rouse the spoil-sport Germans out. It would have been so easy to have cracked off a Very light into their bivouac; and the solemn men would have turned out in ludicrous hurry, and shot hard into the bare, misty hill-side silent at their feet. The identical notion came independently to Nasir, Nuri Said, and myself. We blurted it out together, and each promptly felt ashamed that the others had been as childish. By mutual cautions we managed to keep our respectability. At Mezerib, after midnight, we felt that something must be done to avenge the forfeited bridge. So two parties of my fellows, with guides of Tallal's men, went beyond Shehab, and cut the line twice behind it on deserted gradients. Their echoing explosions gave the German detachment a bad night. Flares were lit and the neighbourhood searched for some brewing attack.

We were glad to give them as tiresome a night as ours, for then they too would be languid in the morning. Our friends were still coming in every minute, to kiss our hands and swear eternal fealty. Their wiry ponies threaded our misted camp, between the hundreds of sleeping men, and the uneasy camels whose great jaws were munching all night at the windy grass swallowed in the day hours.

Before dawn Pisani's other guns and the rest of Nuri Said's troops arrived from Tell Arar. We had written to Joyce that on the morrow we would return southward, by Nisib, to complete the circle of Deraa. I suggested that he move straight back to Umtaiye and there wait for us: for it, with its abundant water, splendid pasture, and equi-distance from Deraa and Jebel Druse and the Rualla Desert, seemed an ideal place in which we might rally and wait news of Allenby's fortune. By holding Umtaiye we as good as cut off the Turkish fourth army of beyond Jordan (our special bird) from Damascus: and were in place quickly to renew our main-line demolitions, whenever the enemy had nearly set them right.

CHAPTER CXII

RELUCTANTLY we pulled ourselves together for another day of effort, called up the army, and moved in a huge straggle through Mezerib station. Our fires had burned out, and the place stood dishevelled. Young and myself leisurely laid tulips, while the troops melted into broken ground towards Remthe, to be out of sight of both Deraa and Shehab. Turkish aeroplanes were humming overhead, looking for us, so we sent our peasants back through Mezerib for their villages. Consequently, the airmen reported that we were very numerous, possibly eight or nine thousand strong, and that our centrifugal movements seemed to be directed towards every direction at once.

To increase their wonderment, the French gunners' long-fused charge blew up the water-tower at Mezerib, loudly, hours after we had passed. The Germans were marching out of Shehab for Deraa, at the moment, and the inexplicable shock sent these humourless ones back there on guard till late afternoon.

Meanwhile we were far away, plodding steadily towards Nisib, whose hill-top we reached about four in the afternoon. We gave the mounted infantry a short rest, while we moved our gunners and machine-guns to the crest of the first ridge, from which the ground fell away hollowly to the railway station.

We posted the guns there in shelter, and asked them to open deliberately upon the station buildings at two thousand yards. Pisani's sections worked in emulation so that, before long, ragged holes appeared in the roofs and sheds. At the same time we pushed our machine-gunners forward on the left, to fire long bursts against the trenches, which returned a hot obstinate fire. However our troops had natural shelter and the advantage of the afternoon sun behind their backs. So we suffered no hurt. Nor did the enemy. Of course, all this was just a game, and the capture of the station not in our plan. Our real objective was the great bridge north of the village. The ridge below our feet curved out in a long horn to this work, serving as one bank of the valley which it was built to span. The village stood on the other bank. The Turks held the bridge by means of a small redoubt, and maintained touch with it by riflemen posted in the village under cover of its walls.

We turned two of Pisani's guns and six machine-guns on the small but deeply-dug bridge-post, hoping to force its defenders out. Five machine-guns directed their fire on the village. In fifteen minutes its elders were out with us, very much perturbed. Nuri put, as the condition of cease-fire, their instant ejectment of the Turks from the houses. They promised. So station and bridge were divided.

We redoubled against these. The firing from the four wings became violent, thanks to our twenty-five machine-guns, the Turks also being plentifully supplied. At last we put all four of Pisani's guns against the redoubt; and, after a few salvoes, thought we saw its guard slipping from their battered trenches through the bridge into cover of the railway embankment.

This embankment was twenty feet high. If the bridge-guard chose to defend their bridge through its arches, they would be in a costly position. However, we reckoned that the attraction of their fellows in the station would draw them away. I told off the half of my bodyguard carrying explosives, to move along the machine-gun crest till within a stone's throw of the redoubt.

It was a noble evening, yellow, mild and indescribably peaceful; a foil to our incessant cannonade. The declining light shone down the angle of the ridges, its soft rays modelling them and their least contour in a delicate complexity of planes. Then the sun sank another second, and the surface became shadow, out of which for a moment there rose, starkly, the innumerable flints strewing it; each western (reflecting) facet tipped like a black diamond with flame.

A very unfit afternoon for dying, seemed to think my men: for the first time their nerves failed, and they refused to quit their shelter for the enemy's clattering bullets. They were tired, and their camels so marched out they could only walk: also they knew that one bullet in the blasting gelatine would send them sky-high.

A try to stir them by jest failed; at last I cast them off; choosing only Hemeid, the young and timid one amongst them, to come up with me on the hill-top. He shook like a man in a sick dream, but followed quietly. We rode down the ridge to its furthest edge, to have a close look at the bridge.

Nuri Said was there, sucking his briar pipe, and cheering the gunners who were keeping a barrage over the darkening roads between the bridge, the village and the station. Nuri, being happy, propounded to me plans of attack and alternative assaults against this station, which we did not wish to assault. We argued theory for ten minutes on the skyline, with Hemeid wincing in his saddle as bullets, some of which were overs, spat past us, or ricochets hummed like slow, angry bees beside our ears. The few proper hits splashed loudly into the flints, kicking up a chalk-dust which hung transparently for a moment in the reflected light.

Nuri agreed to cover my movements to the bridge as well as he could. Then I turned Hemeid back with my camel, to tell the rest that I would hurt them worse than bullets if they did not follow him across the danger-zone to meet me: for I meant to walk round till I could be sure the bridge-post was empty.

While they hesitated, there came up Abdulla, the imperturbable, improvident, adventurous, who feared nothing; and the Zaagi. They, mad with fury that I had been let down, dashed at the shrinkers, who pounded over the shoulder with only six bullet-scratches. The redoubt was indeed abandoned: so we dismounted, and signalled Nuri to cease fire. In the silence we crept discreetly through the bridge-arches, and found them also evacuated.

Hurriedly we piled gun-cotton against the piers, which were about five feet thick and twenty-five feet high; a good bridge, my seventy-ninth, and strategically most critical, since we were going to live opposite it at Umtaiye until Allenby came forward and relieved us. So I had determined to leave not a stone of it in place.

Nuri meanwhile was hurrying the infantry, gunners and machine-gunners down in the thickening light, towards the line, with orders to get a mile beyond into the desert, form up into column and wait.

Yet the passing of so many camels over the track must take tediously long. We sat and chafed under the bridge, matches in hand, to light at once (despite the troops) if there was an alarm. Fortunately every-thing went well, and after an hour Nuri gave me my signal. Half a minute later (my preference for six-inch fuses!) just as I tumbled into the Turkish redoubt, the eight hundred pounds of stuff exploded in one burst, and the black air became sibilant with flying stones. The explosion was numbing from my twenty yards, and must have been heard half-way to Damascus.

Nuri, in great distress, sought me out. He had given the 'all clear' signal before learning that one company of mounted infantry was missing. Fortunately my guards were aching for redeeming service. Talal el Hareidhin took them with him up the hills, while Nuri and I stood by the yawning pit which had been the bridge, and flashed an electric torch, to give them a fixed point for their return.

Mahmud came back in half an hour triumphantly leading the lost unit. We fired shots to recall the other searchers, and then rode two or three miles into the open towards Umtaiye. The going became very broken, over moraines of slipping dolerite: so we gladly called a halt, and lay down in our ranks for an earned sleep.

HOWEVER, it seemed that Nasir and I were to lose the habit of sleeping. Our noise at Nisib had proclaimed us as widely as the flames of Mezerib. Hardly were we still when visitors came streaming in from three sides to discuss the latest events. It was being rumoured that we were raiding, and not occupying; that later we would run away, as had the British from Salt, leaving our local friends to pay the bills.

The night, for hour after hour, was broken by these new-comers challenging round our bivouacs, crying their way to us like lost souls; and, peasant-fashion, slobbering over our hands with protestations that we were their highest lords and they our deepest servants. Perhaps the reception of them fell short of our usual standard; but, in revenge, they were applying the torture of keeping us awake, uneasily awake. We had been at strain for three days and nights; thinking, ordering and executing; and now, on our road to rest, it was bitter to play away this fourth night also, at the old lack-lustre, dubious game of making friends.

And their shaken morale impressed us worse and worse, till Nasir drew me aside and whispered that clearly there existed a focus of discontent in some centre near. I loosed out my peasant bodyguards to mix with the villagers and find the truth; and from their reports it seemed that the cause of distrust lay in the first settlement, at Taiyibe, which had been shaken by the return of Joyce's armoured cars yesterday, by some chance incidents, and by a just fear that they were the spot most exposed in our retreat.

I called Aziz, and we rode straight to Taiyibe, over rough stretches of lava, trackless, and piled across with walls of broken stone. In the head-man's hut sat the conclave which infected our visitors. They were debating whom to send to implore mercy from the Turks; when we walked in unannounced. Our single coming abashed them, in its assumption of supreme security. We talked irrelevantly an hour, of crops and farmyard prices, and drank some coffee: then rose to go. Behind us the babble broke out again; but now their inconstant spirits had veered to what seemed our stronger wind, and they sent no word to the enemy; though next day they were bombed and shelled for such stubborn complicity with us.

We got back before dawn, and stretched out to sleep: when there came a loud boom from the railway, and a shell shattered beyond our sleeping host. The Turks had sent down an armoured train mounting a field-gun. By myself I would have chanced its aim, for my sleep had been just long enough to make me rage for more: but the army had slept six hours and was moving.

We hurried across the horrible going. An aeroplane came over, and circled round to help the gunners. Shells began to keep accurate pace with our line of march. We doubled our speed, and broke into a ragged procession of very open order. The directing aeroplane faltered suddenly, swerved aside towards the line, and seemed to land. The gun put in one more lucky shot, which killed two camels; but for the rest it lost accuracy, and after about fifty shots we drew out of range. It began to punish Taiyibe.

Joyce, at Umtaiye, had been roused by the shooting, and came out to welcome us. Behind his tall figure the ruins were crested by a motley band, samples from every village and tribe in the Hauran, come to do homage and offer at least lip-service. To Nasir's tired disgust I left these to him, while I went off with Joyce and Winterton, telling them of the landed aeroplane, and suggesting that an armoured car beat it up at home. Just then two more enemy machines appeared and landed in about the same place.

However breakfast, our first for some while, was getting ready. So we sat down and Joyce related how the men of Taiyibe had fired at him as he passed by, presumably to show their opinion of strangers who stirred up a hornet's nest of Turks, and then hopped it!

Breakfast ended. We called for a volunteer car to investigate the enemy aerodrome. Everybody came forward with a silent goodwill and readiness which caught me by the throat. Finally Joyce chose two cars — one for Junor and one for me — and we drove for five miles to the valley in whose mouth the planes had seemed to land.

We silenced the cars and crept down its course. When about two thousand yards from the railway, it bent round into a flat meadow, by whose further side stood three machines. This was magnificent, and we leaped forward, to meet a deep ditch with straight banks of cracking earth, quite impassable.

We raced frantically along it, by a diagonal route, till we were within twelve hundred yards. As we stopped two of the aeroplanes started. We opened fire, searching the range by dust spurts, but already they had run their distance and were off, swaying and clattering up across the sky over our heads.

The third engine was sulky. Its pilot and observer savagely pulled the propeller round, while we ranged nearer. Finally they leaped into the railway ditch as we put bullet after bullet into the fuselage till it danced under the rain. We fired fifteen hundred bullets at our target (they burned it in the afternoon) and then turned home.

Unfortunately the two escaped machines had had time to go to Deraa, and return, feeling spiteful. One was not clever and dropped his four bombs from a height, missing us widely. The other swooped low, placing one bomb each time with the utmost care. We crept on defencelessly, slowly, among the stones, feeling like sardines in a doomed tin, as the bombs fell closer. One sent a shower of small stuff through the driving slit of the car, but only cut our knuckles. One tore off a front tyre and nearly lurched the car over.

Of all danger give me the solitary sort. However we reached Umtaiye well and reported success to Joyce. We had proved to the Turks that that aerodrome was not fit for use; and Deraa lay equally open to car attack. Later I lay in the shadow of a car and slept; all the Arabs in the desert, and the Turkish aeroplanes which came and bombed us, having no effect upon my peace. In the clash of events men became feverishly tireless: but to-day we had finished our first round, fortunately; and it was necessary that I rest, to clear my mind about our next moves. As usual when I lay down I dropped asleep, and slept till afternoon.

Strategically, our business was to hold on to Umtaiye, which gave us command at will of Deraa's three railways. If we held it another week we should strangle the Turkish armies, however little Allenby did. Yet tactically Umtaiye was a dangerous place. An inferior force composed exclusively of regulars, without a guerilla screen, could not safely hold it: yet to that we should shortly be reduced, if our air helplessness continued patent.

The Turks had at least nine machines. We were camped twelve miles from their aerodrome, in the open desert, about the only possible water-supply, with great herds of camels and many horses necessarily grazing round us. The Turks' beginning of bombing had been enough to disquiet the irregulars who were our eyes and ears. Soon they would break up and go home, and our usefulness be ended: Taiyibe, too, that first village which covered us from Deraa — it lay defenceless and quivering under repeated attack. If we were to remain in Umtaiye, Taiyibe must be content with us.

Clearly our first duty was to get air reinforcement from Allenby, who had arranged to send a news machine to Azrak on the day after to-morrow. I judged it would be profitable for me to go across and talk with him. I could be back on the twenty-second. Umtaiye would hold out so long, for we might always fox the aeroplanes a while by moving to Um el Surab, the next Roman village.

Whether at Umtaiye or Um el Surab, to be safe we must keep the initiative. The Deraa side was temporarily closed by the suspicion of the peasants: there remained the Hejaz line. The bridge at Kilometre 149 was nearly mended. We must smash it again, and smash another to the south, to deny the repair trains access to it. An effort by Winterton yesterday showed that the first was a matter for troops and guns. The second was objective for a raid. I went across to see if my bodyguard could do it with me on our way to Azrak.

Something was wrong. They were red-eyed, hesitant, trembling: at last I understood that while I was away in the morning the Zaagi, Abdulla and their other chiefs had gone mercilessly through the tally of those who flinched at Nisib. It was their right, for since Tafileh I had left its discipline to the company itself; but the effect for the moment was to make them useless for my purpose. Such punishment was preceded by fear: but the memory of its infliction provoked wilder lawlessness among the stronger victims, and a likelihood of crimes or violence among the witnesses. They would have been dangerous to me, to themselves, or to the enemy, as whim and opportunity provided, had we gone that night into action.

So, instead, I suggested to Joyce that the Egyptians and Ghurkas return to Akaba; proposing further that he lend me an armoured car to go down with them to the railway, their first stage, and do what could be done. We went up to Nasir and Nuri Said, and told them I would be back on the twenty-second with fighting machines, to deliver us from air-scouts and bombing. Meanwhile we would salve Taiyibe with money for the Turkish damage, and Joyce would make landing-grounds, here and at Um el Surab, against my return with our air reinforcements.

The demolition of that night was a fantastic muddle. We moved at sunset to an open valley, three easy miles from the railway. Trouble might threaten from Mafrak station. My armoured car, with Junor attendant in his Ford, would guard that side against hostile advance. The Egyptians would move direct to the line, and fire their charges.

My guiding fell through. We wandered for three hours in a maze of valleys, not able to find the railway, nor the Egyptians, nor our starting-point. At last we saw a light and drove for it, to find ourselves in front of Mafrak. We turned back to get into place, and heard the clank of an engine running northward out of the station. We chased its inter-mittent flame, hoping to catch it between us and the broken bridge: but before we overtook it there came flashes and explosions far up, as Peake fired his thirty charges.

Some mounted men galloped headlong past us, southward. We fired at them, and then the patrolling train returned, backing at its best speed from Peake's danger. We ran alongside, and opened on the tracks with our Vickers, while Junor sent a green shower of tracer bullets from his Lewis across the dark. Above our shooting and the noise of the engine we heard the Turks howling with terror of this luminous attack. They fired back raggedly, but as they did so the big car suddenly sneezed and stood still. A bullet had pierced the un-armoured end of the petrol tank, the only unarmoured spot of all our team of cars. It took us an hour to plug the leak.

Then we drove along the silent line to the twisted rails and gaping culverts, but could not find our friends. So we drew a mile back, and there at last I had my sleep out, three perfect hours of it before the dawn. I awoke fresh, and recognized our place. Probably it was only the fifth sleepless night which had made my wits woolly. We pushed forward, passing the Egyptians with the Ghurkas, and reached Azrak in the early afternoon. There were Feisal and Nuri Shaalan, eager to hear our news. We explained particularly; and then I went over to Marshall, in the temporary hospital. He had all our badly-wounded in his quiet care: but they were fewer than he had expected, so he was able to spare me a stretcher for my bed.

At dawn Joyce unexpectedly arrived. He had made up his mind that in this lull it was his duty to go down to Aba el Lissan to help Zeid and Jaafar before Maan, and to press forward Hornby among the Beni Sakhr. Then the plane from Palestine arrived, and we heard the amazing first chronicle of Allenby's victory. He had smashed and burst through and driven the Turks inconceivably. The face of our war was changed, and we gave hurried word of it to Feisal, with counsels of the general revolt to take profit of the situation. An hour later I was safely in Palestine.

From Ramleh the Air Force gave me a car up to Headquarters; and there I found the great man unmoved, except for the light in his eye as Bols bustled in every fifteen minutes, with news of some wider success. Allenby had been so sure, before he started, that to him the result was almost boredom: but no general, however scientific, could see his intricate plan carried out over an enormous field in every particular with complete success, and not know an inward gladness: especially when he felt it (as he must have felt it) a reward of the breadth and judgement which made him conceive such unorthodox movements; and break up the proper book of his administrative services to suit them; and support them by every moral and material asset, military or political, within his grasp.

He sketched to me his next intentions. Historic Palestine was his, and the broken Turks, in the hills, expected a slackening of the pursuit. Not at all! Bartholomew and Evans were prepared to provision three more thrusts: one across Jordan to Amman, to be done by Chaytor's New Zealanders; one across Jordan to Deraa, to be done by Barrow and his Indians; one across Jordan to Kuneitra, to be done by Chauvel's Australians. Chaytor would rest at Amman; Barrow and Chauvel on attaining the first objectives would converge on Damascus. We were to assist the three: and I was not to carry out my saucy threat to take Damascus, till we were all together.

I explained our prospects, and how everything was being wrecked by air-impotence. He pressed a bell and in a few minutes Salmond and Borton were conferring with us. Their machines had taken an indispensable part in Allenby's scheme: (the perfection of this man who could use infantry and cavalry, artillery and Air Force, Navy and armoured cars, deceptions and irregulars, each in its best fashion!): and had fulfilled it. There were no more Turks in the sky — except on our side, as I hurriedly interpolated. So much the better, said Salmond; they would send two Bristol fighters over to Umtaiye to sit with us while we needed them. Had we spares? Petrol? Not a drop? How was it to be got there? Only by air? An air-contained fighting unit? Unheard of!

However, Salmond and Borton were men avid of novelty. They worked out loads for D.H.9 and Handley-Page, while Allenby sat by, listening and smiling, sure it would be done. The co-operation of the air with his unfolding scheme had been so ready and elastic, the liaison so complete and informed and quick. It was the R.A.F., which had converted the Turkish retreat into rout, which had abolished their telephone and telegraph connections, had blocked their lorry columns, scattered their infantry units.

The Air chiefs turned on me and asked if our landing-grounds were good enough for a Handley-Page with full load. I had seen the big machine once in its shed, but unhesitatingly said 'Yes' though they had better send an expert over with me in the Bristols to-morrow and make sure. He might be back by noon, and the Handley come at three o'clock. Salmond got up: 'That all right, Sir, we'll do the necessary.' I went out and breakfasted.

Allenby's headquarter was a perfect place: a cool, airy, whitewashed house, proofed against flies, and made musical by the moving of the wind in the trees outside. I felt immoral, enjoying white table-cloths, and coffee, and soldier servants, while our people at Umtaiye lay like lizards among the stones, eating unleavened bread, and waiting for the next plane to bomb them. I felt restless as the dusty sunlight which splashed a diaper over the paths, through chinks in the leaves; because,

TURK TROOPS BOMBED IN WADI FARA

after a long spell of the restrained desert, flowers and grass seemed to fidget, and the everywhere-burgeoning green of tilth became vulgar, in its fecundity.

However, Clayton and Deedes and Dawnay were friendliness itself, and also the Air Force staff; while the good cheer and conscious strength of the Commander-in-Chief was a bath of comfort to a weary person after long strained days. Bartholomew moved maps about, explaining what they would do. I added to his knowledge of the enemy, for I was his best served intelligence officer: and in return his perspective showed me the victory sure, whatever happened to our strained little stop-block over there. Yet it seemed to me that in the Arab hands lay an option, whether to let this victory be just one more victory, or, by risking themselves once more, to make it final. Not that, so stated, it was a real option: but, when body and spirit were as wearily sick as mine, they almost instinctively sought a plausible avoidance of the way of danger.

x

BEFORE dawn, on the Australian aerodrome, stood two Bristols and a D.H.9. In one was Ross Smith, my old pilot, who had been picked out to fly the new Handley-Page, the single machine of its class in Egypt, the apple of Salmond's eye. His lending it to fly over the enemy line on so low an errand as baggage carrying, was a measure of the goodwill toward us.

We reached Umtaiye in an hour, and saw that the army had gone: so I waved ourselves back to Um el Surab; and there they were, the defensive group of cars, and Arabs hiding from our suspect noise here, there and everywhere; the cute camels dispersed singly over the plain, filling themselves with the wonderful grazing. Young, when he saw our markings, put a landing-signal and smoke bombs on the turf which his care and Nuri Said's had swept clear of stones.

Ross Smith anxiously paced the length and breadth of the prepared space, and studied its imperfections: but rejoined us, where the drivers were making breakfast with a clear face. The ground was O.K. for the Handley-Page. Young told us of repeated bombings yesterday and the day before, which had killed some regulars and some of Pisani's gunners and tired the life out of everyone, so that they moved in the night to Um el Surab. The idiot Turks were still bombing Umtaiye though men went to it only in the neutral noons and nights to draw water.

Also I heard of Winterton's last blowing up of the railway: an amusing night, in which he had met an unknown soldier and explained to him in broken Arabic how well they were getting on. The soldier had thanked God for His mercies, and disappeared in the dark; whence a moment later, machine-gun fire opened from left and right! Nevertheless, Winterton had fired all his charges, and withdrawn in good order without loss. Nasir came to us, and reported this man hurt, and that killed, this clan getting ready, those already joined, but others gone home — all the gossip of the country. The three shining aeroplanes had much restored the Arabs, who lauded the British, and their own bravery and endurance, while I told them the scarce-credible epic of

Allenby's success — Nablus taken, Afuleh taken, Beisan and Semakh and Haifa. My hearers' minds drew after me like flames. Tallal took fire, boasting; while the Rualla shouted for instant march upon Damascus. Even my bodyguard, still bearing witness of the Zaagi's severity in their muddy eyes and constrained faces, cheered up and began to preen a little before the crowd, with a dawn of happiness. A shiver of self-assertion and confidence ran across the camp. I determined to bring up Feisal and Nuri Shaalan for the final effort.

Meanwhile it was breakfast time with a smell of sausage in the air. We sat round, very ready: but the watcher on the broken tower yelled 'Aeroplane up', seeing one coming over from Deraa. Our Australians, scrambling wildly to their yet-hot machines, started them in a moment. Ross Smith, with his observer, leaped into one, and climbed like a cat up the sky. After him went Peters, while the third pilot stood beside the D.H. 9 and looked hard at me.

I seemed not to understand him. Lewis guns, scarfe mountings, sights, rings which turned, vanes, knobs which rose and fell on swinging parallel bars; to shoot, one aimed with this side of the ring or with that, according to the varied speed and direction of oneself and the enemy. I had been told the theory, could repeat some of it: but it was in my head, and rules of action were only snares of action till they had run out of the empty head into the hands, by use. No: I was not going up to air-fight, no matter what caste I lost with the pilot. He was an Australian, of a race delighting in additional risks, not an Arab to whose gallery I must play.

He was too respectful to speak: only he looked reproach at me while we watched the battle in the air. There were one enemy two-seater and three scouts. Ross Smith fastened on the big one, and, after five minutes of sharp machine-gun rattle, the German dived suddenly towards the railway line. As it flashed behind the low ridge, there broke out a pennon of smoke, and from its falling place a soft, dark cloud. An 'Ah!' came from the Arabs about us. Five minutes later Ross Smith was back, and jumped gaily out of his machine, swearing that the Arab front was the place.

Our sausages were still hot; we ate them, and drank tea (our last English stores, broached for the visitors), but were hardly at the grapes from Jebel Druse when again the watchman tossed up his cloak and screamed, 'A plane!' This time Peters won the race, Ross Smith second, with Traill, disconsolate, in reserve: but the shy enemy turned back so soon that Peters did not catch them till near Arar: there he drove down his quarry, fighting. Later, when the wave of war rolled thither, we found the hopeless crash, and two charred German bodies.

Ross Smith wished he might stay for ever on this Arab front with an enemy every half-hour; and deeply envied Peters his coming days. However, he must go back for the Handley-Page with petrol, food and spares. The third plane was for Azrak, to get the observer marooned there yesterday; and I went in it so far, to see Feisal.

Time became spacious to those who flew: we were in Azrak thirty hours after leaving it. Ghurkas and Egyptians I turned back to rejoin the army, for new demolitions in the north. Then, with Feisal and Nuri Shaalan, I packed into the green Vauxhall, and off we went for Um el Surab to see the Handley-Page alight.

We ran at speed over the smooth flint or mud-flat, letting the strong car throb itself fully: but luck was hostile. A dispute was reported us, and we had to turn aside to a local Serahin camp. However, we made profit of our loss, by ordering their fighting men to Umtaiye: and we had them send word of victory across the railway, that the roads through the Ajlun hills might be closed to the broken Turkish armies, trying to escape into safety.

Then our car flashed northward again. Twenty miles short of Ul em Surab we perceived a single Bedawi, running southward all in a flutter, his grey hair and grey beard flying in the wind, and his shirt (tucked up in his belly-cord) puffing out behind him. He altered course to pass near us, and, raising his bony arms, yelled, 'The biggest aeroplane in the world', before he flapped on into the south, to spread his great news among the tents.

At Um el Surab the Handley stood majestic on the grass, with Bristols and 9.A like fledglings beneath its spread of wings. Round it admired the Arabs, saying, 'Indeed and at last they have sent us THE aeroplane, of which these things were foals'. Before night rumour of Feisal's resource went over Jebel Druse and the hollow of Hauran, telling people that the balance was weighted on our side.

Borton himself had come over in the machine, to concert help. We talked with him while our men drew from her bomb-racks and fuselage a ton of petrol; oil and spare parts for Bristol Fighters; tea and sugar and rations for our men; letters, Reuter telegrams and medicines for us. Then the great machine rose into the early dusk, for Ramleh, with an agreed programme of night-bombing against Deraa and Mafrak, to complete that ruin of the railway traffic which our gun-cotton had begun.

We, for our share, would keep up the gun-cotton pressure. Allenby had assigned us the Turkish Fourth Army, to harass and contain till Chaytor forced them out of Amman; and afterwards to cut up, on their retreat. This retreat was only an affair of days, and it was as certain as things could be in war that we should raise the plains between us and Damascus next week. So Feisal decided to add to our column Nuri Shaalan's Rualla camel men from Azrak. It would increase us to about four thousand strong, more than three-fourths irregular; but reliably so, for Nuri, the hard, silent, cynical old man, held the tribe between his fingers like a tool.

He was that rarity in the desert, a man without sense of argument. He would or would not, and there was no more to it. When others finished talking, he would announce his will in a few flat phrases, and wait calmly for obedience; which came, for he was feared. He was old and wise, which meant tired and disappointed: so old that it was my abiding wonder he should link himself to our enthusiasm.

I rested next day in Nasir's tent, among his peasant visitors; sorting out the too-abundant news furnished by their quick wit and goodwill. During my rest-day, Nuri Said, with Pisani and two guns, Stirling, Winterton, Young, their armoured cars, and a considerable force, went openly to the railway, cleared it by approved military means, destroyed a kilometre of rail, and burnt the tentative wooden structure with which the Turks were mending the bridge blown up by Joyce and myself before our first attack on Deraa. Nuri Shaalan, in black broad-cloth cloak, personally led his Rualla horsemen, galloping with the best of them. Under his eye the tribe showed a valour which drew praise even from Nuri Said.

NURI'S operation of to-day was the Turks' final blow, after which they gave up trying to restore the line between Amman and Deraa. We did not know this, but still had its bogy set over us, and were urgent to put out of action a yet longer stretch. Accordingly, next dawn, Winterton, Jemil and I went out on cars to examine the line south of Mafrak station. We were received with machine-gun fire of a vigour, direction and intensity beyond any of our experience. Later we captured the experts and found they were a German machine-gun unit. For the moment we drew out, puzzled, and went further to a tempting bridge. My plan was to run under it in the car till the vault enabled us to lay the charge against the pier in shelter. So I transferred myself to an armoured car, put sixty pounds of gun-cotton on the back-board, and told the driver to push in under the arch.

Winterton and Jemil came behind in the supporting car. 'It's very hot', groaned Jemil. 'It's going to be still hotter where we're going', replied Winterton, as we drew in slowly over indifferent ground with aimless shells falling about. We were picking our way forward, about fifty yards from the bank, with enough machine-gun bullets for a week's fighting rattling off our armour, when someone from behind the line bowled a hand grenade at us.

This new condition made impossible my plan of getting under the bridge. For one thing, a hit on the back of the car would have set off our guncotton and blown us to blazes; for another, the car was helpless against a lobbed grenade. So we drew off, perplexed to understand this defence lavished on a bit of railway, and much interested, indeed amused, at worthy opposition after so long ease. In our imaginations, Check was a short, compact, furious man, darting glances every way from beneath tangled eyebrows, for an end to his troubles; beside him Victory seemed a lanky, white-skinned, rather languid woman. We must try again after dark. At Um el Surab we found that Nasir wished to fix camp once more at Umtaiye. It was a first stage of our journey to Damascus, so his wish delighted me, and we moved; winning thereby good excuse for doing nothing this night to the line. Instead, we sat and told stories of experience and waited for midnight, when the Handley-Page was to bomb Mafrak station. It came, and hundred-pound bomb after hundred-pound bomb crashed into the packed sidings till they caught fire, and the Turks' shooting stopped.

We slept, having given prize of the night to a tale of Enver Pasha, after the Turks re-took Sharkeui. He went to see it, in a penny steamer, with Prince Jemil and a gorgeous staff. The Bulgars, when they came, had massacred the Turks; as they retired the Bulgar peasants went too. So the Turks found hardly any one to kill. A greybeard was led on board for the Commander-in-Chief to bait. At last Enver tired of this. He signed to two of his bravo aides, and throwing open the furnace door, said, 'Push him in'. The old man screamed, but the officers were stronger and the door was slammed-to on his jerking body. 'We turned, feeling sick, to go away, but Enver, his head on one side, listening, halted us. So we listened, till there came a crash within the furnace. He smiled and nodded, saying, "Their heads always pop, like that".'

All night, and next day, the fire among the trucks burned greater and greater. It was proof of the breakdown of the Turks, which the Arabs had been rumouring since yesterday. They said the Fourth Army was streaming up from Amman in a loose mob. The Beni Hassan, who were cutting off stragglers and weak detachments, compared them to gipsies on the march.

We held a council. Our work against the Fourth Army was finished. Such remnants as avoided out of the hands of the Arabs would reach Deraa as unarmed stragglers. Our new endeavour should be to force the quick evacuation of Deraa, in order to prevent the Turks there reforming the fugitives into a rearguard. So I proposed that we march north, past Tell Arar, and over the railway at dawn to-morrow, into Sheikh Saad village. It lay in familiar country with abundant water, perfect observation, and a secure retreat west or north, or even south-west, if we were directly attacked. It cut off Deraa from Damascus; and Mezerib also.

Tallal seconded me with fervour. Nuri Shaalan gave his nod: Nasir and Nuri Said. So we prepared to strike camp. The armoured cars could not come with us. They had better stay in Azrak, till Deraa fell and we wanted them to help us into Damascus. The Bristol Fighters, likewise, had done their work, clearing the air of Turkish aeroplanes. They might return to Palestine with news of our move to Sheikh Saad.

Off they circled. We, watching their line of flight, noticed a great cloud of dust added to the slow smoke from ruined Mafrak. One machine turned back and dropped a scribble that a large body of hostile cavalry were heading out from the railway towards us.

This was unwelcome news, for we were not in trim for a fight. The cars had gone, the aeroplanes had gone, one company of the mounted infantry had marched, Pisani's mules were packed and drawn up in column. I went off to Nuri Said, standing with Nasir on an ash heap at the head of the hill, and we wavered whether to run or stand. At last it seemed wiser to run, since Sheikh Saad was a more profitable stop-block. So we hurried the regulars away.

Yet things could hardly be left like that. Accordingly Nuri Shaalan and Tallal led the Rualla horse and the Hauran horse back to delay the pursuit. They had an unexpected ally for our cars, on their way to Azrak, had seen the enemy. After all, the Turks were not cavalry coming to attack us, but deluded elements seeking a shorter way home. We took some hundreds of thirsty prisoners and much transport; causing such panic that the main rout in the plain cut the traces of their limbers and rode off on the bare horses. The infection of terror spread down the line, and troops miles from any Arab interference threw away all they had, even to their rifles, and made a mad rush towards supposed safety in Deraa.

However, this interruption delayed us; for we could hardly march a khaki-clad body of regular camel corps across Hauran at night without enough local cavalry to go bail to the suspicious villagers that we were not Turks. So late in the afternoon we halted for Tallal and Nasir and Nuri Shaalan to catch up.

This halt gave some people time to review the proceedings, and new questions arose as to the wisdom of crossing the railway again, to put ourselves in the dangerous position of Sheikh Saad, astride the retreat of the main Turkish forces. Finally, near midnight, Sabin appeared where I lay awake in the midst of the army on my carpet. He suggested that we had done enough. Allenby had appointed us watchmen of the Fourth Army. We had just seen its disordered flight. Our duty was completed; and we might honourably fall back to Bosra, twenty miles out of the way to the east, where the Druses were collecting under Nesib el Bekri to help us. We might wait with them for the British to take Deraa, and for our reward, in the victorious close of the campaign.

This attitude passed me by, since, if we withdrew to Jebel Druse, we ended our active service before the game was won, leaving the last brunt on Allenby. I was very jealous for the Arab honour, in whose service I would go forward at all costs. They had joined the war to win freedom, and the recovery of their old capital by force of their own arms was the sign they would best understand.

'Duty', like people who praised it, was a poor thing. Evidently, by thrusting behind Deraa into Sheikh Saad we put more pressure on the Turks than any British unit was in place to put. It would forbid the Turks fighting again this side of Damascus; for which gain our few lives would be cheap payment. Damascus meant the end of this war in the East, and, I believed, the end of the general war, too; because the Central Powers being inter-dependent, the breaking of their weakest link — Turkey — would swing the whole cluster loose. Therefore, for every sensible reason, strategical, tactical, political, even moral, we were going on.

Sabin's stubborn resistant mind was not to be convinced. He returned with Pisani and Winterton, and began to debate; speaking slowly because Nuri Said was lying on the next rug only half asleep, and he wanted to include him in the conference.

Accordingly he stressed the military aspect: our fulfilled purpose and the danger of the Hejaz Railway. This delay made us too late to cross to-night. To-morrow it would be madness to attempt the operation. The line would be guarded from end to end by tens of thousands of Turks pouring out of Deraa. If they let us over we would only be in still greater danger. Joyce, he said, had appointed him military adviser to the expedition; and it was his duty to point out, reluctantly, that as a regular officer he knew his business.

Had I been a regular officer I might have found Sabin's upsetting the

x*

others irregular. As it was I endured his complaints, patiently sighing whenever I thought it would irritate the protestant. At the end wanderingly I said I wanted to sleep, since we would have to be up early to cross the line, and it was my intention to go in front with my bodyguard among the Beduin, wherever they were, for it was odd that Nuri Shaalan and Tallal had not overtaken us. Anyway, I was going to sleep now.

Pisani, whose long military life had been all as subordinate, said with correctness that he took his orders and would follow. I liked him for that, and tried to soothe his honest doubts by reminding him that we had worked for eighteen months together without his ever finding cause to call me rash. He replied with a French laugh that he thought it all very rash, but was a soldier.

Winterton's instinct joined him to the weaker and more sporting side in any choice but fox-hunting. Nuri Said had lain silently through our talk, pretending to be asleep; but, when Sabin went away, he rolled over whispering, 'Is it true?' I replied that I saw no unusual risk in crossing the line in mid-afternoon, and with care we should avoid traps at Sheikh Saad. He lay back satisfied.

CHAPTER CXVI

NASIR, Nuri Shaalan and Talal had overshot us in the dark. Our joined forces marched, with a heady breeze in the teeth, northward across the ploughlands' fat, happy villages. Over the harvested fields, whose straw had been rather plucked than reaped, grew thistles, tall as a child, but now yellow and dried and dead. The wind snapped them off at the hollow root, and pitch-polled their branchy tops along the level ground, thistle blowing against thistle and interlocking spines, till in huge balls they careered like run-away haycocks across the fallow.

Arab women, out with their donkeys to fetch water, ran to us, crying that an aeroplane had landed a while since, near by. It bore the round rings of the Sherifian camel brand upon its body. Peake rode across, to find two Australians whose Bristol had been hit in the radiator over Deraa. They were glad, though astonished, to meet friends. After the leak had been plugged, we levied water from the women, to fill them up, and they flew home safely.

Men rode up every minute and joined us, while from each village the adventurous young ran out afoot to enter our ranks. As we moved on, so closely knit in the golden sunlight, we were able, in rare chance, to see ourselves as a whole: quickly we became a character, an organism, in whose pride each of us was uplifted. We cracked bawdy jokes to set off the encompassing beauty.

At noon we entered water-melon fields. The army ran upon them, while we spied out the line, which lay desertedly quivering in the sunlight ahead. As we watched a train passed down. Only last night had the railway been mended: and this was the third train. We moved without opposition upon the line in a horde two miles across, and began hastily to blow up things, anyone who had explosive using it as he fancied. Our hundreds of novices were full of zeal and the demolitions, albeit uninstructed, were wide.

Clearly our return had surprised the dazed enemy: we must extend and improve this chance. So we went to Nuri Shaalan, Auda, and

Talal, and asked what local effort each would undertake. Talal, the energetic, would attack Ezraa, the big grain depot to the north: Auda was for Khirbet el Ghazala, the corresponding station southward: Nuri would sweep his men down the main road, towards Deraa, on chance of Turkish parties.

These were three good ideas. The chiefs went to put them into being, while we, pulling our column to its shape again, pursued our road past the ruined colony of Sheikh Miskin, very gaunt in the moonlight. Its obstacle of water ditches muddled our thousands, so that we halted on the stubble plain beyond, for dawn. Some made fires against the penetrating mist of this clay Hauran: others slept as they were on the dew-slimy ground. Lost men went about calling their friends, in that sharp, full-throated wail of the Arab villager. The moon had set, and the world was black and very cold.

I roused my bodyguard, who rode so briskly that we entered Sheikh Saad with the dawn. As we passed between the rocks into the field behind the trees, the earth sprang to life again with the new sun. The morning airs flashed the olive-yards to silver, and men from a great goat-hair tent on the right called us to guest with them. We asked whose camp it was. 'Ibn Smeir's' they replied. This threatened complications. Rashid was an enemy of Nuri Shaalan's, unreconciled, chance-met. At once we sent a warning to Nasir. Fortunately Ibn Smeir was absent. So his family would be our temporary guests, and Nuri, as host, must observe the rules.

It was a relief, for already in our ranks we had hundreds of deadly enemies, their feuds barely suspended by Feisal's peace. The strain of keeping them in play, and employing their hot-heads in separate spheres, balancing opportunity and service that our direction might be esteemed as above jealousy — all that was evil enough. Conduct of the war in France would have been harder if each division, almost each brigade of our army had hated every other with a deadly hatred and fought when they met suddenly. However, we had kept them quiet for two years, and it would be only a few days now.

The parties of the night returned, full of spoil. Ezraa had been feebly held by Abd el Kader, the Algerian, with his retainers, some volunteers and troops. When Talal came the volunteers joined him, the troops fled, and the retainers were so few that Abd el Kader had to abandon the place without fighting. Our men were too heavy with their great booty to catch him.

Auda came, boasting. He had taken el Ghazale by storm, capturing a derelict train, guns and two hundred men, of whom some were Germans. Nuri Shaalan reported four hundred prisoners with mules and machine-guns. The rank and file of Turks had been farmed out to remote villages, to earn their keep.

An English aeroplane flew round and round, wondering if we were the Arab force. Young spread out ground signals, and to him they dropped a message that Bulgaria had surrendered to the Allies. We had not known there was an offensive in the Balkans, so the news came orphaned, and as it were insignificant to us. Undoubtedly the end, not only of the great war, but of our war, was near. A sharp effort, and our trial would be over and everyone loosed back to his affairs, forgetting the madness: since for most of us it was the first war, and we looked to its end as rest and peace.

The army had arrived. The groves became thronged as each detachment picked out the best vacant place and unsaddled, whether beside fig-trees, or under palms, or olives, from which the birds burst out in frightened clouds, with a multitudinous crying. Our men took their animals to the stream meandering through green bushes and flowers and cultivated fruits, things strange to us during the years of our wandering in the flinty desert.

The people of Sheikh Saad came shyly to look at Feisal's army, which had been a whispered legendary thing, and was now in their village, led by renowned or formidable names — Talal, Nasir, Nuri, Auda. We stared back, in secret envy of their peasant life.

While the men stretched the saddle-stiffness of riding from their legs, we went up, five or six of us, above the ruins, whence across the southern plain we should see the measure of security in store for us. To our astonishment we perceived, just over the walls, a thin company of regulars in uniform — Turks, Austrians, Germans — with eight machine-guns on pack-animals. They were toiling up from Galilee towards Damascus after their defeat by Allenby; hopeless, but care-free, marching at ease, thinking themselves fifty miles from any war.

We did not give an alarm, to spare our tired troops pains: just Durzi ibn Dughmi, with the Khaffaji and others of the family, mounted quietly and fell on them from a narrow lane. The officers showed fight and were instantly killed. The men threw down their arms, and in five minutes had been searched and robbed and were being shepherded in file along the water-paths between the gardens to an open pound which seemed fit for our prison. Sheikh Saad was paying soon and well.

Away to the east appeared three or four black knots of people, moving northward. We loosed the Howeitat on them, and after an hour they returned in laughter, each man leading a mule or pack-horse; poor, tired, galled brutes, showing all too clearly the straits of the beaten army. Their riders had been unarmed soldiers fleeing from the British. The Howeitat disdained to make such prisoners. 'We gave them to the boys and girls of the villages for servants,' sneered Zaal, with his thin-lipped smile.

News came to us from the west that small companies of Turks were retiring into the local villages from Chauvel's attacks. We sent against them armed parties of Naim, a peasant tribe which had joined us last night at Sheikh Miskin, as appointed by Nasir, to do what they could. The mass rising we had so long prepared was now in flood, rising higher as each success armed more rebels. In two days' time we might have sixty thousand armed men in movement.

We snapped up further trifles on the Damascus road; and then saw heavy smoke above the hill which hid Deraa. A man cantered in, to inform Tallal that the Germans had set fire to aeroplanes and store-houses, and stood ready to evacuate the town. A British plane dropped word that Barrow's troops were near Remtha, and that two Turkish columns, one of four thousand, one of two thousand, were retiring towards us from Deraa and Mezerib respectively.

It seemed to me that these six thousand men were all that remained of the Fourth Army, from Deraa, and of the Seventh Army, which had been disputing Barrow's advance. With their destruction would end our purpose here. Yet, till we knew, we must retain Sheikh Saad. So the larger column, the four thousand, we would let pass, only fastening to them Khalid and his Rualla, with some northern peasantry, to harry their flanks and rear.

CHAPTER CXVII

THE nearer two thousand seemed more our size. We would meet them with half our regulars, and two of Pisani's guns. Tallal was anxious, for their indicated route would bring them through Tafas, his own village. He determined us to make speed there and seize the ridge south of it. Unfortunately speed was only a relative term with men so tired. I rode with my troop to Tafas, hoping to occupy a shadow position beyond it and fight a retiring action till the rest came up. Half-way on the road, there met us mounted Arabs, herding a drove of stripped prisoners towards Sheikh Saad. They were driving them mercilessly, the bruises of their urging blue across the ivory backs; but I left them to it, for these were Turks of the police battalion of Deraa, beneath whose iniquities the peasant-faces of the neighbourhood had run with tears and blood, innumerable times.

The Arabs told us that the Turkish column — Jemal Pasha's lancer regiment — was already entering Tafas. When we got within sight, we found they had taken the village (from which sounded an occasional shot) and were halted about it. Small pyres of smoke were going up from between the houses. On the rising ground to this side, knee-deep in the thistles, stood a remnant of old men, women and children, telling terrible stories of what had happened when the Turks rushed in an hour before.

We lay on watch, and saw the enemy force march away from their assembly-ground behind the houses. They headed in good order towards Miskin, the lancers in front and rear, composite formations of infantry disposed in column with machine-gun support as flank guards, guns and a mass of transport in the centre. We opened fire on the head of their line when it showed itself beyond the houses. They turned two field-guns upon us, for reply. The shrapnel was as usual over-fused, and passed safely above our heads.

Nuri came with Pisani. Before their ranks rode Auda abu Tayi, expectant, and Tallal, nearly frantic with the tales his people poured out of the sufferings of the village. The last Turks were now quitting it.

We slipped down behind them to end Tallal's suspense, while our infantry took position and fired strongly with the Hotchkiss; Pisani advanced his half battery among them; so that the French high explosive threw the rearguard into confusion.

The village lay stilly under its slow wreaths of white smoke, as we rode near, on our guard. Some grey heaps seemed to hide in the long grass, embracing the ground in the close way of corpses. We looked away from these, knowing they were dead; but from one a little figure tottered off, as if to escape us. It was a child, three or four years old, whose dirty smock was stained red over one shoulder and side, with blood from a large half-fibrous wound, perhaps a lance thrust, just where neck and body joined.

The child ran a few steps, then stood and cried to us in a tone of astonishing strength (all else being very silent), 'Don't hit me, Baba'. Abd el Aziz, choking out something — this was his village, and she might be of his family — flung himself off his camel, and stumbled, kneeling, in the grass beside the child. His suddenness frightened her, for she threw up her arms and tried to scream; but, instead, dropped in a little heap, while the blood rushed out again over her clothes; then, I think, she died.

We rode past the other bodies of men and women and four more dead babies, looking very soiled in the daylight, towards the village; whose loneliness we now knew meant death and horror. By the outskirts were low mud walls, sheepfolds, and on one something red and white. I looked close and saw the body of a woman folded across it, bottom upwards, nailed there by a saw bayonet whose haft stuck hideously into the air from between her naked legs. She had been pregnant, and about her lay others, perhaps twenty in all, variously killed, but set out in accord with an obscene taste.

The Zaagi burst into wild peals of laughter, the more desolate for the warm sunshine and clear air of this upland afternoon. I said, 'The best of you brings me the most Turkish dead', and we turned after the fading enemy, on our way shooting down those who had fallen out by the roadside, and came imploring our pity. One wounded Turk, half naked, not able to stand, sat and wept to us. Abdulla turned away his camel's head, but the Zaagi, with curses, crossed his track and whipped three bullets from his automatic through the man's bare chest. The blood came out with his heart beats, throb, throb, throb, slower and slower.

Tallal had seen what we had seen. He gave one moan like a hurt animal; then rode to the upper ground and sat there awhile on his mare, shivering and looking fixedly after the Turks. I moved near to speak to him, but Auda caught my rein and stayed me. Very slowly Tallal drew his head-cloth about his face; and then he seemed suddenly to take hold of himself, for he dashed his stirrups into the mare's flanks and galloped headlong, bending low and swaying in the saddle, right at the main body of the enemy.

It was a long ride down a gentle slope and across a hollow. We sat there like stone while he rushed forward, the drumming of his hoofs unnaturally loud in our ears, for we had stopped shooting, and the Turks had stopped. Both armies waited for him; and he rocked on in the hushed evening till only a few lengths from the enemy. Then he sat up in the saddle and cried his war-cry, 'Tallal, Tallal', twice in a tremendous shout. Instantly their rifles and machine-guns crashed out, and he and his mare, riddled through and through with bullets, fell dead among the lance points.

Auda looked very cold and grim. 'God give him mercy; we will take his price.' He shook his rein and moved slowly after the enemy. We called up the peasants, now drunk with fear and blood, and sent them from this side and that against the retreating column. The old lion of battle waked in Auda's heart, and made him again our natural, inevitable leader. By a skilful turn he drove the Turks into bad ground and split their formation into three parts.

The third part, the smallest, was mostly made up of German and Austrian machine-gunners grouped round three motor-cars, and a handful of mounted officers or troopers. They fought magnificently and repulsed us time and again despite our hardiness. The Arabs were fighting like devils, the sweat blurring their eyes, dust parching their throats; while the flame of cruelty and revenge which was burning in their bodies so twisted them, that their hands could hardly shoot. By my order we took no prisoners, for the only time in our war.

At last we left this stern section behind, and pursued the faster two.

They were in panic; and by sunset we had destroyed all but the smallest pieces of them, gaining as and by what they lost. Parties of peasants flowed in on our advance. At first there were five or six to a weapon: then one would win a bayonet, another a sword, a third a pistol. An hour later those who had been on foot would be on donkeys. Afterwards every man had a rifle, and a captured horse. By nightfall the horses were laden, and the rich plain was scattered over with dead men and animals. In a madness born of the horror of Tafas we killed and killed, even blowing in the heads of the fallen and of the animals; as though their death and running blood could slake our agony.

Just one group of Arabs, who had not heard our news, took prisoner the last two hundred men of the central section. Their respite was short. I had gone up to learn why it was, not unwilling that this remnant be let live as witnesses of Tallal's price; but a man on the ground behind them screamed something to the Arabs, who with pale faces led me across to see. It was one of us — his thigh shattered. The blood had rushed out over the red soil, and left him dying; but even so he had not been spared. In the fashion of to-day's battle he had been further tormented by bayonets hammered through his shoulder and other leg into the ground, pinning him out like a collected insect.

He was fully conscious. When we said, 'Hassan, who did it?' he drooped his eyes towards the prisoners, huddling together so hopelessly broken. They said nothing in the moments before we opened fire. At last their heap ceased moving; and Hassan was dead; and we mounted again and rode home slowly (home was my carpet three or four hours from us at Sheikh Saad) in the gloom, which felt so chill now that the sun had gone down.

However, what with wounds and aches and weariness I could not rest from thinking of Tallal, the splendid leader, the fine horseman, the courteous and strong companion of the road; and after a while I had my other camel brought, and with one of my bodyguard rode out into the night to join our men hunting the greater Deraa column.

It was very dark, with a wind beating in great gusts from the south and east; and only by the noise of shots it tossed across to us and by occasional gun flashes, did we at length come to the fighting. Every field and valley had its Turks stumbling blindly northward. Our men were clinging on. The fall of night had made them bolder, and they were now closing with the enemy. Each village, as the fight rolled to it, took up the work; and the black, icy wind was wild with rifle-fire, shoutings, volleys from the Turks, and the rush of gallops, as small parties of either side crashed frantically together.

The enemy had tried to halt and camp at sunset, but Khalid had shaken them again into movement. Some marched, some stayed. Many dropped asleep in their tracks with fatigue. They had lost order and coherence, and were drifting through the blast in lorn packets, ready to shoot and run at every contact with us or with each other; and the Arabs were as scattered, and nearly as uncertain.

Exceptions were the German detachments; and here, for the first time, I grew proud of the enemy who had killed my brothers. They were two thousand miles from home, without hope and without guides, in conditions mad enough to break the bravest nerves. Yet their sections held together, in firm rank, sheering through the wrack of Turk and Arab like armoured ships, high-faced and silent. When attacked they halted, took position, fired to order. There was no haste, no crying, no hesitation. They were glorious.

At last I found Khalid, and asked him to call off the Rualla and leave this rout to time and the peasantry. Heavier work, perhaps, lay to the southward. At dusk a rumour had passed across our plain that Deraa was empty, and Trad, Khalid's brother, with a good half of the Anazeh, had ridden off to see. I feared a reverse for him, since there must still be Turks in the place, and more struggling towards it up the railway and through the Irbid Hills. Indeed, unless Barrow, last reported to us as delayed in Remthe, had lost contact with his enemy, there must be a fighting rearguard yet to follow.

I wanted Khalid to support his brother. After an hour or two of shouting his message down the wind, hundreds of horsemen and camel men had rallied to him. On his way to Deraa he charged through and over several detachments of Turks in the star-blink, and arrived to find Trad in secure possession. He had won through in the later twilight, taking the station at a gallop, jumping trenches and blotting out the scanty Turkish elements which still tried to resist.

With local help the Rualla plundered the camp, especially finding booty in the fiercely burning storehouses whose flaming roofs imperilled their lives; but this was one of the nights in which mankind went crazy, when death seemed impossible, however many died to the right and left, and when others' lives became toys to break and throw away.

Sheikh Saad passed a troubled evening of alarms and shots and shouts, with threatenings from the peasantry to murder the prisoners as added price of Tallal and his village. The active sheikhs were out hunting the Turks, and their absence with their retainers deprived the Arab camp of its experienced chiefs and of its eyes and ears. Sleeping clan-jealousies had awaked in the blood thirst of the afternoon of killing, and Nasir and Nuri Said, Young and Winterton, had to strain every nerve in keeping peace.

I got in after midnight and found Trad's messengers just arrived from Deraa. Nasir left to join him. I had wished to sleep, for this was my fourth night of riding; but my mind would not let me feel how tired my body was, so about two in the morning I mounted a third camel and splashed out towards Deraa, down the Tafas track again, to windward of the dark village.

Nuri Said and his staff were riding the same road in advance of their mounted infantry, and our parties hurried together till the half-light came. Then my impatience and the cold would not let me travel horse-pace any longer. I gave liberty to my camel — the grand, rebellious Baha — and she stretched herself out against the field, racing my wearied followers for mile upon mile with piston-strides like an engine, so that I entered Deraa quite alone in the full dawn.

Nasir was at the Mayor's house, arranging a military governor, and police; and for an inquisition of the place; I supplemented his ideas, putting guards over the pumps and engine sheds and what remained of tool shops or stores. Then in an hour of talk I built up publicly a programme of what the situation would demand of them, if they were not to lose hold. Poor Nasir stared in bewilderment.

I inquired about General Barrow. A man just ridden in from the west told us he had been fired on by the English, as they deployed to attack the town. To prevent such an accident the Zaagi and I rode up the Buweib, on whose crest was visible a strong post of Indian machine-gunners. They trained their weapons on us, proud of such splendidly dressed prizes. However, an officer showed himself, with some British troopers, and to them I explained myself. They were indeed in the midst of an enveloping movement against Deraa, and, while we watched, their aeroplanes bombed the luckless Nuri Said as he rode into the railway station. This was his penalty for losing the race from Sheikh Saad: but, to stop it, I hurried down to where General Barrow was inspecting outposts in a car.

I told him we had spent the night in the town, and the shooting he heard was joy-firing. He was short with me; but I had little pity for him, because he had delayed a day and night watering at the poor wells of Remthe, though his map showed the lake and river of Mezerib in front, on the road by which the enemy were escaping. However his orders were Deraa, and to Deraa he would go.

He told me to ride beside him: but his horses hated my camel, so the General Staff bucked along the ditch, while I soberly paced the crown of the road. He said he must post sentries in the village to keep the populace in order. I explained gently that the Arabs had installed their military governor. At the wells he said his sappers must inspect the pumps. I replied welcoming their assistance. We had lit the furnaces and hoped to begin watering his horses in an hour. He snorted that we seemed to be at home; he would take charge only of the railway station. I pointed to the engine moving out towards Mezerib (where our little Sheikh had prevented the Turks from blowing up the Tell el Shehab bridge, now become Arab property) and asked that his sentries be instructed not to interfere with our proper working of the line.

He had had no orders as to the status of the Arabs. Clayton did us this service, thinking we should deserve what we could assert: so Barrow, who had come in thinking of them as a conquered people, though dazed at my calm assumption that he was my guest, had no option but to follow the lead of such assurance. My head was working full speed in these minutes, on our joint behalf, to prevent the fatal first steps by which the unimaginative British, with the best will in the world, usually deprived the acquiescent native of the discipline of responsibility, and created a situation which called for years of agitation and successive reforms and riotings to mend.

I had studied Barrow and was ready for him. Years before, he had published his confession of faith in Fear as the common people's main incentive to action in war and peace. Now I found fear a mean, over-rated motive; no deterrent, and, though a stimulant, a poisonous stimulant, whose every injection served to consume more of the system to which it was applied. I could have no alliance with his pedant belief of scaring men into heaven: better that Barrow and I part at once. My instinct with the inevitable was to provoke it. Therefore, I was very spiny and high.

Barrow surrendered himself by asking me to find him forage and food-stuffs. Indeed, soon we got on well. In the square I showed him Nasir's little silk pennon, propped on the balcony of the charred Government office, with a yawning sentry underneath. Barrow drew himself up and saluted sharply, while a thrill of pleasure at the General's compliment ran round Arab officers and men.

In return we strove to keep self-assertion within the bounds of political necessity. On all Arabs we impressed that these Indian troops were guests, and must be permitted, nay helped, to do anything they wished. The doctrine took us into unexpected places. Every chicken disappeared from the village, and three sowars carried off Nasir's pennon, having coveted the silver knobs and spike of its dainty staff. This pointed a contrast between the English General who saluted and the Indian trooper who stole: a contrast welcome to the Arab race-hesitation towards the Indians.

Meanwhile, everywhere we were taking men and guns. Our prisoners could be counted in thousands. Some we handed over to the British, who counted them again: most we boarded-out in the villages. Azrak heard the full news of victory. Feisal drove in a day later, our string of armoured cars following his Vauxhall. He installed himself in the station. I called with my record of stewardship: as the tale ended the room shook with a gentle earthquake.

CHAPTER CXVIII

BARROW, now watered and fed, was due to leave for his meeting with Chauvel near Damascus, that they might enter the city together. He asked us to take the right flank, which suited me, for there, along the Hejaz line, was Nasir, hanging on to the main Turkish retreat, reducing its numbers by continuous attack day and night. I had still much to do, and therefore waited in Deraa another night, savouring its quiet after the troops had gone; for the station stood at the limit of the open country, and the Indians round it had angered me by their out-of-placeness. The essence of the desert was the lonely moving individual, the son of the road, apart from the world as in a grave. These troops, in flocks like slow sheep, looked not worthy of the privilege of space.

My mind felt in the Indian rank and file something puny and confined; an air of thinking themselves mean; almost a careful, esteemed subservience, unlike the abrupt wholesomeness of Beduin. The manner of the British officers toward their men struck horror into my bodyguard, who had never seen personal inequality before.

I had felt man's iniquity here: and so hated Deraa that I lay each night with my men upon the old aerodrome. By the charred hangars my guards, fickle-surfaced as the sea, squabbled after their wont; and there to-night for the last time Abdulla brought me cooked rice in the silver bowl. After supping, I tried in the blankness to think forward: but my mind was a blank, my dreams puffed out like candles by the strong wind of success. In front was our too-tangible goal: but behind lay the effort of two years, its misery forgotten or glorified. Names rang through my head, each in imagination a superlative: Rum the magnificent, brilliant Petra, Azrak the remote, Batra the very clean. Yet the men had changed. Death had taken the gentle ones; and the new stridency, of those who were left, hurt me.

Sleep would not come, so before the light, I woke Stirling and my drivers, and we four climbed into the Blue Mist, our Rolls tender, and set out for Damascus, along the dirt road which was first rutted, and then blocked by the transport columns and rearguard of Barrow's division. We cut across country to the French railway, whose old ballast gave us a clear, if rugged road; then we put on speed. At noon we saw Barrow's pennon at a stream, where he was watering his horses. My bodyguard were near by, so I took my camel and rode over to him. Like other confirmed horsemen, he had been a little contemptuous of the camel; and had suggested, in Deraa, that we might hardly keep up with his cavalry, which was going to Damascus in about three forced marches.

So when he saw me freshly riding up he was astonished, and asked when we left Deraa. 'This morning.' His face fell. 'Where will you stop to-night?' 'In Damascus,' said I gaily; and rode on, having made another enemy. It a little smote me to play tricks, for he was generous towards my wishes: but the stakes were high, beyond his sight, and I cared nothing what he thought of me so that we won.

I returned to Stirling, and drove on. At each village we left notes for the British advance guards, telling them where we were, and how far beyond us the enemy. It irked Stirling and myself to see the caution of Barrow's advance; scouts scouting empty valleys, sections crowning every deserted hill, a screen drawn forward so carefully over friendly country. It marked the difference between our certain movements and the tentative processes of normal war.

There could be no crisis till Kiswe, where we were to meet Chauvel, and where the Hejaz line approached our road. Upon the railway were Nasir, Nuri Shaalan and Auda, with the tribes; still harrying that column of four thousand (but in truth nearer seven) marked by our aeroplane near Sheikh Saad three busy days ago. They had fought ceaselessly throughout this time of our ease.

As we drove up we heard firing, and saw shrapnel behind a ridge to our right, where the railway was. Soon appeared the head of a Turkish column of about two thousand men, in ragged groups, halting now and then to fire their mountain guns. We ran on to overtake their pursuers, our great Rolls very blue on the open road. Some Arab horsemen from behind the Turks galloped towards us, bucketing unhandily across the irrigation ditches. We recognized Nasir on his liver-coloured stallion, the splendid animal yet spirited after its hundred

miles of a running fight: also old Nuri Shaalan and about thirty of their
servants. They told us these few were all that remained of the seven
thousand Turks. The Rualla were hanging desperately on to both
flanks, while Auda abu Tayi had ridden behind Jebel Mania to gather
the Wuld Ali, his friends, and lie in wait there for this column, which
they hoped to drive over the hill into his ambush. Did our appearance
mean help at last?

I told them the British, in force, were just behind. If they could
delay the enemy only an hour . . . Nasir looked ahead and saw a walled
and wooded farmstead barring the level. He called to Nuri Shaalan,
and they hastened thither to check the Turks.

We drove back three miles to the leading Indians, and told their
ancient, surly Colonel what a gift the Arabs brought. He seemed not
pleased to upset the beautiful order of his march, but at last opened out
a squadron and sent them slowly across the plain towards the Turks,
who turned the little guns their way. One or two shells burst nearly
among the files, and then to our horror (for Nasir had put himself in
jeopardy, expecting courageous help) the Colonel ordered a retirement,
and fell back quickly to the road. Stirling and myself, hopping mad,
dashed down and begged him not to be afraid of mountain guns, no
heavier than Very pistols: but neither to kindness nor to wrath did
the old man budge an inch. We raced a third time back along the road
in search of higher authority.

A red-tipped Aide told us that over there was General Gregory.
We blessed him, Stirling's professional pride nearly in tears at the mis-
management. We pulled our friend aboard and found his General, to
whom we lent our car that the brigade major might take hot orders to
the cavalry. A galloper hurtled back for the horse artillery, which
opened first just as the last of the light fled up the hill to its summit and
took refuge in the clouds. Middlesex Yeomanry appeared and were
pushed in among the Arabs, to charge the Turkish rear; and, as the
night fell, we saw the break-up of the enemy, who abandoned their
guns, their transport and all their stuff and went streaming up the col
towards the two peaks of Mania, escaping into what they thought was
empty land beyond.

However, in the empty land was Auda; and in that night of his last battle the old man killed and killed, plundered and captured, till dawn showed him the end. There passed the Fourth Army, our stumbling-block for two years.

Gregory's happy vigour heartened us to face Nasir. We drove to Kiswe, where we had agreed to meet him before midnight. After us came the press of Indian troops. We sought a retired spot; but already there were men by the thousand everywhere.

The movement and cross-currents of so many crowded minds drove me about, restlessly, like themselves. In the night my colour was unseen. I could walk as I pleased, an unconsidered Arab: and this finding myself among, but cut off from, my own kin made me strangely alone. Our armoured-car men were persons to me, from their fewness and our long companionship; and also in their selves, for these months unshieldedly open to the flaming sun and bullying wind had worn and refined them into individuals. In such a mob of unaccustomed soldiery, British, Australian and Indian, they went as strange and timid as myself; distinguished also by grime, for with weeks of wearing their clothes had been moulded to them by sweat and use and had become rather integuments than wrappings.

But these others were really soldiers, a novelty after two years' irregularity. And it came upon me freshly how the secret of uniform was to make a crowd solid, dignified, impersonal: to give it the single-ness and tautness of an upstanding man. This death's livery which walled its bearers from ordinary life, was sign that they had sold their wills and bodies to the State: and contracted themselves into a service not the less abject for that its beginning was voluntary. Some of them had obeyed the instinct of lawlessness: some were hungry: others thirsted for glamour, for the supposed colour of a military life: but, of them all, those only received satisfaction who had sought to degrade themselves, for to the peace-eye they were below humanity. Only women with a lech were allured by those witnessing clothes; the soldiers' pay, not sustenance like a labourer's, but pocket-money, seemed most profitably spent when it let them drink sometimes and forget.

Convicts had violence put upon them. Slaves might be free, if they could, in intention. But the soldier assigned his owner the twenty-four hours' use of his body; and sole conduct of his mind and passions.

A convict had licence to hate the rule which confined him, and all humanity outside, if he were greedy in hate: but the sulking soldier was a bad soldier; indeed, no soldier. His affections must be hired pieces on the chess-board of the king.

The strange power of war which made us all as a duty so demean ourselves! These Australians, shouldering me in unceremonious horse-play, had put off half civilization with their civil clothes. They were dominant to-night, too sure of themselves to be careful: and yet: — as they lazily swaggered those quick bodies, all curves with never a straight line, but with old and disillusioned eyes: and yet: — I felt them thin-tempered, hollow, instinctive; always going to do great things; with the disquieting suppleness of blades half-drawn from the scabbard. Disquieting: not dreadful.

The English fellows were not instinctive, nor negligent like the Australians, but held themselves, with a slow-eyed, almost sheepish care. They were prim in dress, and quiet; going shyly in pairs. The Australians stood in groups and walked singly: the British clung two and two, in a celibate friendliness which expressed the level of the ranks: the commonness of their Army clothes. 'Holding together' they called it: a war-time yearning to keep within four ears such thoughts as were deep enough to hurt.

About the soldiers hung the Arabs: gravely-gazing men from another sphere. My crooked duty had banished me among them for two years. To-night I was nearer to them than to the troops, and I resented it, as shameful. The intruding contrast mixed with longing for home, to sharpen my faculties and make fertile my distaste, till not merely did I see the unlikeness of race, and hear the unlikeness of language, but I learned to pick between their smells: the heavy, standing, curdled sourness of dried sweat in cotton, over the Arab crowds; and the feral smell of English soldiers: that hot pissy aura of thronged men in woollen clothes: a tart pungency, breath-catching, ammoniacal; a fervent fermenting naphtha-smell.

CHAPTER CXIX

OUR war was ended. Even though we slept that night in Kiswe, for the Arabs told us the roads were dangerous, and we had no wish to die stupidly in the dark at the gate of Damascus. The sporting Australians saw the campaign as a point-to-point, with Damascus the post; but in reality we were all under Allenby now, and the victory had been the logical fruit solely of his genius, and Bartholomew's pains.

Their tactical scheme properly put the Australians north and west of Damascus, across its railways, before the southern column might enter it: and we, the Arab leaders, had waited for the slower British partly because Allenby never questioned our fulfilling what was ordered. Power lay in his calm assumption that he would receive as perfect obedience as he gave trust.

He hoped we would be present at the entry, partly because he knew how much more than a mere trophy Damascus was to the Arabs: partly for prudential reasons. Feisal's movement made the enemy country friendly to the Allies as they advanced, enabling convoys to go up without escort, towns to be administered without garrison. In their envelopment of Damascus the Australians might be forced, despite orders, to enter the town. If anyone resisted them it would spoil the future. One night was given us to make the Damascenes receive the British Army as their allies.

This was a revolution in behaviour, if not in opinion; but Feisal's Damascus committee had for months been prepared to take over the reins when the Turks crashed. We had only to get in touch with them, to tell them the movements of the Allies, and what was required. So as dusk deepened Nasir sent the Rualla horse into the town, to find Ali Riza, the chairman of our committee, or Shukri el Ayubi, his assistant, telling them that relief would be available on the morrow, if they constructed a government at once. As a matter of fact it had been done at four o'clock in the afternoon, before we took action. Ali Riza was absent, put in command at the last moment by the Turks of the retreat of their army from Galilee before Chauvel: but Shukri found unexpected support from the Algerian brothers, Mohammed Said and Abd el Kader. With the help of their retainers the Arab flag was on the Town Hall before sunset as the last echelons of Germans and Turks defiled past. They say the hindmost general saluted it, ironically.

I dissuaded Nasir from going in. This would be a night of confusion, and it would better serve his dignity if he entered serenely at dawn. He and Nuri Shaalan intercepted the second body of Rualla camel men, who had started out with me from Deraa this morning; and sent them all forward into Damascus, to support the Rualla sheikhs. So by midnight, when we went to rest, we had four thousand of our armed men in the town.

I wanted to sleep, for my work was coming on the morrow; but I could not. Damascus was the climax of our two years' uncertainty, and my mind was distracted by tags of all the ideas which had been used or rejected in that time. Also Kiswe was stifling with the exhalations of too many trees, too many plants, too many human beings: a microcosm of the crowded world in front of us.

As the Germans left Damascus they fired the dumps and ammunition stores, so that every few minutes we were jangled by explosions, whose first shock set the sky white with flame. At each such roar the earth seemed to shake; we would lift our eyes to the north and see the pale sky prick out suddenly in sheaves of yellow points, as the shells, thrown to terrific heights from each bursting magazine, in their turn burst like clustered rockets. I turned to Stirling and muttered 'Damascus is burning', sick to think of the great town in ashes as the price of freedom.

When dawn came we drove to the head of the ridge, which stood over the oasis of the city, afraid to look north for the ruins we expected: but, instead of ruins, the silent gardens stood blurred green with river mist, in whose setting shimmered the city, beautiful as ever, like a pearl in the morning sun. The uproar of the night had shrunk to a stiff tall column of smoke, which rose in sullen blackness from the store-yard by Kadem, terminus of the Hejaz line.

We drove down the straight banked road through the watered fields, in which the peasants were just beginning their day's work. A galloping horseman checked at our head-cloths in the car, with a merry salutation, holding out a bunch of yellow grapes. 'Good news: Damascus salutes you.' He came from Shukri.

Nasir was just beyond us: to him we carried the tidings, that he might have the honourable entry, a privilege of his fifty battles. With Nuri Shaalan beside him, he asked a final gallop from his horse, and vanished down the long road in a cloud of dust, which hung reluctantly in the air between the water splashes. To give him a fair start, Stirling and I found a little stream, cool in the depths of a steep channel. By it we stopped, to wash and shave.

Some Indian troopers peered at us and our car and its ragged driver's army shorts and tunic. I was in pure Arab dress; Stirling, but for his head-covering, was all British staff officer. Their N.C.O., an obtuse and bad-tempered person, thought he had taken prisoners. When delivered from his arrest we judged we might go after Nasir.

Quite quietly we drove up the long street to the Government buildings on the bank of the Barada. The way was packed with people lined solid on the side-walks, in the road, at the windows and on the balconies or house-tops. Many were crying, a few cheered faintly, some bolder ones cried our names: but mostly they looked and looked, joy shining in their eyes. A movement like a long sigh from gate to heart of the city, marked our course.

At the Town Hall things were different. Its steps and stairs were packed with a swaying mob: yelling, embracing, dancing, singing. They crushed a way for us to the antechamber, where were the gleaming Nasir, and Nuri Shaalan, seated. On either side of them stood Abd el Kader, my old enemy, and Mohammed Said, his brother. I was dumb with amazement. Mohammed Said leaped forward and shouted that they, grandsons of Abd el Kader, the Emir, with Shukri el Ayubi, of Saladin's house, had formed the government and proclaimed Hussein 'King of the Arabs' yesterday, into the ears of the humbled Turks and Germans.

While he ranted I turned to Shukri, who was no statesman, but a beloved man, almost a martyr in the people's eyes, because of what he had suffered from Jemal. He told me how the Algerians, alone of all Damascus, had stood by the Turks till they saw them running. Then, with their Algerians, they had burst in upon Feisal's committee where it sat in secret, and brutally assumed control.

They were fanatics, whose ideas were theological, not logical; and I turned to Nasir, meaning through him to check their impudence now from the start; but there came a diversion. The screaming press about us parted as though a ram drove through, men going down to right and left among ruined chairs and tables, while the terrific roaring of familiar voice triumphed, and stilled them dead.

In the cleared space were Auda abu Tayi and Sultan el Atrash, chief of the Druses, tearing one another. Their followers bounded forward, while I jumped in to drive them apart; crashing upon Mohammed el Dheilan, filled with the same purpose. Together we broke them, and forced Auda back a pace, while Hussein el Atrash hustled the lighter Sultan into the crowd, and away to a side room.

Auda was too blind with rage to be fairly conscious. We got him into the great state-hall of the building; an immense, pompous, gilded room, quiet as the grave, since all doors but ours were locked. We pushed him into a chair and held him, while in his fits he foamed and shouted till his voice cracked, his body twitching and jerking, arms lunging wildly at any weapon within reach, his face swollen with blood, bareheaded, the long hair streaming over his eyes.

The old man had been hit first, by Sultan, and his ungovernable spirit, drunk with a life-time's wine of self-will, raved to wash out the insult in Druse blood. Zaal came in, with the Hubsi; and the four or five of us united to restrain him: but it was half an hour before he calmed enough to hear us speaking, and another half-hour before we had his promise to leave his satisfaction, for three days, in the hands of Mohammed and myself. I went out and had Sultan el Atrash taken secretly from the town with all speed; and then looked round for Nasir and Abd el Kader, to set in order their Government.

They were gone. The Algerians had persuaded Nasir to their house for refreshment. It was a good hap, for there were more pressing public things. We must prove the old days over, a native government in power: for this Shukri would be my best instrument, as acting Governor. So in the Blue Mist, we set off to show ourselves, his enlargement in authority itself a banner of revolution for the citizens.

When we came in there had been some miles of people greeting us: now there were thousands for every hundred then. Every man, woman and child in this city of a quarter-million souls seemed in the streets, waiting only the spark of our appearance to ignite their spirits. Damascus went mad with joy. The men tossed up their tarbushes to cheer, the women tore off their veils. Householders threw flowers, hangings, carpets, into the road before us: their wives leaned, screaming with laughter, through the lattices and splashed us with bath-dippers of scent.

Poor dervishes made themselves our running footmen in front and behind, howling and cutting themselves with frenzy; and over the local cries and the shrilling of women came the measured roar of men's voices, chanting, 'Feisal, Nasir, Shukri, Urens', in waves which began here, rolled along the squares, through the market down long streets to East gate, round the wall, back up the Meidan; and grew to a wall of shouts around us by the citadel.

They told me Chauvel was coming; our cars met in the southern outskirts. I described the excitement in the city, and how our new government could not guarantee administrative services before the following day, when I would wait on him, to discuss his needs and mine. Meanwhile I made myself responsible for public order: only begging him to keep his men outside, because to-night would see such carnival as the town had not held for six hundred years, and its hospitality might pervert their discipline.

Chauvel unwillingly followed my lead, his hesitations ruled by my certainty. Like Barrow, he had no instructions what to do with the captured city; and as we had taken possession, knowing our road, with clear purpose, prepared processes, and assets in hand, he had no choice but to let us carry on. His chief of staff who did his technical work, Godwin, a soldier, was delighted to shelve the responsibility of civil government. His advocacy confirmed my assumption.

Indeed, it was confirmed in Chauvel's next words, which asked liberty for himself to drive round the town. I gave it so gladly that he asked if it would be convenient for him to make formal entry with his troops on the morrow. I said certainly, and we thought a little of the route. There flashed into my head the pleasure of our men at Deraa

ENTERING DAMASCUS

when Barrow saluted their flag — and I quoted it as an example good to follow before the Town Hall when he marched past. It was a casual thought of mine, but he saw significance in it: and a grave difficulty if he saluted any flag except the British. I wanted to make faces at his folly: but instead, in kindness I kept him company, seeing equal difficulty in his passing the Arab flag deliberately not noticed. We stumbled round this problem, while the joyful, unknowing crowd cheered us. As a compromise I suggested we leave out the Town Hall, and invent another route, passing, let us say, by the Post Office. I meant this for farce, since my patience had broken down; but he took it seriously, as a helpful idea; and in return would concede a point for my sake and the Arabs. In place of an 'entry' he would make a 'march through': it meant that instead of going in the middle he would go at the head, or instead of the head, the middle. I forgot, or did not well hear, which: for I should not have cared if he had crawled under or flown over his troops, or split himself to march both sides.

Y

CHAPTER CXX

WHILE we discussed ceremonial antics a world of work waited, inside and outside, for each of us. It was bitter, playing down to such a part: also the won game of grab left a bad taste in my mouth, spoiling my entry much as I spoiled Chauvel's. The airy birds of promise so freely sent to the Arabs in England's day of need were homing now, to her confusion. However, the course I mapped for us was proving correct. Another twelve hours, and we should be safe, with the Arabs in so strong a place that their hand might hold through the long wrangle and appetite of politics about to break out about our luscious spoil.

We sneaked back to the Town Hall, to grapple with Abd el Kader: but he had not returned. I sent for him, and for his brother, and for Nasir: and got a curt reply that they were sleeping. So should I have been: but instead four or five of us were eating a snatch-meal in the gaudy salon, sitting on gold chairs, which writhed, about a gold table whose legs also writhed obscenely.

I explained pointed to the messenger what I meant. He disappeared, and in a few minutes a cousin of the Algerians came up, very agitated, and said they were on their way. This was an open lie, but I replied that it was well, since in half an hour I should have fetched British troops and looked carefully for them. He ran off in haste; and Nuri Shaalan asked quietly what I meant to do.

I said I would depose Abd el Kader and Mohammed Said, and appoint Shukri in their place till Feisal came; and I did it in this gentle fashion because I was loath to hurt Nasir's feelings, and had no strength of my own if men resisted. He asked if the English would not come. I replied Certainly; but the sorrow was that afterwards they might not go. He thought a moment and said, 'You shall have the Rualla if you do all your will, and quickly'. Without waiting, the old man went out to muster me his tribe. The Algerians came to the tryst with their bodyguards, and with murder in their eyes: but, on the way, saw Nuri Shaalan's massed lowering tribesmen; Nuri Said, with his regulars in the square; and within, my reckless guardsmen lounging in the antechamber. They saw clearly that the game was up: yet it was a stormy meeting.

In my capacity as deputy for Feisal I pronounced their civil government of Damascus abolished, and named Shukri Pasha Ayubi as acting Military Governor. Nuri Said was to be Commandant of troops; Azmi, Adjutant General; Jemil, Chief of Public Security. Mohammed Said, in a bitter reply, denounced me as a Christian and an Englishman, and called on Nasir to assert himself.

Poor Nasir, far out of his depth, could only sit and look miserable at this falling out of friends. Abd el Kader leaped up and cursed me virulently, puffing himself to a white heat of passion. His motives seemed dogmatic, irrational: so I took no heed. This maddened him yet more: suddenly he leaped forward with drawn dagger.

Like a flash Auda was on him, the old man bristling with the chained-up fury of the morning, and longing for a fight. It would have been heaven, for him, to have shredded someone there and then with his great fingers. Abd el Kader was daunted; and Nuri Shaalan closed the debate by saying to the carpet (so enormous and violent a carpet it was) that the Rualla were mine, and no questions asked. The Algerians rose and swept in high dudgeon from the hall. I was persuaded they should be seized and shot; but could not make myself fear their power of mischief, nor set the Arabs an example of precautionary murder as part of politics.

We passed to work. Our aim was an Arab Government, with foundations large and native enough to employ the enthusiasm and self-sacrifice of the rebellion, translated into terms of peace. We had to save some of the old prophetic personality upon a substructure to carry that ninety per cent of the population who had been too solid to rebel, and on whose solidity the new State must rest.

Rebels, especially successful rebels, were of necessity bad subjects and worse governors. Feisal's sorry duty would be to rid himself of his war-friends, and replace them by those elements which had been most useful to the Turkish Government. Nasir was too little a political philosopher to feel this. Nuri Said knew, and Nuri Shaalan.

Quickly they collected the nucleus of a staff, and plunged ahead as a team. History told us the steps were humdrum: appointments, offices, and departmental routine. First the police. A commandant and assistants were chosen: districts allotted: provisional wages, indents, uniform, responsibilities. The machine began to function. Then came a complaint of water-supply. The conduit was foul with dead men and animals. An inspectorate, with its labour corps, solved this. Emergency regulations were drafted.

The day was drawing in, the world was in the streets: riotous. We chose an engineer to superintend the power-house, charging him at all pains to illuminate the town that night. The resumption of street lighting would be our most signal proof of peace. It was done, and to its shining quietness much of the order of the first evening of victory belonged: though our new police were zealous, and the grave sheikhs of the many quarters helped their patrol.

Then sanitation. The streets were full of the debris of the broken army, derelict carts and cars, baggage, material, corpses. Typhus, dysentery and pellagra were rife among the Turks, and sufferers had died in every shadow along the line of march. Nuri prepared scavenger gangs to make a first clearing of the pestilent roads and open places, and rationed out his doctors among the hospitals, with promises of drugs and food next day, if any could be found.

Next a fire-brigade. The local engines had been smashed by the Germans, and the Army storehouses still burned, endangering the town. Mechanics were cried for; and trained men, pressed into service, sent down to circumscribe the flames. Then the prisons. Warders and inmates had vanished from them together. Shukri made a virtue of that, by amnesties, civil, political, military. The citizens must be disarmed — or at least, dissuaded from carrying rifles. A proclamation was the treatment, followed up by good-humoured banter merging into police activity. This would effect our end without malice in three or four days.

Relief work. The destitute had been half-starved for days. A distribution of the damaged food from the Army storehouses was arranged. After that food must be provided for the general. The city might be starving in two days: there were no stocks in Damascus. To get temporary supplies from the near villages was easy, if we restored confidence, safe-guarded the roads, and replaced the transport animals, which the Turks had carried off, by others from the pool of captures. The British would not share out. We parted with our own animals: our Army transport.

The routine feeding of the place needed the railway. Pointsmen, drivers, firemen, shopmen, traffic staff had to be found and re-engaged immediately. Then the telegraphs: the junior staff were available: directors must be found, and linesmen sent out to put the system in repair. The post could wait a day or two: but quarters for ourselves and the British were urgent: and so were the resumption of trade, the opening of shops, and their corollary needs of markets and acceptable currency.

The currency was horrible. The Australians had looted millions in Turkish notes, the only stuff in use, and had reduced it to no value by throwing it about. One trooper gave a five hundred pound note to a lad who held his horse three minutes. Young tried his prentice-hand at bolstering it with the last remnant of our Akaba gold: but new prices had to be fixed, which involved the printing press; and hardly was that settled when a newspaper was demanded. Also, as heirs of the Turkish Government, the Arabs must maintain its records of fisc and property: with the register of souls. Whereas the old staffs were taking jubilant holiday.

Requisitions plagued us while we were yet half-hungry. Chauvel had no forage and he had forty thousand horses to feed. If forage was not brought him he would go seek it and the new-lit freedom puff out like a match. Syria's status hung on his satisfaction; and we should find little mercy in his judgements.

Taken all in all, this was a busy evening. We reached an apparent end by sweeping delegation of office (too often, in our haste, to hands unworthy), and by drastic cutting down of efficiency. Stirling the suave, Young the capable, and Kirkbride the summary backed to their best, the open-minded power of the Arab officers.

Our aim was a façade rather than a fitted building. It was run up so furiously well that when I left Damascus on October the fourth the Syrians had their *de facto* Government, which endured for two years, without foreign advice, in an occupied country wasted by war, and against the will of important elements among the Allies.

Later I was sitting alone in my room, working and thinking out as firm a way as the turbulent memories of the day allowed, when the Muedhdhins began to send their call of last prayer through the moist night over the illuminations of the feasting city. One, with a ringing voice of special sweetness, cried into my window from a near mosque. I found myself involuntarily distinguishing his words: 'God alone is great: I testify there are no gods, but God: and Mohammed his Prophet. Come to prayer: come to security. God alone is great: there is no god — but God.'*

At the close he dropped his voice two tones, almost to speaking level, and softly added: 'And He is very good to us this day, O people of Damascus.' The clamour hushed, as everyone seemed to obey the call to prayer on this their first night of perfect freedom. While my fancy, in the overwhelming pause, showed me my loneliness and lack of reason in their movement: since only for me, of all the hearers, was the event sorrowful and the phrase meaningless.

---

* I have not seen this cry put exactly into English; indeed it will not go, for hidden in the Arabic there lurks a quantification of the predicate for which our accidence has failed to provide.

QUIVERINGLY a citizen woke me, with word that Abd el Kadir was making rebellion. I sent over to Nuri Said, glad the Algerian fool was digging his own pit. He had called his men, told them these Sherifs were only English creatures, and conjured them to strike a blow for religion and the Caliph while there was yet time. They, simple retainers with an ingrained habit of obedience, took his word for it, and set out to make war on us.

The Druses, for whose tardy services I had this night sharply refused reward, listened to him. They were sectaries, caring nothing for Islam or Caliph or Turk, or Abd el Kadir: but an anti-Christian rising meant plunder, and perhaps Maronites to kill. So they ran to arms, and began to burst open shops.

We held our hands till day, for our numbers were not so great that we could throw away our advantage in weapons, and fight in the dark which made a fool and a man equal. But when dawn hinted itself we moved men to the upper suburb, and drove the rioters towards the river districts of the town's centre, where the streets crossed bridges, and were easy to control.

Then we saw how small the trouble was. Nuri Said had covered the parades with machine-gun sections, who, in one long rattle of fire, barraged them across to blank walls. Past these our sweeping parties urged the dissident. The appalling noise made the Druses drop their booty and flee down side alleys. Mohammed Said, not so brave as his brother, was taken in his house, and gaoled in the Town Hall. Again I itched to shoot him, but waited till we had the other.

However, Abd el Kader broke back into the country. At noon it was all over. When things began I had called up Chauvel, who at once offered his troops. I thanked him, and asked that a second company of horse be drafted to the Turkish barracks (the nearest post) to stand by against call: but the fighting was too petty for that call.

Its best consequence was among the pressmen in an hotel whose wall was the stop-block of one barrage. They had not dipped their pens in much blood during this campaign, which had run faster than their cars; but here was a godsend at their bedroom windows, and they wrote and telegraphed till Allenby, away in Ramleh, took fright, sending me a Press despatch which recalled two Balkan wars and five Armenian massacres, but never carnage like to-day's: the streets paved with corpses, the gutters running blood, and the swollen Barada spouting crimson through all the fountains in the city! My reply was a death-roll, naming the five victims, and the hurts of the ten wounded. Of the casualties three fell to Kirkbride's ruthless revolver.

The Druses were expelled from the city, and lost horses and rifles at the hands of the citizens of Damascus, whom we had formed for the emergency into civic guards. These gave the town a warlike look, patrolling till afternoon, when things grew quiet again, and street traffic normal; with sweetmeats, iced drinks, flowers, and little Hejaz flags being hawked round by their pedlars as before.

We returned to the organization of the public services. An amusing event for me, personally, was an official call from the Spanish Consul, a polished English-speaking individual, who introduced himself as Chargé d'Affaires for seventeen nationalities (including all combatants except the Turks) and was in vain search of the constituted legal authority of the town.

At lunch an Australian doctor implored me, for the sake of humanity, to take notice of the Turkish hospital. I ran over in my mind our three hospitals, the military, the civil, the missionary, and told him they were cared for as well as our means allowed. The Arabs could not invent drugs, nor could Chauvel give them to us. He enlarged further; describing an enormous range of filthy buildings without a single medical officer or orderly, packed with dead and dying; mainly dysentery cases, but at least some typhoid; and it was only to be hoped, no typhus or cholera.

In his descriptions I recognized the Turkish barracks, occupied by two Australian companies of town reserve. Were there sentries at the gates? Yes, he said, that was the place, but it was full of Turkish sick. I walked across and parleyed with the guard, who distrusted my single appearance on foot. They had orders to keep out all natives lest they massacre the patients—a misapprehension of the Arab fashion of making war. At last my English speech got me past the little lodge whose garden was filled with two hundred wretched prisoners in exhaustion and despair.

Through the great door of the barrack I called, up the dusty echoing corridors. No one answered. The huge, deserted, sun-trapping court was squalid with rubbish. The guard told me that thousands of prisoners from here had yesterday gone to a camp beyond the town. Since then no one had come in or out. I walked over to the far thoroughfare, on whose left was a shuttered lobby, black after the blazing sunlight of the plastered court.

I stepped in, to meet a sickening stench: and, as my eyes grew open, a sickening sight. The stone floor was covered with dead bodies, side by side, some in full uniform, some in underclothing, some stark naked. There might be thirty there, and they crept with rats, who had gnawed wet red galleries into them. A few were corpses nearly fresh, perhaps only a day or two old: others must have been there for long. Of some the flesh, going putrid, was yellow and blue and black. Many were already swollen twice or thrice life-width, their fat heads laughing with black mouth across jaws harsh with stubble. Of others the softer parts were fallen in. A few had burst open, and were liquescent with decay.

Beyond was the vista of a great room, from which I thought there came a groan. I trod over to it, across the soft mat of bodies, whose clothing, yellow with dung, crackled dryly under me. Inside the ward the air was raw and still, and the dressed battalion of filled beds so quiet that I thought these too were dead, each man rigid on his stinking pallet, from which liquid muck had dripped down to stiffen on the cemented floor.

I picked forward a little between their lines, holding my white skirts about me, not to dip my bare feet in their puddled running: when suddenly I heard a sigh and turned abruptly to meet the open beady eyes of an outstretched man, while 'Aman, Aman' (pity, pity, pardon) rustled from the twisted lips. There was a brown waver as several tried to lift their hands, and a thin fluttering like withered leaves, as they vainly fell back again upon their beds.

No one of them had strength to speak, but there was something which made me laugh at their whispering in unison, as if by command.

Y*

No doubt occasion had been given them to rehearse their appeal all the last two days, each time a curious trooper had peered into their halls and gone away.

I ran through the arch into the garden, across which Australians were picketed in lines, and asked them for a working-party. They refused. Tools? They had none. Doctors? Busy. Kirkbride came; the Turkish doctors, we heard, were upstairs. We broke open a door to find seven men in night-gowns sitting on unmade beds in a great room, boiling toffee. We convinced them quickly that it would be wise to sort out living and dead, and prepare me, in half an hour, a tally of their numbers. Kirkbride's heavy frame and boots fitted him to oversee this work: while I saw Ali Riza Pasha, and asked him to detail us one of the four Arab army doctors.

When he came we pressed the fifty fittest prisoners in the lodge as labour party. We bought biscuits and fed them: then armed them with Turkish tools and set them in the backyard to dig a common grave. The Australian officers protested it was an unfit place, the smell arising from which might drive them from their garden. My jerky reply was that I hoped to God it would.

It was cruelty to work men so tired and ill as our miserable Turks, but haste gave us no choice. By the kicks and blows of their victor-serving non-commissioned officers they were at last got obedient. We began operations on a six-foot hole to one side of the garden. This hole we tried to deepen, but beneath was a cement floor; so I said it would do if they enlarged the edges. Near by was much quicklime, which would cover the bodies effectually.

The doctors told us of fifty-six dead, two hundred dying, seven hundred not dangerously ill. We formed a stretcher party to carry down the corpses, of which some were lifted easily, others had to be scraped up piecemeal with shovels. The bearers were hardly strong enough to stand at their work: indeed, before the end, we had added the bodies of two to the heap of dead men in the pit.

The trench was small for them, but so fluid was the mass that each newcomer, when tipped in, fell softly, just jellying out the edges of the pile a little with his weight. Before the work finished it was midnight, and I dismissed myself to bed, exhausted, since I had not slept three hours since we left Deraa four days ago. Kirkbride (a boy in years, doing two men's work these days) stayed to finish the burying, and scatter earth and lime over the grave.

At the hotel waited a bunch of urgent matters: some death sentences, a new justiciary, a famine in barley for the morrow if the train did not work. Also a complaint from Chauvel that some of the Arab troops had been slack about saluting *Australian* officers!

B Y morning, after the sudden fashion of troubles, they were ended and our ship sailing under a clear sky. The armoured cars came in, and the pleasure of our men's sedate faces heartened me. Pisani arrived, and made me laugh, so bewildered was the good soldier by the political hubbub. He gripped his military duty as a rudder to steer him through. Damascus was normal, the shops open, street merchants trading, the electric tramcars restored, grain and vegetables and fruits coming in well.

The streets were being watered to lay the terrible dust of three war-years' lorry traffic. The crowds were slow and happy, and numbers of British troops were wandering in the town, unarmed. The telegraph was restored with Palestine, and with Beyrout, which the Arabs had occupied in the night. As long ago as Wejh I had warned them, when they took Damascus to leave Lebanon for sop to the French and take Tripoli instead; since as a port it outweighed Beyrout, and England would have played the honest broker for it on their behalf in the Peace Settlement. So I was grieved by their mistake, yet glad they felt grown-up enough to reject me.

Even the hospital was better. I had urged Chauvel to take it over, but he would not. At the time I thought he meant to overstrain us, to justify his taking away our government of the town. However, since, I have come to feel that the trouble between us was a delusion of the ragged nerves which were jangling me to distraction these days. Certainly Chauvel won the last round, and made me feel mean, for when he heard that I was leaving he drove round with Godwin and thanked me outright for my help in his difficulties. Still, the hospital was improving of itself. Fifty prisoners had cleaned the courtyard, burning the lousy rubbish. A second gang had dug another great grave-pit in the garden, and were zealously filling it as opportunity offered. Others had gone through the wards, washing every patient, putting them into cleaner shirts, and reversing their mattresses to have a tolerably decent side up. We had found food suitable for all but critical cases, and each ward had some Turkish-spoken orderly within hearing, if a sick man called. One room we had cleared, brushed out and disinfected, meaning to transfer into it the less ill cases, and do their room in turn.

At this rate three days would have seen things very fit, and I was proudly contemplating other benefits when a medical major strode up and asked me shortly if I spoke English. With a brow of disgust for my skirts and sandals he said, 'You're in charge?' Modestly I smirked that in a way I was, and then he burst out, 'Scandalous, disgraceful, outrageous, ought to be shot . . .' At this onslaught I cackled out like a chicken, with the wild laughter of strain; it did feel extraordinarily funny to be so cursed just as I had been pluming myself on having bettered the apparently hopeless.

The major had not entered the charnel house of yesterday, nor smelt it, nor seen us burying those bodies of ultimate degradation, whose memory had started me up in bed, sweating and trembling, a few hours since. He glared at me, muttering 'Bloody brute'. I hooted out again, and he smacked me over the face and stalked off, leaving me more ashamed than angry, for in my heart I felt he was right, and that anyone who pushed through to success a rebellion of the weak against their masters must come out of it so stained in estimation that afterward nothing in the world would make him feel clean. However, it was nearly over.

When I got back to the hotel crowds were besetting it, and at the door stood a grey Rolls-Royce, which I knew for Allenby's. I ran in and found him there with Clayton and Cornwallis and other noble people. In ten words he gave his approval to my having impertinently imposed Arab Governments, here and at Deraa, upon the chaos of victory. He confirmed the appointment of Ali Riza Rikabi as his Military Governor, under the orders of Feisal, his Army Commander, and regulated the Arab sphere and Chauvel's.

He agreed to take over my hospital and the working of the railway. In ten minutes all the maddening difficulties had slipped away. Mistily I realized that the harsh days of my solitary battling had passed. The lone hand had won against the world's odds, and I might let my limbs relax in this dreamlike confidence and decision and kindness which were Allenby.

Then we were told that Feisal's special train had just arrived from Deraa. A message was hurriedly sent him by Young's mouth, and we waited till he came, upon a tide of cheering which beat up against our windows. It was fitting the two chiefs should meet for the first time in the heart of their victory; with myself still acting as the interpreter between them.

Allenby gave me a telegram from the Foreign Office, recognizing to the Arabs the status of belligerents; and told me to translate it to the Emir: but none of us knew what it meant in English, let alone in Arabic: and Feisal, smiling through the tears which the welcome of his people had forced from him, put it aside to thank the Commander-in-Chief for the trust which had made him and his movement. They were a strange contrast: Feisal, large-eyed, colourless and worn, like a fine dagger; Allenby, gigantic and red and merry, fit representative of the Power which had thrown a girdle of humour and strong dealing round the world.

When Feisal had gone, I made to Allenby the last (and also I think the first) request I ever made him for myself — leave to go away. For a while he would not have it; but I reasoned, reminding him of his year-old promise, and pointing out how much easier the New Law would be if my spur were absent from the people. In the end he agreed; and then at once I knew how much I was sorry.

DAMASCUS *had not seemed a sheath for my sword, when I landed in Arabia: but its capture disclosed the exhaustion of my main springs of action. The strongest motive throughout had been a personal one, not mentioned here, but present to me, I think, every hour of these two years. Active pains and joys might fling up, like towers, among my days: but, refluent as air, this hidden urge re-formed, to be the persisting element of life, till near the end. It was dead, before we reached Damascus.*

Next in force had been a pugnacious wish to win the war: yoked to the conviction that without Arab help England could not pay the price of winning its Turkish sector. When Damascus fell, the Eastern war — probably the whole war — drew to an end.

Then I was moved by curiosity. 'Super flumina Babylonis', read as a boy, had left me longing to feel myself the node of a national movement. We took Damascus, and I feared. More than three arbitrary days would have quickened in me a root of authority.

There remained historical ambition, insubstantial as a motive by itself. I had dreamed, at the City School in Oxford, of hustling into form, while I lived, the new Asia which time was inexorably bringing upon us. Mecca was to lead to Damascus; Damascus to Anatolia, and afterwards to Bagdad; and then there was Yemen. Fantasies, these will seem, to such as are able to call my beginning an ordinary effort.

APPENDIX I

NOMINAL ROLL:
HEJAZ ARMOURED CAR COMPANY

M.G.C.

Gilman	Dowsett	Grisenthwaite	Wade	Greenhill
D. M. Grant	E. Palmer		H. Comery	
G. V. P. Kenknight	J. L. Pender		R. Fairgrave	
G. S. Bond	W. Rowe		W. A. Holdsworth	
F. J. Davies	H. M. Shackleton		V. Holden	
A. Frost	A. Tunnicliffe		R. P. Jones	
H. Mann	G. Westwater		D. M. Murray	
D. Anderson	J. Wilson		R. McKenzie	
G. Barton	J. Goodchild		H. E. Parker	
T. W. Beaumont	H. Wareham		G. A. Pikett	
H. W. Bailey	G. Williams		E. Stoller	
G. A. Draper	H. J. Ingram		W. Thacker	
A. Hancock	E. Featherstone		H. W. Twiner	
J. H. Hurd	F. Wilson		F. Whitelegg	
Jackson	W. Axup		A. Woodburn	
E. Lowe	C. J. Bird			
W. McDonald	F. Brander			

R.A.S.C.

H. Monks	J. W. Ramsbottom	W. Hurst
A. Barnes	S. E. Rolls	W. W. Kidd
W. Coxon	T. R. Robinson	E. J. Keslake
A. Duff	J. O. Seddon	L. Matthews
S. Evans	J. E. Wadland	J. McKechnie
F. Garnett	A. Wainwright	W. Page
S. Haymes	R. B. Arnott	E. Rawcliffe
R. W. Hurst	G. Buckle	S. D. Ross
H. H. Helme	D. Dickson	J. E. Sanderson
A. Knowles	G. T. Elphick	C. W. Thomas
J. Mackay	J. E. Exton	W. E. Wells
O. McCarnen	H. R. Green	
F. Mudd	H. Hosker	

NOMINAL ROLL:
TEN-POUNDER TALBOT BATTERY

R.F.A.

Brodie

Pascoe

L. W. Parsonage	J. Black	T. Richardson
W. Bassett	A. Catley	C. W. Sorton
H. Iverson	H. E. Drewitt	J. Smail
H. B. Eccles	E. Garrett	R. Sneddon
W. Stanford	C. H. Hare	P. Stokes
J. Shaw	A. Lynn	A. Fawcett
R. Nicol	W. McInnes	
J. Baxter	H. M. Palmer	

R.A.S.C.

J. Bourne	A. Davies	R. Guthrie
M. Harper	Harrison	Draycuf
A. G. Frankis	A. Bentley	Puffer
J. Douglas	D. P. Quentin	J. W. Holyoak
W. Johnson	Heysed	

APPENDIX II

The following table of our movements or position-at-night is from my skeleton diary. Accident, preoccupations, and prudence were responsible for gaps. My book follows the strict order of time: but leaves out many by-plays. The dates here do not altogether agree with its text. Memory sometimes assists me with moonlight, on a new-moon night: and I have preferred memory to the calendar. Arabic names are spelt anyhow, to prevent my appearing an adherent of one of the existing 'systems of transliteration'.

1917

Jan.	1 Nakhl Mubarak	Apr.	1 Abu Markha	June	1 Wadi Bair
	2 Nagb Dhifran		3 Magrah el Semn		2 Ageila
	3 Yenbo		4 El Fershah		3 Nebk, etc.
	14 In *Suva*, etc.		5 Km. 1121		19 El Wagf
	17 Bir Waheidi		6 El Fershah		20 Bair
	18 Semna		7 Bir el Amri		21 El Ghadaf
	19 Harrat Gelib		8 Abu Markha		22 Wadi Mishnag
	20 Wadi Dhulm		10 Wadi Geraia		23 Hemme
	21 Abu Zereibat		11 Wadi Hamdh		24 Minifir
	23 Kurna		14 Wejh		25 Ifdein
	24 Habban		27 Magrah Raal		26 Dhaba
	25 Wejh		28 W. Hamdh		27 W. Maghara
	27 In *Hardinge*	May	1 Mellaha, etc.		28 Bair
	28 Cairo, etc.		3 Wejh		29 Rijt el Herar
Feb.	1 Suez		6 Wadi Hamdh		30 El Jefer
	4 In *Arethusa*		7 Wejh	July	1 Km. 479
	6 Wejh, etc.		9 Kalaat el Zereib		2 Fuweileh
	20 In *Arethusa*		10 El Kurr		3 Nagb el Shtar
	22 Cairo, etc.		12 Wadi Arnoua		4 Guweira
Mar.	2 In *Lama*		13 Abu Saad		5 W. Yitm
	3 Wejh, etc.		14 Abu Raga		6 Akaba
	10 Seil Arja		17 El Shegg		7 Bir Mohammed
	11 Abu Zereibat		18 Wadi Aish		8 Sudr Heidan
	12 Wadi Kitan		19 Dizaad		9 Suez
	13 Wadi Gara		20 Wadi Abu Arad		10 Cairo
	14 Wadi Tleih		21 Bir Fejr		12 Alexandria
	15 Abu Markha		22 Khabrat Ajaj		13 Cairo, etc.
	26 Wadi Serum		23 El Jaala		15 Alexandria
	27 Wadi Meseij		24 Kaseim Arfaja		16 Cairo
	28 El Jurf		25 Arfaja		17 In *Dufferin*
	29 Aba el Naam		26 Maiseri		19 Jeida
	30 Wadi Turaa		27 Isawiya		20 In *Dufferin*
	31 Bir el Amri		30 Abu Tarfeiyat		22 Jidda

Aug.	1	Jidda
	2	In *Hardinge*
	4	Wadi Itm, etc.
	6	In *Hardinge*
	7	Cairo
	14	Alexandria
	16	In *Hardinge*
	17	Akaba, etc.
	21	Kuntilla
	22	Akaba, etc.
Sept.	7	Wadi Itm
	8	Wadi Medeifein
	9	Guweira
	10	Hesma
	11	Rumm
	12	Akaba
	13	Rumm, etc.
	16	Wadi Dumna
	17	Mudowwara
	18	Km. 587
	19	Mudowwara
	20	Rumm
	21	Itm el Imran
	22	Akaba
	26	Wadi Itm
	27	Hawara
	28	Rumm, etc.

Oct.	1	Wadi Hafir
	2	Batra
	3	Shedia
	4	Km. 489
	5	El Kasr
	6	Imshash Hesma
	7	Rumm
	8	Wadi Itm
	9	Akaba
	11	Suez
	12	Kelab
	13	Ismailia
	14	Suez
	15	Akaba, etc.
	24	Wadi Itm
	25	Rumm
	26	Wadi Hafir
	27	Shedia
	28	El Jefer, etc.
	30	Shegg
	31	Bair
Nov.	1	Wadi Dhirwa
	2	Ammri
	3	Ain el Beidha
	4	Hamad
	5	Kseir 'Hallaḥat
	6	Ghadir Abyadh

Nov.	7	Tell el Shahab
	8	Abu Sawana
	9	Minifir
	11	Abu Sawana
	12	Azrak, etc.
	23	Wadi Butm
	24	Bair
	25	Jefer
	26	Akaba
	30	Wadi Itm
Dec.	1	Wadi Hawara
	2	Wadi Itm
	3	Akaba
	8	Kantara
	9	Gaza
	10	Suafa
	11	G.H.Q., etc.
	12	Gaza
	13	Cairo
	21	Suez, etc.
	25	Akaba
	26	Guweira
	27	Abu Sawana
	28	Akaba
	29	Guweira
	30	Ramleh
	31	Tell el Shahm

1918

Jan.	1	Abu Tarfeiya
	2	Akaba, etc.
	10	Wadi Itm
	11	Guweira
	15	Nagb Shtar
	16	Aba el Lissan
	18	Wadi Musa
	19	Shobek
	20	Tafileh, etc.
	28	Mezra, etc.
Feb.	4	Odroh
	5	Guweira
	8	Khabr el Abid
	9	Basta
	10	Shobek
	11	Tafileh, etc.
	13	Buseira
	14	Ghor el Safi
	16	Wadi Dhahal
	17	Seil Hesa
	18	Hesban, etc.
	19	Tafileh

Feb.	20	Wadi Araba
	21	Beersheba
	22	Ramleh, etc.
	27	Jerusalem
	28	Rafa
Mar.	1	Cairo
	4	Akaba
	6	In *Borulos*
	8	Cairo
	12	Suez
	13	In *Borulos*
	15	Akaba
	16	Guweira
	17	Akaba
	18	Nagb Shtar
	19	Shobek
	20	Sadaka
	21	Akaba, etc.
	30	Guweira
Apr.	1	Khabr el Abid
	2	Aba el Lissan
	3	Aneyza

Apr.	4	Wadi el Jinz
	5	Wadi el Hafir
	6	El Atara, etc.
	11	Jurf el Derawish
	12	Odroh
	13	Guweira
	14	Waheida
	18	Retm
	19	Shahm
	20	Ramleh
	21	Disi
	22	Aba el Lissan
	23	Waheida
	25	Aba el Lissan
	27	In *Arethusa*
	29	Cairo
May	1	Sinai
	2	G.H.Q.
	3	Jerusalem
	4	Aba el Lissan
	5	G.H.Q.
	6	Sinai

May 7 Cairo	June 21 In *Mansurah*	Aug. 21 Kusair el Amr
14 Sinai	25 Jidda	22 Azrak
15 G.H.Q.	July 1 In *Mansurah*	23 Ammari
16 Wadi Hafira	3 Wejh	24 Um Kharug
17 Cairo	4 In *Mansurah*	25 Thlaithukhwat
19 In *Imogen*	6 Cairo	26 Aba el Lissan
21 Akaba	8 Alexandria	Sept. 1 Aba el Lissan
22 Aba el Lissan	9 Cairo	5 Bair
23 Akaba	11 Palestine	6 Azrak, etc.
24 Disi	13 Cairo	13 Gian Khunna
25 Mudowwara	26 In *Borulos*	14 Umtaiye, etc.
26 Akaba	28 Akaba	16 Mezerib
27 Aba el Lissan	29 Aba el Lissan	17 Nasib
28 Fagair	31 Akaba	18 Umtaiye
29 Towani	Aug. 1 Akaba	19 Ifdein
30 Hesa, etc.	2 Wadi Itm	20 Azrak
June 1 Sultani	3 Wadi Nejd	21 Ramleh
2 Um el Rusas	4 Rumm	22 Um el Surab
5 Themed	5 Akaba	24 Umtaiye
6 Wadi Mojeb	6 Aba el Heiran	25 Nueime
7 Jurf	7 Akaba	26 Shekh Miskin
8 Aba el Lissan	8 Aba el Lissan	27 Sheikh Saad
10 In *Arethusa*	11 Jefer	28 Deraa
12 Suez	12 Um Kharug	30 Kiswe
13 Cairo	13 Amri, etc.	Oct. 1 Damascus
15 Alexandria	15 Bair	4 Kuneitra
17 Cairo	17 El Hadi	5 Sebaste
18 Sinai	18 Wadi Ghadaf	6 Ramleh
19 G.H.Q.	19 El Umdeisisat	7 Sinai
20 Cairo	20 Muaggar	8 Cairo

INDEX TO PLACE NAMES

PERSONAL INDEX

696